HURRICANE

THE ILLUSTRATED HISTORY

PHILIP J. BIRTLES

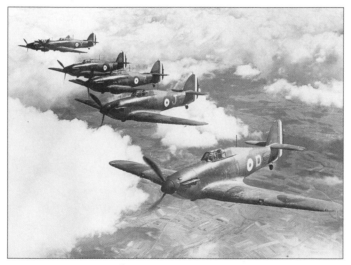

PSL

Patrick Stephens Limited

AN IMPRINT OF HAYNES PUBLISHING

First published in the United Kingdom in 2001 by
Patrick Stephens Limited, an imprint of
Haynes Publishing, Sparkford, Nr Yeovil,
Somerset BA22 7JJ, UK.

British Library Cataloguing in Publication Data
A catalogue record for this book is available from the British Library

ISBN 1-85260-604-5

Title page photograph: In August 1938, Digby based 73 Squadron received their first Hurricanes, which had the fixed pitch wooden Watts propeller. These were soon replaced by aircraft with three-blade variable pitch propellers. (*IWM*)
Endpapers: Final assembly of Hurricane Mk IIcs at Langley.

Typeset in 10/13pt Sabon.
Typesetting and origination by Sutton Publishing Limited.
Printed and bound in England by
J.H. Haynes & Co. Ltd, Sparkford.

CONTENTS

DEDICATION

To John Scott
And all who served in Hurricanes

ACKNOWLEDGEMENTS

I should like to thank Jonathan Falconer of Sutton Publishing for supporting me in the concept of this book and Rod Priddle for sharing some of his information. This book would not have been possible without the help of my old colleague Chaz Bowyer, who made his large collection of photos available to me. Photographs have come from many other sources, including BAE Systems, The RAF Museum, Imperial War Museum, FAA Museum and the Aviation Heritage Museum of Western Australia. My thanks to the staff of all these organizations for their assistance.

In Luftwaffe raids on Middle Wallop and Worthy Down late on 'Eagle Day', 87 Squadron was one of the defending units. A formation of Hurricane Mk IIcs, some armed with four 20 mm cannons. (*Author's Collection*)

804 Squadron Hurricanes over Strangford Lough with John Scott's Hurricane V7048 S7L closest. (*John Scott picture*)

INTRODUCTION

Designed principally by Sydney Camm, the Hawker Hurricane was a direct monoplane development of the 1930s technology Hawker high performance biplane fighters, although it owed its genesis to the earlier designs of Tom Sopwith, tested in the arduous combat conditions of the First World War. Retaining the same rugged structure as the biplanes, but gaining from the greater power of the Rolls-Royce Merlin engine, the Hurricane was fortunately available in sufficient numbers to delay the enemy forces in the Battle of France, when there was no other effective air defence to hand. More importantly, despite being often outclassed in performance by the Messerschmidt Bf109s, Hurricanes were responsible for the destruction of more enemy aircraft in the Battle of Britain than all other British fighters and defences combined.

By the time the Battle of Britain had been won, forestalling a German invasion, Spitfires with improved performance had taken over most of the air defence role. However, the Hurricane was not finished. It continued to prove its worth in overseas operations, where the enemy was frequently struggling for air superiority. Hurricanes also adapted very well to the ground attack role as a fighter-bomber and anti-armour aircraft, supporting Allied ground forces in the Mediterranean, North Africa, Middle East and Asia theatres. Its rugged construction made maintenance and repair relatively easy, and its positive handling made the Hurricane a steady but manoeuvrable weapons platform.

Despite the success of Hurricanes with the RAF and Allied air forces, not many survived for long after the war; and, of those that did, few remain in flying condition, apart from two with the Battle of Britain Memorial Flight and one or two other examples around the world. Now, with increasing interest in warbirds, more Hurricanes have taken to the air, some having their origins in Canada and others as wrecks recovered from the frozen north of Russia (see Appendix 4) and restored by enthusiasts, sometimes with a bare minimum of original parts.

*

I have dedicated this book to my good friend and ex-boss at Hawker Siddeley Aviation and British Aerospace at Hatfield, the late John Scott. That is not to forget all the other pilots who shivered in freezing cockpits on ship's catapults ready to be shot off in Hurricanes to defend convoys against enemy raiders, with no hope of landing again; or those who sweated on makeshift runways in the tropical heat. But John was a special friend.

He was trained to fly Sea Hurricanes off Catapult Ships with the 804 Squadron FAA from May 1941. Although he was not fired off in anger, he made one training launch from Maplin in Bangor Bay on 2 July 1941 in Hurricane V7048, and returned to land at Sydenham airfield in Belfast. He left 804 Squadron on 30 October 1941 to join 888 Squadron at Lee-on-Solent and HMS *Formidable*, making his first deck landing on 4 February 1942, and later flew Martlets in combat. Following a short time with 1832 Squadron at Speke, he joined 846 Squadron on 1 December 1943, again seeing combat, until 31 August 1944. He then flew a variety of aircraft with 787 (NAFDU) Squadron until ending his service on 30 November 1945.

John did not talk much about his exploits, except to joke that he would never again complain about how much tax he had to pay, seeing as he and his fellow pilots had been responsible for the destruction of a great many expensive aircraft during the Second World War, mostly of Allied manufacture! He commented wryly that their Lordships at the Admiralty had had a good idea about how to bring air defence to Allied convoys, but had neglected to devise a scheme for the recovery of the aircraft.

Despite his unorthodox views, John was awarded the DSC in 1944.

John Scott taught me how to be effective in public relations, which has been a good foundation for my working life. Before he signed up in the FAA as a naval aviator, he studied art; and, while serving, kept private diaries containing some outstanding line drawings, which survive him, and which are reproduced below and on the previous page. Sea Hurricane V7048 is the aircraft in which John made his one and only launch from a ship, on 2 July 1941.

Philip Birtles
Stevenage, December 2001

A picture by John Scott of HMS *Maplin*, the Fighter Catapult ship used to launch Hurricanes for convoy protection, manned by 804 Squadron FAA. (*Mrs A.B. Scott*)

CHAPTER 1

THE FIGHTER FAMILY

SOPWITH, HAWKER & SYDNEY CAMM

The development of the Hawker Hurricane was not an isolated event, but the culmination of a long process of combat-tested engineering solutions that began during the First World War with the Sopwith Camel, brainchild of the British aviation pioneer, Tom Sopwith. Sopwith's remarkable history (he lived to fly in Concorde) goes back further still, to the halcyon days of Edwardian England and the very first intrepid aviators in their 'canvas-and-string' powered kites.

Among such names as A.V. Roe, Blackburn, de Havilland, Handley Page and the Short brothers, Sir Thomas 'Tom' Sopwith was surely one of Britain's greatest aviation pioneers. Remarkably, he lived to over 100 years of age, seeing aerospace progress from modest beginnings into the space age, just over half a century later. Among his many achievements, he will be remembered as one of the founders of Hawker Siddeley Aviation, which was largely responsible for the development and production of the Hawker Hurricane. In any history of the aircraft, it is worth recounting his story, as he played such a seminal role in the British aviation industry pre- and post-Second World War.

Sopwith's first time in the air, while still a teenager, was in a balloon. This 'uplifting' experience was followed by a flight in a Henry Farman at Brooklands in September 1910. He then bought his first aeroplane, a

Howard Wright monoplane, but his first adventurous attempt to fly it without an instructor on 22 October 1910 at Brooklands ended with his losing control, going into a stall and crash landing, damaging the aircraft. After making repairs, and with considerably more care, one imagines, he flew again on 4 November, initially making short hops, then building up to circuits. After another month he switched to a Howard Wright biplane and, on 21 November, achieved his Royal Aero Club Certificate, No. 31.

Sopwith followed this rapid achievement by gaining the British record for distance and endurance, flying 107.75 miles in 3 hours and 12 minutes around a closed circuit on 10 December 1910. The Michelin Tyre Company was offering a £500 prize for the longest flight made before 31 December 1910, provided the pilot was British and flying a British built aeroplane. Sopwith just failed to gain the prize when Cody flew 195 miles in 4 hours 50 minutes on the last day of the year.

However, he did succeed that year in making the longest flight from Britain to the Continent. The prize was £4,000, a very large sum of money in those days, offered by Baron de Forest and promoted by the *Daily Mail*. Once again, it had to be a British pilot flying a British aircraft, and the deadline was also 31 December. While most of the contestants gathered at Dover, Sopwith took off from Eastchurch in the Howard Wright biplane on

Tom Sopwith gained his Royal Aero Club Certificate in a Howard Wright biplane on 21 November 1910. (*BAE Systems*)

18 December, flying over Dover and heading out across the Channel. His compass was not working and visibility deteriorated, resulting in Sopwith becoming lost. With only 11 gallons remaining in the fuel tank, gusting winds caused him problems maintaining control, and he made a landing at what turned out to be Beaumont in Belgium, nine miles from the French frontier. The total distance flown was 177 miles in 3 hours 40 minutes and, with most of his competitors grounded by bad weather at Dover, Sopwith gained the prize.

During 1911, Sopwith and his technical team, led by Fred Sigrist, spent some time in the USA attending aviation meetings. As well as winning prizes, there was the occasional drama: while attempting a forced landing with engine trouble off Manhattan Beach, for

instance, Sopwith and his passenger ended up hitting the water and overturning. Both survived, but the Howard Wright biplane was wrecked. His original intention had been to attempt to fly across America from the Atlantic to the Pacific coast, but the idea was shelved and Sopwith returned to Britain in October.

On 1 February 1912, the announcement was made of the opening of The Sopwith School of Flying at Brooklands. The school was equipped with a Howard Wright biplane, an American Burgess Wright biplane, a Bleriot monoplane and a Howard Wright monoplane, offering a wide range of flying experience, all four aircraft being available for instruction by early March. Fred Raynham was appointed chief pilot, manager and instructor, and his first pupil qualified on

Tom Sopwith made his first solo flight in a Howard Wright monoplane from Brooklands in November 1910. (*BAE Systems*)

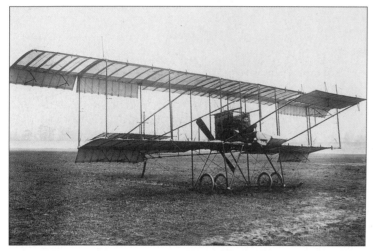

Tom Sopwith was the winner of the £4,000 Baron de Forest prize when he made the longest flight to date from Britain to Europe on 18 December 1910 covering a distance of 177 miles. (*BAE Systems*)

16 April. Other successful pupils included Major Hugh Trenchard, who, not long after, would become the commander of the Royal Flying Corps and 'founding father' of the Royal Air Force; and Harry Hawker, who went on to have a great influence in the Sopwith organization, and whose career began with test flying a new Sopwith Wright biplane on 15 October 1912.

On top of all the flying activities, including testing, instruction, competition and carrying passengers, Sopwith also found the time to design aeroplanes. His first effort was a tractor biplane powered by a 70hp Gnome rotary engine, with biplane wings based on the Wright camber and form. The aircraft was built by the flying school staff and first flown by Sopwith on 4 July 1912. Just over a week later, it was wrecked on take-off from Brooklands when it sideslipped into the ground, but was rebuilt and flying again by September.

As well as aviation, Sopwith was deeply interested in boats and cars. This led him to the idea of an amphibious aircraft. Boatbuilders S.E. Saunders Ltd of Cowes agreed to make the hull, designed by Sopwith, while Sigrist directed the building of the wings in the flying school. Their joint efforts resulted in a very early example of a 'flying boat' type of aircraft.

With increasing competition from other flying schools, Sopwith decided to stop training and concentrate on aircraft design, with Sigrist supervising the construction and the Australian, Hawker, being the test and demonstration pilot. A draughtsman, R.J. Ashfield, was appointed on 21 October at a salary of £3 per week, and the partners' first business success was confirmed shortly afterwards, with the sale to the Admiralty of a Sopwith tractor biplane, delivered to Eastchurch on 23 November 1912.

With the proceeds of the sale of this and a second aircraft, the Sopwith Aviation Company was formed in early 1913, and a redundant skating rink in Canbury Park Road, Kingston-on-Thames acquired as a production centre. Brooklands continued in use for flight testing and experimental work. Among the early aircraft to be built at Kingston were the 'Bat Boat', using the hull produced by Saunders with the Sigrist wings fitted, and a new, unnamed three-seater tractor biplane, the latter being the first entirely original Sopwith design.

A prize of £500 was at that time being offered for the first aircraft to operate from both water and land, a role for which the Bat Boat could be adapted. The workforce was therefore increased by six fitters and carpenters. Both the new aircraft were exhibited at the Olympia Aero Exhibition, which opened on 14 February 1913. After the exhibition, the Bat Boat was taken to Cowes for trials, but neither Sopwith nor Hawker could coax it off the water, and the hull was damaged in the process. It was then wrecked by an overnight storm. The biplane was collected from Brooklands on 1 March by two Royal Navy pilots and flown to Hendon. The aircraft exhibited excellent performance, achieving a British altitude record of 11,450

ft on 31 May. Meanwhile, the Bat Boat was being reconstructed and became the first British amphibian, winning the £500 Mortimer Singer Prize on 8 July 1913. The success of both types resulted in modest orders from the British government, and was soon followed by the Tabloid, the first wholly Sopwith production type.

The Sopwith Aviation Co. Ltd was formally constituted in March 1914 and new premises acquired in Canbury Park Road, about 100 yards from the skating rink. In addition to supplying the Admiralty and War Office with aircraft, the first seaplanes were sold to the Greek Naval Air Service.

Britain was not represented in the first Schneider Trophy contest in 1913, but a Tabloid fitted with floats was entered by Sopwith in the following year's contest, held at Monaco. It was flown by Howard Pixton to win the Trophy on 20 April 1914, the rest of the contestants having dropped out mainly because of engine problems. Pixton flew 28 laps, covering 280 km in 2 hours 13 seconds, averaging 85.5 mph; and, despite having his own engine difficulties, continued for another two laps to beat the 300 km speed record. Gaining the record at 92 mph made the Tabloid the fastest seaplane in the world.

With the declaration of war on Germany on 4 August 1914, to avoid conflict with the War Office, the Sopwith Company became an exclusive contractor to the Admiralty. The two Canbury Park Road premises began to expand, both in size and workforce; while Brooklands became a military airfield, as all civilian training was being replaced by training of pilots for the RFC. Early production consisted of Tabloids and float-planes, the former being put into service with the RFC in France, but by the end of the year no Sopwith aircraft remained in service on

The Sopwith School of Flying opened at Brooklands on 1 February 1912. Amongst the aircraft for training was an American Burgess Wright biplane. (*BAE Systems*)

Hangars were occupied by Sopwith at Brooklands for the operation of his own aircraft and the flying school. (*BAE Systems*)

One of the early students with the Flying School was Australian Harry Hawker, who became a test pilot with the company from October 1912. He is seen here with a Tabloid. (*BAE Systems*)

The 1½ Strutter was the first Sopwith type to be put into production for combat duties in World War I. It was armed with a single fixed forward firing Vickers gun firing through the propeller arc using an interrupter gear. (*RAF Museum*)

the Western Front, as they had not been designed to withstand the rigours of front line combat.

He had more luck with the Admiralty, however. When HMS *Ark Royal*, the first ship to be designated as a seaplane carrier, sailed from Sheerness on 1 February 1915, there were more Sopwith types than any other on board, including three Folder Seaplanes and four crated Tabloids. Their destination was the Dardanelles, where the aircraft were used for observation, directing the naval gunnery against land-based targets.

By December 1915, three experimental aircraft were planned and the design side was expanding. The first new type, which became known as the 1½ Strutter two seater biplane, was cleared for production in December. It was armed with a fixed forward aiming Vickers gun firing through the propeller arc using an interrupter gear. This was followed by a single seater Scout, later named the Pup, which was cleared for production early in 1916, and by the Sopwith Triplane a month later. To cope with increasing production orders, the factory was enlarged and a number of component manufacturers moved into the area to supply Sopwith.

So successful was the 1½ Strutter that the RFC expressed an urgent requirement; but because the company was still an exclusive supplier to the RNAS, the type had to be built under sub-contract by other manu-facturers, the first being Ruston Proctor at Lincoln, who made their first delivery on 11 July 1916. They were followed by many other contractors, effectively putting Sopwith at the hub of a major industrial network. As well as building seaplanes in their own factory, Sopwith then became specialists in fighter aircraft, initially known as Scouts.

The Sopwith Pup was a major early success as a scout and was popular with the pilots. N5180 is preserved in flying condition by the Shuttleworth Trust and was restored from a civil Dove. (*Author's Collection*)

The first 1½ Strutters entered service with 5 Wing RNAS in France on 24 April 1916, followed by the Pup, the first production batch being produced by Beardmore in Scotland. The Triplane was first flown on 30 May and was in action over France by mid-June. The Pup was extremely easy to handle and could fly higher than 18,000 ft on the power of an 80 hp Le Rhône or Clerget engine. German combat aircraft were superior in level speed and dive, but the Pup was more manoeuvrable.

During 1916, Sopwith Aviation had expanded rapidly, and production was concentrated on Triplanes and Pups, with the earlier 1½ Strutter tailing off. Despite the small number built, the Triplane achieved remarkable results. The Pup however was so effective that it remained in production with sub-contractors until the end of the war, following which it continued for some time in a training role.

Because the Sopwith works in Canbury Park Road was unsuited to mass production the company was asked to concentrate on the production of spares, while complete aircraft were to be produced by sub-contractors, who were erecting new assembly buildings. In 1917, the situation improved, as Sopwith were able to lease a new factory at Ham, within two miles of the existing factory. This allowed the company to become a large production centre as well as a design organization.

However, the outstanding Sopwith aircraft of the First World War was the Camel, with its record of shooting down more enemy aircraft than any other British fighter.

The original design for the Camel was to an Admiralty requirement, but the type served with both air arms, since the RFC's need for fighters was much greater. The first order was placed by the Admiralty in January 1917, followed in May by orders for the RFC, placed with both Sopwith and its subcontractors. By June 1917, the Royal Naval Air Service (RNAS) was operational, with Camels armed with two fixed forward firing Vickers guns synchronised to fire through the propeller arc. Unfortunately, the guns suffered from early teething troubles, often shooting off the propellor blades; while the RFC found that the 130 hp Clerget engines were losing power through wear and were unable to attain sufficient altitude to gain an advantage over the enemy. The RNAS Camels, on the other hand, were powered by Bentley BR1 rotary engines which gave less trouble. The aircraft was also demanding to handle, with sensitive controls; and, being prone to spinning, required experienced pilots who could make the most of its performance.

The Camels entered service with the RFC in July. The mechanics worked hard to keep the engines tuned and the aircraft performing successfully, both as fighters and in a ground attack role with four 20 lb bombs mounted on under-fuselage racks. As production rapidly increased, the aircraft were used for bombing for the first time by 70 Squadron RFC and 10 Squadron RNAS on 19 September, the eve of the Third Battle of Ypres.

Sopwith aircraft were also involved in the development of shipboard operations. A Sopwith Schneider floatplane fitted with a detachable wheel unit made a successful take-off from a ramp on HMS *Campania* on 6 August 1915. There was no provision to land back on board again, however. On 2 August 1917, a Pup was landed successfully for the first time on HMS *Furious* by Sqn Cdr Dunning but, on the third attempt, the Pup burst a tyre and fell over the side. Dunning was drowned. Despite this mishap, from June 1917 Pups were regularly flying from the decks of warships; but, as would again be the case with the Hurricane-carrying Camships in the Second World War (see Chapter 5), there was no provision for landing back on board. Eventually, though, in March 1918 a landing after-deck was fitted to *Furious*.

Following on from the Camel came the faster Dolphin, the world's first multi-gun single seater fighter. This aircraft, with backward staggered wings, was armed with twin fixed Vickers machine guns firing through the propeller arc, and a pair of elevated Lewis machine guns. These were ideal for attacks against Zeppelins. The prototype was flown from Brooklands by Harry Hawker in late May 1917.

In view of its combat potential the Dolphin attracted the largest order to date, in June 1917, 500 aircraft for the RFC, with deliveries commencing in November. The original Hispano engine, however, was giving a number of problems and, with no support forthcoming from the engine manufacturer, Sopwith's chief designer Herbert Smith proposed adapting the Dolphin to be powered by the more reliable Bentley BR2 engine.

The first Dolphins, still with Hispano engines, were issued to 19 Squadron RFC in France in January 1918, and scored their first victory in aerial combat on 8 March. Although the aircraft was initially committed to ground support, it was soon found that the high altitude performance of the Dolphin enabled the Allies to intercept high flying German reconnaissance aircraft. The upward firing guns, designed for balloon-bursting, were rarely used in combat, and were useless against ground forces, so they were adapted to fit under the wings outside the propeller arc, giving a greater concentration of fire. The versatile Dolphins were used for ground

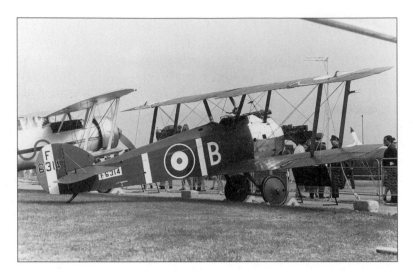

The Sopwith Camel was the outstanding fighter of the First World War in the hands of experienced pilots. Powered by a Bentley BR1 rotary engine it was used to destroy more enemy aircraft than any other British fighter. F6314 is preserved in the RAF Museum. (*Author's Collection*)

The Sopwith Dolphin, with backwards staggered wings giving a better view for the pilot, was the world's first multi-gun fighter. First deliveries were in November 1917 with 19 Squadron RFC receiving the first aircraft in France in January 1918. (*RAF Museum*)

The Sopwith Snipe was designed to replace Camels in service with what had now become the RAF, but only three units were equipped before the Armistice in November 1918. The type remained in service with the RAF until 1927. (*RAF Museum*)

attack, interception, line patrols, balloon bursting and bomber escort, the last major operation being flown on 30 October 1918 by 19 Squadron. But despite its effectiveness, only four squadrons on the Western Front were ever equipped with the aircraft.

The mainstay of the RFC was, however, the Camel. By the end of the war, 15 squadrons were flying Camels; Sopwith types altogether accounted for over 50 per cent of the total fighter aircraft strength.

The next major design, the Snipe was powered by the 234 hp Bentley BR2 rotary engine and was designed as a single seater fighter to replace the Camel, an aircraft which it closely resembled. The armament was identical. An initial version of the Snipe, fitted with single-bay wings, underwent official trails in December 1917 and, although it performed well, it was considered desirable to have the greater strength of two-bay wings. At the beginning of 1918, the first Snipes were being prepared for service trials at Martlesham Heath. The two-bay Snipe was tested in February 1918. Due to its increased drag it was no faster than the Camel, but the rate of climb was superior. The handling was also much improved over the Camel, making the Snipe less demanding in inexperienced hands.

More than 1,800 Snipes were ordered from six different contractors, with the first deliveries arriving in the summer of 1918. By the end of September, 161 Snipes had been completed, but only 97 were in France by 31 October 1918, and by the Armistice in November, only three squadrons had been equipped. Although the aircraft saw little action, Major W.G. Barker was awarded the VC for gallantry while flying a Snipe on 27 October 1918. Despite being wounded in one arm and both legs, he successfully crash-landed after destroying four enemy aircraft in the air. Following the end of the war, Snipes remained in service with the RAF until 1927.

With a massive offensive expected from the Germans in 1918, there was a need for an armoured trench fighter, among other equipment; the initial proposal being to adapt a Camel with 700 lb of armour plate and a downward firing gun. The first conversion flew on 15 February. However, the Sopwith design office was already working on an adaptation of the Snipe, which became known as the Salamander. It was armed with two fixed forward firing synchronised Vickers guns, giving much more effective cover than the adapted, downward firing Lewis guns.

The anticipated German offensive was launched on 21 March but the first Salamander did not commence flight trials at Brooklands until 27 April. After favourable trials, the aircraft was ordered into production in early June. With a full load of fuel, armament and armour, but without ammunition, on service trials the Salamander could reach 125mph at 3,000 ft and climb to 6,000 ft in less than six minutes. The armour plating was designed to protect against German armour piercing bullets at 150 ft range, as well as stopping shrapnel from AA fire. Unfortunately, production Salamanders did not enter service before the Armistice but, unlike the Camel, the Salamander was not declared obsolete at the end of 1918. Although the type never reached squadron service, about 50 were stored until the early 1920s before being scrapped.

*

The creative team of Sopwith as Chairman, with particular interest in test and experimental programmes; Smith, the chief designer since March 1914, Sigrist the engineer and Hawker the test pilot had produced a world beating series of single seater, single-engined high performance fighters. This formula was to become a speciality of the future Hawker Company, through the economic ups and downs of the 1920s and 1930s, in preparation, had they but known it, for the Second World War, and on into the jet age.

In addition to the major types already mentioned, during the 1920s and '30s the Sopwith team produced a number of other designs in their 'menagerie', including the Cuckoo, Bulldog, Rhino, Sparrow, Snail, Swallow, Buffalo, Dragon, Snark and Snapper; and finally, the Cobham twin engine bomber, which had no connection with any animal, real or fictional.

At the end of the war, the four Sopwith facilities – the original skating rink, the workshops in Canbury Park Road, the production factory at Ham and the Brooklands flight test facility – employed around 3,500 people. Many of the older employees and the women now left, having made their contributions to the war effort; the workload dropped drastically, despite efforts to diversify into civil aviation and other products. The first civil aircraft to come out of the factory was a two seater adaptation of the Pup, called the Dove, in which HRH The Prince of Wales, later to become the Duke of Windsor, was given an impromptu flight at Hounslow in May 1919.

The economic slump of 1920 was the final straw, however, and it was announced that the works would close for two weeks, starting 3 September. A week later, the business was wound up by voluntary liquidation, with the creditors paid in full. In place of Sopwith, a new organization was formed on 15 November 1920, named H.G. Hawker Engineering Company. Located at the same premises, its main activity was the design and manufacture of motorcycles. Some aviation work continued, however, including spares and the reconditioning of Snipes for home defence.

Hawker himself was not a man to be grounded. He entered the Aerial Derby of 1921 in a Nieuport Goshawk, powered by an ABC Dragonfly engine. Four days before the event, on 12 July, he took the aircraft on a test flight from Hendon, but owing to what was said to have been 'pilot incapacitation', although this was never explained, the aircraft crashed and Hawker was killed.

Nevertheless, his name lived on in the business. The first Hawker aircraft, the unsuccessful Duiker, appeared in 1923, and the first production contract to be awarded was for 64 Woodcocks, which replaced Snipes with 3 and 17 Squadrons in the mid-1920s. In 1924, W.G. Carter took over as chief designer and, in November 1923, Sydney Camm joined Hawker as a draughtsman. A move was made towards metal airframe construction, which Camm and Sigrist developed as a system of bolted duralumin tubes, soon adopted as the standard Hawker method. As the old machinery was being replaced by metal tooling, the Hawker Horsley, which had started as a wooden construction, was then specified as composite wood and metal, and finished production as an all-metal aircraft, total orders exceeding 100.

Camm was given the task by Carter of revamping the Sopwith Tabloid with half the weight and half the power, the resulting design being the Cygnet, which was the winning entry in the 1924 Lympne Light Aircraft Competition. When Carter resigned from Hawker in 1925, later to become chief designer at Gloster, Camm, with only 11 years' aviation industry experience since starting on a woodworker's bench, was appointed chief designer. He was domineering, a hard taskmaster who could be very difficult to work with. A complete perfectionist, he personally checked every drawing to ensure it met his high standards.

Camm's first design brief inaugurated the classic Hawker biplane series, which included the Heron, Hornbill, Hawkfinch, Hart and

In November 1923 Sydney Camm joined Hawker Aircraft as a draughtsman, later to become Chief Designer, and responsible for the Hurricane as well as many other types. (*Flight*)

Fury, and eventually the Hurricane, the first monoplane fighter, which was to become the country's main air defence in the Battle of Britain. The Hart of 1928 and the Fury of 1931, however, established Camm's reputation as the pre-eminent designer of high performance biplanes, and he was appointed to the Board of Directors in 1935.

The Hawker Hart was built to a day bomber specification, powered by a 450 hp Rolls-Royce Falcon engine giving a top speed of 160 mph. The first flight was made by George Bulman, the chief test pilot, in June 1928 from Brooklands; and, after service trials at Martlesham, an initial order was placed for 15 development Harts in June 1929 with 12 of the first batch delivered to 33 Squadron in January 1933. Such was the performance of the Hart that it was also developed as a fighter and trainer, and was exported as both wheeled undercarriage and float versions.

The Hawker Hart became the basis for a family of high performance biplane bombers between the two World Wars. The Hart bomber prototype J9052 was a two seater biplane powered by a Rolls-Royce Kestrel engine and was first flown from Brooklands by George Bulman in June 1928. (*BAe*)

The Hawker Fury was developed from the Hart family as a single seater fighter powered by a 525 hp Kestrel engine. As well as being exported it was further developed into the High Speed Fury K3586 a private venture with the Kestrel VI engine. This was later replaced by a Rolls-Royce PV12, which was to become the Merlin. (*RAF Museum*)

A two seater fighter development of the Hart bomber was the Demon powered by a 485 hp Kestrel engine. The type first entered service with 23 Squadron at Kenley in March 1931. (*RAF Museum*)

The final biplane Hawker design was the Hind bomber, powered by a 640 hp Kestrel V engine. It entered service with the RAF in 1935 and was exported to six countries. This example recovered in Afghanistan was restored for the RAF Museum in 1968. (*Author's Collection*)

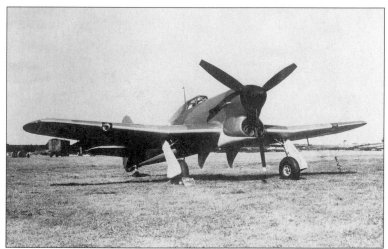

Following the Hurricane's success in the ground attack role, the Hawker Typhoon powered by a Napier Sabre engine was developed. The prototype was first flown on 24 February 1940, with main production by Gloster. Typhoon Ia R7580 is seen at the Air Fighting Development Unit at Duxford in September 1941. (*RAF Museum*)

The Tempest was developed from the Typhoon and, entered service in 1944. Owing to its high speed at low level it was instrumental in combating the V-1 flying bombs. The production version was the Tempest V powered by the Napier Sabre engine but the prototype HM595 is seen here, in February 1943. (*RAF Museum*)

The Sea Fury was a lighter weight development of the Tempest II powered by the 2,480 hp Bristol Centaurus radial engine. Adopted by the FAA and RAN, a two seater trainer version was produced. A two seater Sea Fury, 253, had been used in Germany for support of a number of single seater Sea Furies used for target towing duties. (*Author's Collection*)

The Gloster part of Hawker Siddeley was given the responsibility for producing the pioneer E28/39 Whittle jet aircraft. Meanwhile Sydney Camm designed the elegant R-R Nene-powered P1040 which was developed into the Sea Hawk for the FAA and German Navy. The majority were built by Armstrong Whitworth at Coventry, another part of Hawker Siddeley Aviation. (*MOS*)

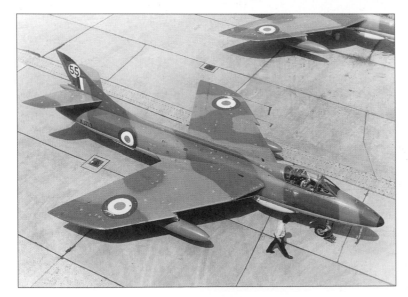

The sleek Hawker Hunter was progressively developed from the Sea Hawk, through the P1052 and P1081, powered by either a single Rolls-Royce Avon or Armstrong Siddeley Sapphire jet engine. Supersonic in a shallow dive, the Hunter became the backbone of the RAF day fighter force as well as achieving exports worldwide. (*Author's Collection*)

Powered by a 525 hp Rolls-Royce Kestrel engine, the first of an initial order for 21 single seater Fury aircraft made its maiden flight from Brooklands, piloted by Gerry Sayer, on 25 March 1931. Production was already in hand for the RAF and Yugoslavia. The first RAF unit to be equipped was 43 Squadron at Tangmere, where 16 were delivered in May 1931, soon followed by 25 Squadron at Hawkinge, and 1 Squadron, also at Tangmere, in May 1932. In addition to serving with the RAF, Furies were exported to a number of countries, including Portugal, Persia and Spain.

Using the Fury experience, the Nimrod was developed as a two seater fleet fighter powered initially by a 477 hp Kestrel and first flown by Sayer on 14 October 1931. This was later followed by the Osprey fleet spotter/reconnaissance aircraft. As a result of the success of the Hart Fighter, the two seater Demon was produced, powered by a supercharged 485 hp Kestrel engine. The first flight was on 10 February 1933, and the aircraft entered service with 23 Squadron that April. The final Hawker biplane design of any importance was the Hind bomber, powered by a 640hp Kestrel V engine, which made its maiden flight on 12 September 1934. Hinds saw service with the RAF and were exported to Switzerland, Portugal, Yugoslavia, Latvia, Persia and Afghanistan

Using the new method of construction, the Hart family of single engine biplane fighters and light bombers was developed, with large orders placed for the RAF and export. The increased prosperity of the organization required additional capital, and Hawker Aircraft Limited was formed in 1933. In 1934 the Gloster Aircraft Company was bought, and its factory at Hucclecote used for the production of some Hawker types. In 1935, the Hawker Siddeley Aircraft Co. Ltd was formed, which brought together Armstrong Siddeley Motors, Armstrong Whitworth Aircraft, A.V.

Roe (Avro) and Air Service Training with Hawker and Gloster. The scene was now set for the arrival of the Hurricane.

The first steps in development of the Hurricane were taken some six years before the outbreak of the Second World War, despite some in the Air Ministry who believed that monoplane fighters were inherently unsound. In August 1933, proposals were put forward for a monoplane fighter based on the Fury, initially with a spatted fixed undercarriage, powered by a Rolls-Royce Goshawk engine and armed by four fixed guns in the wings. Later refinements included a retractable undercarriage and power from what was to become the Merlin engine.

With the pre-war RAF Expansion Scheme underway, further floor space was required by Hawker and a new factory and airfield were built at Langley, where Hurricane production would be centred. By the start of the Second World War, the Hawker part of the Group employed some 4,000 workers, growing overall to 12,500 people during the war. The Hurricane remained in production at Langley until 1944, by which time Typhoons were already coming off the line, to be followed by Tempests. When the 20-year lease held by Leyland Motors expired on the Richmond Road factory in 1948, Hawkers moved in quickly to produce Hawker jet fighters, in the very place where Sopwith types had been built during the First World War.

Work on Britain's first jet aircraft was allocated to Hawker's partner company, Gloster. Camm started design of the Hawker P1040 powered by a Rolls-Royce Nene jet engine. With folding wings, it was later developed into the Sea Hawk for the FAA. By progressively giving the wings sweepback in the Nene engined P1052, and with the addition of a swept tail and straight through jet pipe on the P1081, the Hawker Hunter was produced. Supersonic in a shallow dive, the Hunter was powered by a single Rolls-

Royce Avon or Armstrong Siddeley Sapphire jet engine, and first flew on 20 July 1951. Modified as the Mark 3 with a reheat Avon RA7R developing up to 9,600 lb thrust, the Hunter was flown by Neville Duke to achieve a World Absolute Speed Record of 727.6 mph at low level on 7 September 1953. On 19 September, the same pilot flew the aircraft round a 100 km circuit to set up another world record speed of 709.2 mph. Hunters were progressively developed for the RAF and for export into potent fighter ground attack aircraft, and a two seater side-by-side version was produced for advanced pilot training as well as other duties.

Sydney Camm's last design was the revolutionary P1127, a single seater VSTOL (Vertical & Short Take-Off and Landing) jet combat aircraft. It was produced in close co-operation with Dr Stanley Hooker of Bristol-Siddeley Engines, who designed the BS53 Pegasus VSTOL jet engine. Bill Bedford made the first flight from Dunsfold, starting with tethered flights on 21 October 1960, untethered hovering on 19 November, and the first conventional take-off from Bedford on 13 March 1961. This unique concept was developed into the Harrier, the world's only successful VSTOL combat aircraft, which is still in development for the RAF, FAA and US Navy. The autocratic Camm continued to head the field in innovative aerospace technology until his death in 1966, after 41 years of design leadership at Kingston.

Meanwhile, in 1953 Tom Sopwith had received a Knighthood in the Queen's Coronation Honours List for services to aviation. He stayed on for a further ten years as chairman of the Hawker Siddeley Group, which absorbed yet more manufacturers in 1960, including de Havilland, Blackburn and Folland. By this time, the Group had become a major industrial undertaking, with Hawker Siddeley Aviation responsible for its aerospace interests. In 1963, Sir Thomas resigned as Chairman and took over as President, a position he retained until his death on 24 January 1989, at the age of 101.

Thanks to the work of men like Sopwith, Smith, Camm and Hawker, their companies built up an outstanding world reputation for combat aircraft, from the early Scouts and Pups to the sophisticated VSTOL Harriers of half a century later. This book will focus on only one type, however; as, more than any other, the Hawker Hurricane can be said to have played a pivotal role historically in the defence of the Free World.

In conjunction with Dr Stanley Hooker of Bristol Siddeley, who designed the Pegasus engine, the final design by Sir Sydney Camm was the P1127 VSTOL fighter which became the world-beating Harrier. The first prototype, XP831 was first flown by Bill Bedford from Dunsfold on 21 October 1960 and served with the Aero Flight at Bedford before retirement to the RAF Museum in October 1972. (*Author's Collection*)

CHAPTER 2

HURRICANE

DESIGN, DEVELOPMENT AND PRODUCTION

With the political temperature mounting in Europe, where Hitler and the National Socialist Party had been voted to power in Germany, in 1933 Sydney Camm and his staff began thinking about a monoplane successor to the Fury. This was in response to the challenge thrown out by the Air Ministry to UK manufacturers to design a frontline fighter for service with the RAF. At this stage, the Rolls-Royce Goshawk engine was pencilled in, while the tubular braced fuselage structure would be along similar lines to the Fury in external shape and layout, but enlarged to suit the new concept and with provision for a single, low wing. To obtain the required increase in performance, the wing would be the most fundamental change. Initial discussions were held with Air Staff member Air Cdr Cave-Brown-Cave and Major Buchanan, the Deputy Director of Technical Development, to define the Fury Monoplane, as it was then known, as a single seater fighter with two machine guns in the fuselage and two more in the wings, all firing forward. Eventually, eight wing-mounted Browning machine guns were specified.

To maintain the required strength the wing had to be relatively thick, with a thickness/chord ratio of 19 per cent and a maximum thickness of 18 inches at 30 per cent chord.* The wing area was established

in December as 257.5 sq ft, and remained the same for the subsequent Hurricane. The main undercarriage was fixed, faired over with spats, and the rear fuselage protected by a tail skid. The pilot was enclosed beneath a raised cockpit canopy. The all-up weight was estimated to be 3,807 lb with 50 gallons of fuel and 4.5 gallons of oil.

In early 1934, the decision was taken to replace the Goshawk engine with the Rolls-Royce PV12 in the 1,000 hp class, later to become the Merlin. The Goshawk had been suffering problems with the steam cooling system, and it was also vulnerable to battle damage. The Merlin was glycol cooled, allowing higher operating temperatures and smaller radiators with less drag. In January, a new layout was drawn, incorporating the Merlin and introducing a retractable undercarriage, including a tail wheel which, in the prototype, was also a retractable unit. To improve slow speed control on the approach to land and to assist with take-off, large area split trailing edge flaps were fitted to the wing between the ailerons.

By May 1934, a start had been made on the first manufacturing drawings for the fuselage and engine mountings. The wing design was more demanding, to provide adequate strength and stiffness and a smooth enough basis for fabric covering. By this stage, the project was being referred to as the Interceptor Monoplane. Wind tunnel testing commenced with a 1/10th scale model in the National Physical

---

* 'Chord' is the distance from the wing leading edge to the trailing edge at any point along its length.

The prototype Hurricane K5080 at Brooklands in the original form with reduced cockpit canopy frames and additional hinged doors on the main undercarriage legs. (*BAe*)

Hurricane prototype K5080 with modified cockpit canopy, retractable tail wheel and tailplane struts. (*Flight*)

Hurricane prototype K5083 in formation with Henley prototype K5115. The Hurricane is being flown by George Bulman wearing a trilby hat and the tailplane struts have been removed. (*Author's Collection*)

Laboratory (NPL) in August and, the following month, design proposals for the PV12 powered aircraft were submitted to the Air Ministry. Although a contract was not awarded until February 1935, drawings of the fuselage structure were released for manufacture as a private venture in October 1934, and construction was begun of a cockpit mock-up.

A meeting was held with Rolls-Royce in mid-December 1934 on progress with the PV12 engine. It was estimated that maximum power in level flight at 15,000 ft would be 1,025 hp at 2,900 rpm with a dry weight of no more than 1,200 lb. By this time, the predicted normal loaded weight of the aircraft would be 4,600 lb. Last minute changes to the wing design required revisions to the manufacturing drawings. Because the armament decision had not been made in time, the prototype wing had no provision for guns. However, the decision was soon made

to fit four .303 in Browning machine guns in each wing, firing outside the propeller arc. The existing wing structure was easily adapted to incorporate the guns and ammunition feeds.

The spar booms were fabricated from the traditional Hawker high tensile steel (HTS) strip polygon section, produced by a multi-rolling process. The booms were joined with a corrugated stiffened web plate also of rolled HTS. Similar boom sections were used across the separate wing centre section and enveloping reinforced rolled sections were also developed with tubular liners inserted into the booms as required. Fastening was commonly by blind and open-ended pop rivets. The web plates used thicker light alloy for the webs between the top and bottom booms, a mixture of rivets and bolts being used for fixing. Some reduction in weight was achieved with flanged lightening holes.

21

The gap between the main spars of the outer wings was braced in a zigzag pattern, in a spanwise manner. The diagonal bracing also was fabricated from smaller section HTS rolled tube with light alloy web plates and lightening holes. This robust structure had a high degree of torsional stiffness, while effectively taking the bending and drag loads. Some modest modifications were required to the inboard pair of diagonal members to accommodate the ammunition feed for the guns. It was not practical to curve the HTS rolled section booms, so a thicker light alloy section was used. The ailerons were of the Frise balanced type with tubular steel spars and light alloy ribs. The wing centre-section was bolted to the fuselage at four locations on the front and rear spars. The spars had plug end fittings, as did the outer wing spar ends, and the units were joined by bushed and tapered joint pins.

To present a smooth, low drag surface the booms of the wing ribs were provided with a channel in the light alloy rolled material. The fabric, with inner and outer reinforcing tape, was pulled down into the recess by a small flanged channel section, and held by close pitch light alloy screws into self-locking nuts on the underside of the recess. The external channel and exposed screw heads were covered with a doped-on fabric strip, giving a smooth surface. All the remaining flying surfaces and controls were similarly designed, but with a smaller recess and channel fixed with pop rivets.

Fuel was carried in two 34.5 gal. metal tanks situated between the centre-section spars with a further 28 gal. tank in front of the pilot behind the engine fireproof bulkhead. Engine oil was located in part of the outer leading edge of the port wing centre section.

The main undercarriage had Vickers oleo legs hinged on a low-mounted fore and aft member which bridged the spars at each outboard end on the centre section. Bracing was by fore and aft and sideways struts. The legs and wheels retracted hydraulically into the wing and fuselage centre section, with fairings attached to the legs completing the aerofoil surface after retraction. Although there were additional hinged flaps on the bottoms of the doors to complete the covering of the wheel aperture, they were not stiff enough and were removed after early test flights, leaving the wheels partly uncovered. The wide span split trailing edge flaps were operated by hydraulic jacks, but owing to cooling problems with the radiator, the centre section of the flaps was later removed. The hydraulic jacks and many of the undercarriage components were supplied by Dowty.

*

By New Year 1935, Hawker's design staff had reached 100, and on 10 January Air Ministry representatives inspected the mock-up at Kingston. The predicted maximum speed of the new aircraft at 15,000 ft was then estimated to be 330 mph.

After all the private venture work had been done by Hawker, the official order was finally placed on 21 February 1935 for a High Speed Monoplane to the design submitted in September 1934. The 'Specification for a Single Seater Fighter' was F36/34 and the serial K5083 was allocated. On 20 July, a contract amendment was issued to cover the work on the second set of wings carrying the eight Browning guns. At the same time, early investigations were begun on using metal stressed skin covering for the wings. A mock-up was built of the four gun installation in the port wing, which was inspected and approved on 23 August, by which time the predicted loaded weight with guns had increased to 5,200 lb.

The prototype was rapidly taking shape at Canbury Park Road and, from mid-1935

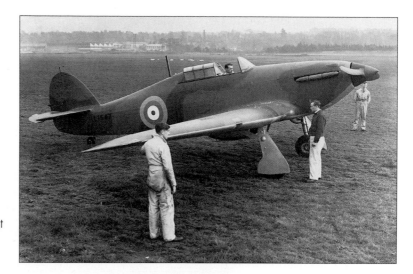

First production Hurricane Mk1 L1547 which flew from Brooklands on 12 October 1937. After service with 111 Squadron it was lost on 10 October 1940 when abandoned by Sgt Hanzlicek of 312 Squadron at Speke and crashed in the River Mersey. (*Flight*)

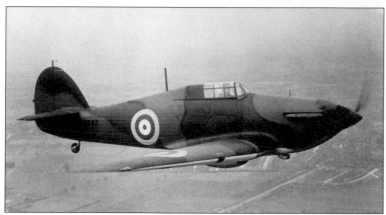

Early production Hurricane I L1582 which served with 3 Squadron. (*Author's Collection*)

Hurricane I L1648, clearly showing the wing shape, served with 85 Squadron in France in 1940. (*Flight*)

Hurricane I L1683 with the extended lower fin and rudder and still fitted with a wooden Watts fixed pitch two-blade propeller. (*RAF Museum*)

A later production standard Hurricane I with a variable pitch three-blade propeller, bullet-proof windscreen and metal wings. (*Flight*)

One of the last Hurricane Is V7826, built by Hawker, seen at Brooklands with a tropical filter under the engine and fixed 44 gal. underwing fuel tanks. (*HSA*)

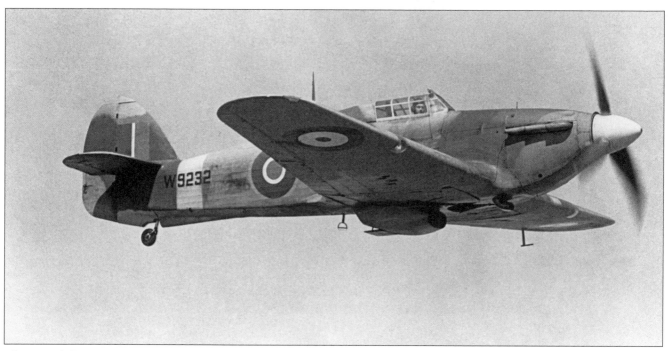

Full service standard Hurricane I W9232 built by Gloster powered by Merlin III engine. (*MOD*)

onwards, the Design Office and Experimental Department were busy finalizing assembly and systems design to obtain approval of the company from AID inspectors. The hydraulic undercarriage and flaps required a new series of retraction and ground operation tests, as this was new technology at the time. On 23 October, the first aircraft was dismantled and taken by road to Brooklands, where assembly started, ready for weighing on the 30th. This was followed by the maiden flight on 6 November by George Bulman, only 11½ months from the first issue of manufacturing drawings.

Early in the test flying programme the cockpit canopy blew off, slightly damaging the surrounding structure, so a replacement was fitted with additional stiffening frames. Although the tailplane was stressed as a cantilever structure, Camm insisted on adding struts from the underside to the base of the fuselage. When the autocratic Camm had to

go into hospital to have his appendix removed in early 1936, however, the struts were quietly removed, never to return.

Before a production order could be confirmed, the prototype had to complete its basic airworthiness testing prior to service evaluation at the A&AEE at Martlesham Heath. The situation was becoming urgent with the build-up of the German Air Force, especially the Bf109 fighter, which was initially powered by a Rolls-Royce Kestrel engine. How the Germans came to fit a British engine is not really known, especially as the Luftwaffe was operating under Allied restrictions following the Treaty of Versailles; but it is thought that some old technology Kestrels may have come on to the European market at the right time, and were snapped up, being soon after replaced by the intended 950 hp Daimler-Benz engines which were to give the Bf109 such a fearsome reputation in combat.

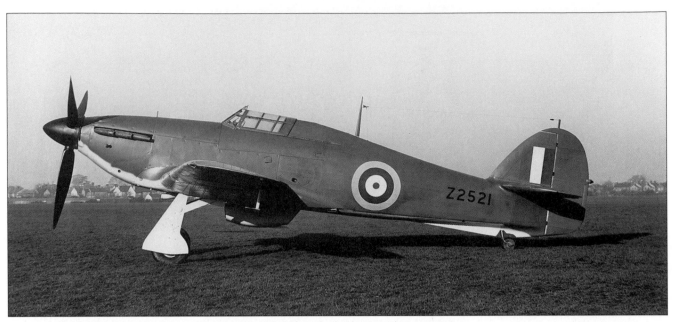

Hawker built Hurricane Mk II Z2521 at Langley powered by a Merlin XX engine and armed with eight .303 machine guns. (*HSA*)

Following the shock appearance of the Bf109, the Hurricane prototype was hurriedly delivered to Martlesham Heath on 7 February after only ten flights by Hawker test pilots, totalling some eight hours. The overall impression was favourable, but teething problems were experienced with the new PV12 engine, including the loss of coolant owing to internal leaks. The high level of unserviceability of the PV12 meant that further development was needed, requiring many engine changes.

When the prototype, K5083, returned to Brooklands, flying was curtailed as there were no Merlin I engines available for production aircraft. The Merlin was simply not reliable enough as a power plant. One of the major design changes that caused the delay was a new cylinder head, which had yet to undergo rig, test bed and flight testing. The developed version, known as the Merlin II, was not expected to be available until Autumn of 1937 and, with Hurricane production already authorized, it would be

some months after the first Hurricane was due to come off the production line that Merlins would be available.

Test flying of the prototype was restricted owing to the poor availability of the unreliable Merlin Is but spinning trials were carried out by Philip Lucas and resulted in a small under-fin being located forward of the fixed tailwheel, together with a downward extension of the rudder.

The first production contract for 600 aircraft was placed on 3 June 1936, and on 27 June the name Hurricane was formally approved by the Air Ministry.

During the middle of 1936, many new drawings were issued, and others revised, including the prototype drawings. On 20 July, Production Standard Specification P15/36 was issued to cover this work. In addition, the engine installation had to be modified to accommodate the improved Merlin II, slowing up the production

Hurricane IIa Z3451 powered by a Merlin XX fitted with underwing incendiary bombs on racks in March 1942. (*IWM*)

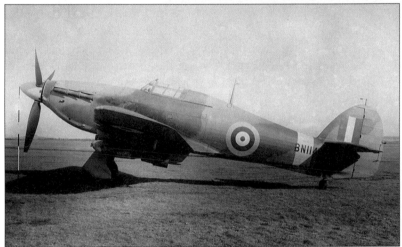

Hawker built Hurricane IIb BN114 in March 1942. (*RAF Museum*)

Hawker built Hurricane IIc prototype Z2905 fitted with long-range underwing fuel tanks and an armament of four 20 mm cannons, February 1942. (*IWM*)

deliveries with all the detail changes. A Merlin II was installed in the first production aircraft on 19 April 1937. L1547 was transported to Brooklands on 8 September, where it is variously reported to have made its first flight on 12 or 13 October. The new sliding canopy was fitted, together with a standard blind flying panel and full night flying equipment. An engine-driven hydraulic pump replaced the hand pump for undercarriage and flap operation used on the prototype. The aircraft still did not have any armament, and there was no radio fitted.

The prototype and early Mk I Hurricanes were fitted with a Watts fixed pitch wooden propeller, which had been in widespread service for more than a decade with biplane fighters but was only suitable for speeds of up to 360mph. To improve performance, a three-blade de Havilland-licensed two-pitch propeller produced by Hamilton Standard was fitted to Hurricane Mk I L1562, first flown on 29 August 1938. This was followed by the Rotol three-blade constant speed propeller, first fitted to L1606 for trials. To accommodate the Rotol propeller with its hydraulic controls, Rolls-Royce produced the Merlin III with a universal airscrew shaft to accept any propeller available. Following repairs to L1606 after an accident while serving with 56 Squadron, the aircraft was registered by Hawker as G-AFKX and flown in the new configuration by Philip Lucas on 24 January 1939. A speed of 344 mph was recorded soon after at 15,100 ft, the fastest to date in a Hurricane.

In the early stages of Hurricane production, once ready for testing, the company test pilots flew about six flights to check handling, performance and systems, to allow any necessary adjustments to be made. Before the establishment of RAF maintenance units (MU) the company pilots were responsible for the delivery of the aircraft to the squadrons or training units, and only then did ownership pass to the Air Ministry. Any loss of an aircraft before delivery had to be made good by the manufacturer. Once MUs were established, some of the service equipment could be fitted after delivery, reducing work on production testing.

In late 1937, the Air Ministry began putting on pressure to equip the first unit and, before Martlesham had even approved the aircraft, 111 Squadron based at Northolt was selected. The location west of London was convenient for both Kingston and Brooklands, from where the manufacturer could easily provide technical support for the new aircraft. The third and subsequent production aircraft were delivered to Northolt by Christmas 1937, complementing the test flying of the first two production Hurricanes at Brooklands. Despite three unfortunate accidents early on in the programme, squadron pilots overall adapted well to the new monoplane fighter.

With initial production Hurricanes in service and faults being rectified through the test programme, the time was ripe to consider some early development, one of the simplest ideas being to fit ejector exhausts to the Merlin engines, giving 5mph increase in speed. To help defend against the 20 mm cannon fitted to the Messerschmidt Bf109, armoured windscreens and armour plate were fitted fore and aft in the cockpit. Although the early units did not have these improvements, they were incorporated in time for the Battle of Britain. Jettisonable canopies were developed to avoid pilots being trapped by damage to the sliding rail, and rearward facing mirrors were fitted to the top of the windscreen. Self-sealing tanks were introduced to reduce the risk of fire or loss of fuel through combat damage and, for Middle East operations, long-range tanks could be fitted under the wings, each carrying a further 45 gallons, later increased to 90 gallons, jettisonable when empty.

Merlin XX powered, Hawker built Hurricane IIc KZ466 armed with four 20 mm cannons, April 1943. (*RAF Museum*)

Demand from the Services was almost immediate, so that it was often difficult to allocate sufficient suitable aircraft to the testing of these developments. After the Battle of Britain, there were enough Spitfires available to allow Hurricanes to be used in a variety of roles, including convoy protection and fighter-bomber duties on low level attack in Europe. They were also used as fighter and ground attack aircraft in North Africa and Asia, especially as tank busters in North Africa when the two x 40 mm cannon Mk IId entered service in 1942. We will examine the varied roles adopted by Hurricanes in a later chapter.

The Hurricane Mk II, in its various guises, powered by the Merlin XX, offering performance improvements and greater weapons load capability, was proposed in February 1940. The armament was increased to 12 x .303 in machine guns firing 300 rounds each. With a two speed supercharger fitted, the Merlin XX developed 1,060 hp, against 860 hp from the Merlin II. This gave an increase in speed from 300 mph to 330 mph at 20,000 ft. The coolant was changed to the non-flammable mix of 30 per cent glycol and 70 per cent water. Modifications to the airframe were modest but the engine was more reliable, with a longer life between overhauls.

The go-ahead was given rapidly and the first Mk II was flown from Brooklands on 11 June 1940, with deliveries starting in the

Hawker built Hurricane IId HW719 powered by a Merlin XX and armed with a pair of Vickers 40 mm cannons for anti-armour operations. (*IWM*)

Autumn. The first production aircraft with the 12 gun wing flew in August, while a Mk I had its machine guns replaced by 20 mm Hispano cannons in order to help determine the armament for the Typhoon. A trial installation was made on the fabric covered wings of L1750, delivered to Boscombe Down in October 1940, where the A&AEE had moved after the outbreak of war.

All production now concentrated on the Hurricane Mk II as Merlin XXs became increasingly available, the main service deliveries beginning in January 1941. These aircraft formed the basis of the first modern ground attack and close support aircraft, known as fighter-bombers. The Hurricane already had the capability of carrying a pair of 250 lb or 500 lb bombs under the wings and, in 1942, design work commenced on a universal wing which would allow any

combination of internal or external armament to be carried, including 3 in rocket projectiles (RP). The Hurricane IIb was typically armed with 12 x .303 internally wing mounted Browning machine guns; the Mk IIc was armed with four internally wing mounted 20 mm Hispano cannons, and the IId had a pair of underwing mounted Vickers 40 mm S guns. Fitted with the more powerful Merlin 24 or 27 engines, the Hurricane IV was introduced into service from the Spring of 1943.

From September 1939, until the end of the fighting in Asia six years later, some 14,500 Hurricanes were built, serving in all combat zones from Russia to Asia, on land and afloat. By 1941, although becoming outclassed as a fighter in Europe, it still packed a mighty punch as a fighter-bomber, and its successors – the Typhoon and Tempest

– were already entering service or in development. So, let's go back and look at how this tremendous rate of production was achieved.

*

At the time plans were being laid for Hurricane production in 1933, the total floor space available in densely populated Kingston was 250,000 sq ft, with a further 30,000 sq ft assembly and flight test facility in a 1914–18 Belfast truss double hangar at Brooklands nearby. The planes were built at Kingston, then dismantled and transported to Brooklands for re-assembly. In May 1935, the first stage in the expansion of production floor space opened at Brooklands within a long, narrow building of some 46,000 sq ft. It was built alongside the banking of the old car racing circuit and therefore had a slight curve, and could accommodate five rows of Hurricane fuselages in assembly with a separate fabric and dope shop at the Byfleet end. After 2,815 Hurricanes had been assembled there, this facility was replaced in 1941 by a new purpose-built factory and airfield at Langley in Buckinghamshire.

In early 1935 the prototype Interceptor Monoplane, later to become the Hurricane, was in assembly in the Experimental Department at Canbury Park Road in Kingston. The employees in the department were mainly fitters and assemblers, with many of the detail and sub-assemblies made in the Kingston workshops, all under the supervision of the design office.

The prototype wings were assembled on trestles in the traditional Hawker manner. By trammeling the spar webs, the experienced operators were able to achieve the required accuracy without the use of assembly jigs, to allow the close fitting bushes and taper pins to fit without difficulty. The new wings were considerably deeper in section than the earlier biplane wings, and had greater stiffness requiring closer tolerances for the accuracy of alignment. For production purposes, major wing jigs were designed and built to allow production by relatively inexperienced personnel.

In March 1936, the Hawker directors confirmed their confidence in the new Monoplane Fighter by agreeing that preparations should be made for major production ahead of the placing of the official contract. Tooling and facilities were set up, initially for 1,000 Hurricanes; and, three months later, their confidence was rewarded with an order for 600 aircraft, 558 with engines and the remaining 42 airframe-only, for completion by 31 March 1939. To cope with this large number of aircraft it was realised that considerably larger facilities would be required and, in 1936, a request was made to the Hawker test pilots to look out for a suitable site in the surrounding area for a new factory and airfield.

The site selected was on Parlaunt Park Farm at Langley, where construction of a 600,000 sq ft factory was begun in 1937, ready for the first occupation in June 1939. This became the main assembly factory for Hurricanes throughout the war, with the first aircraft being completed in October 1939. Further expansion became necessary at Langley to accommodate increased wing production, and aircraft repairs requiring a new four bay flight shed complex, taking the total covered area to 750,000 sq ft.

Meanwhile, production was steadily increasing at Brooklands, with the first production aircraft making its maiden flight on 12 October 1937. A total of 545 Hurricane Mk Is were delivered from Brooklands by 31 October 1939, of which some 50 were delivered to Belgium, Canada, Persia (Iran), Poland, Romania and Yugoslavia before the outbreak of war.

Hurricane Z2326 was originally built as a Mk II, but later converted to the Mk IV prototype. (*Author's Collection*)

Hawker built Hurricane IV KX877 powered by a Merlin XX engine, in April 1943. (*RAF Museum*)

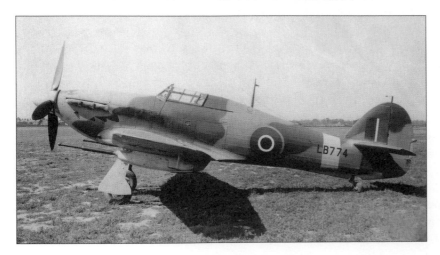

Hawker built Hurricane IV LB774 armed with a pair of anti-armour 40 mm Vickers cannons in underwing fairings, June 1943. (*RAF Museum*)

Hurricane BP173 was built at Langley as a tropical Mk IIb and later modified as a Mk IV for RP trials at A&AEE Boscombe Down from July 1942. The Hurricane was the first RAF fighter to be armed with RP, which was first in action with 137 Squadron over Holland on 2 September 1943. (*HSA*)

To achieve the planned high output, the use of raw materials had to be tightly controlled. For instance, the Hurricanes that were built in Belgium under licence, referred to later in the chapter, had wings made with a high proportion of locally available steel structure. These wings had an 80mph speed reduction in the dive, compared with the later metal covered wings available in Britain. Even in Britain, difficulties, both with the availability of materials and caused by the new manufacturing techniques required to produce all-metal wings, resulted in the first production batch of 500 Hurricane Mk Is being completed with fabric covered wings. By September 1939, the last of the fabric covered wings was completed at Brooklands and the

new metal covered wings were being completed at the rate of 15 a month by Gloster Aircraft, who were also manufacturing similar metal wings for the Henley.

The construction of the wings, centre section and tail surfaces was by an entirely new method to Hawker's, based on rolled high tensile strip steel tubular spar sections with a series of flats and lipped edges for attachment to the spar or rib web. This method was pioneered in the 1920s by Armstrong Whitworth and Boulton & Paul and was used in the production of the original fabric covered wings. As already described, in the design process these wings had diagonal ribs between the two spars to help give a smooth, low drag finish.

The first aircraft on the line at Brooklands to be fitted with metal skinned rather than fabric covered wings was L2027: these wings, for the 481st Mk I Production Hurricane and subsequent aircraft, were produced at Kingston, although the majority were built at Langley. The metal skinned wing, initially with eight machine gun armament, followed by 12 guns and then four 20 mm cannons, was common to the majority of the production aircraft, and interchangeable with the earlier, fabric covered wings. Both the design and method of construction were completely new, hence the anticipated delays in establishing production justified keeping the fabric covered wings in build.

With the new wings, the old rolled HTS spar booms and diagonal girders were replaced by light alloy extruded angle sections forming the booms of the main and intermediate spars and ribs with aluminium alloy webs. A variety of sections rolled from strip were used for the stringers and for the top and bottom booms of the trailing edge ribs, with diagonals of light alloy tube. Nose ribs, inter-spar diaphragms and many of the detail fittings were light alloy pressings. The structure was covered with wing panels with the stringers already attached by flush rivets. As with the earlier wings, assembly was carried out in pairs in fixtures, with the wing vertical, leading edge down. The leading edge was then completed with the wings mounted horizontally on trestles. The gun bay for the cannon wing had to be modified, and the 'universal' wing later developed for the Mk IV had to be adapted for carriage of the full variety of armaments. These fixtures were developed accordingly, to allow ease of access.

Moving to the fuselage, as we have seen, the primary structure utilized the Hawker patented system of metal tubular construction similar to the earlier method of construction of the Hart and Fury biplane families. A spaceframe of high tensile steel tubes was connected with stainless steel fishplates and machined fittings at the joints. The tubes were locally rolled to square or rectangle section where the plates were fitted. The joints were held together by bolts or tubular rivets passing through ferrules fitted in reamed holes, with distance tubes between the squared-off tube walls.

The fuselage was built in four sections, starting at the front with the engine mounting, which was later attached to the centre fuselage and wing centre section. The centre section of the fuselage was a rectangular constant width section and provided the basis for the alignment of the rear fuselage. The rear portion, which is tapered in plan view, was built up from top and bottom longerons and diagonal struts, which formed the two separate side frames. Behind this was the small tail section with tailplane, fin and tail-wheel attachment points. The fuselage was assembled with the centre section located on a jig representing the wing centre section spars. The assembly process consisted of fitting the cross tubes and bracing wires and the tail section, with adjustment of the tensions to achieve the correct alignment which was checked with a plumb bob to a datum plate on the floor. The fuselage was then ready for mounting on the wing centre section, attached at the four main fittings on the lower longerons. The engine mounts, complete with fireproof bulkhead, were then attached and the primary structure completed with the attachment of diagonal struts to the wing centre section.

Much of the installation work on the fuselage was carried out from floor level, prior to the fitting of wooden formers and stringers, which faired the centre section and rear fuselage to an oval section. When complete, the fuselage was lifted on to the wing centre section for joining and engine mounts. The Merlin, radiator and cowlings

Female labour was used extensively during Hurricane production. Women are seen here installing the engine firewall bulkhead. (*RAF Museum*)

An early Hurricane Mk I fuselage frame assembled to the wing centre-section. The metal tubular construction contrasts with the wooden stringers giving shape to the rear fuselage, which was fabric covered. (*Flight*)

Fuselage and wing centre-sections were moved to the final assembly area at Langley. (*HSA*)

Before the wings are attached the Merlin engine and cowlings are installed. (*RAF Museum*)

Hurricane Mk IIc MW336 moves along the Langley production line with the wings ready for attachment. (*HSA*)

Hurricane Mk IIcs LF772, LF773 & LF774 move down the production line at Langley. (*RAF Museum*)

were fitted and the aircraft was jacked up for undercarriage tests. The aircraft could then be moved on its own wheels to the fabric and paint shop. It was returned to the line for the completion of systems assembly, fitting of panels, windscreen, sliding cockpit canopy and tail surfaces. Finally, the aircraft was transferred to the flight shed for the fitting of the outer wings, armament, radio and preparation for flight testing.

*

The production policy set by the Hawker directors had seemed ambitious at first, but with the developing political situation in Europe between 1936 and 1937 it became obvious that further expansion still would be required. In September 1937, Gloster Aircraft was awarded a direct contract, initially for 500 Hurricanes, with the first one making its maiden flight from Hucclecote on 20 October 1939. A year later, 1,000 Gloster built Hurricanes had been completed and, eventually, 2,750 were built by the company, the last being delivered on 21 March 1942. Gloster then replaced Hurricanes with Typhoon production.

The Austin Motor Company was the other major UK source of Hurricane production, building 300 Mk IIas at Longbridge between 1940 and 1941. This is not necessarily an explanation for why so few examples have survived!

Overseas, the majority of Hurricanes were produced in Canada, where the government had agreed to build the aircraft in 1938 and issued Specification P3 on 4 January 1939 for work to start on the programme with the Canadian Car & Foundry Co. in Montreal. A

When the Hurricane wing centre-section structure was complete, systems and equipment were installed, including undercarriage and fuel tanks, before main assembly to the fuselage. (*RAF Museum*)

Final assembly of Hurricane Mk IIcs at Langley.

The Merlin engine installation in an early Mk I Hurricane. (*Flight*)

To help protect the aircraft against enemy defences during low level air attack, the ground attack Hurricane MkIV had additional armour plating including protection of the engine. (*HSA*)

The Hurricane cockpit was easily accessible for maintenance through a removable panel giving access to systems and structure.

Hurricane cockpit. (*Public Archives of Canada*)

Early production Canadian Hurricane I 328, with the Test & Development Flight at RCAF Rockcliffe on 26 August 1939. (*Public Archives of Canada*)

pattern Hurricane was supplied from the UK, together with a set of Hawker component and tool drawings and one set of Hawker-made parts. With the minimum of contact between the companies, much of the detail tooling was ready by February 1939 and the first fuselage structure was out of the jigs in July. Transported to the airfield on 8 January 1940, the first Canadian Hurricane was flown just two days later.

Canadian production concentrated on Hurricane Mks X, XI and XII, which were similar to the British produced Mk I and II, but adapted for local conditions and equipment, as well as obtaining their power from the American built Packard Merlin engines, driving Hamilton propellers. A total of 1,451 Hurricanes were built in Canada before production was halted in 1943.

Before the start of the Second World War, arrangements had been made for Hurricanes to be licence built by Avions Fairey in Belgium but, after only two had been completed, work was stopped by the German invasion. Licence production by Rogarsky in Belgrade was well established by the time of the German occupation of Yugoslavia in 1941, with about 20 Hurricanes delivered to the RYAF, but then production stopped.

Not all Hurricanes were built in one place. Output was maintained and increased by the Hawker policy of sub-contracting 50 per cent of detail and sub-assembly manufacture, ranging from single details to complete wings. As already mentioned, Gloster was producing metal covered wings for Hawker at the rate of up to 25 sets per month, in addition to the wings for their own Hurricane line. Wing production lines were also set up at Henry Balfour and Scottish Motor Traction at Airdrie, and at the LMS Railway works in Derby, with additional wings coming from Austin Motors.

At Kingston, where a night shift was worked in most areas, there was always a need for more production space. Various small premises were taken over around Kingston and further afield, including a factory at Acton for sheet metal work, starting at the end of 1938; and the Sanderson wallpaper factory at Perivale for additional machine and press shop capacity, together with some sub-assembly. On the Slough Trading Estate, one factory manufactured components for the metal wings and another produced some fuselage assemblies before the work was transferred to Langley.

As the new Langley factory began manufacturing operations in 1939, Hurricane production at Brooklands was reduced, until in 1941, after 2,815 aircraft had been completed by Hawkers, the buildings were handed over to Vickers Aircraft.

During the period of Hurricane production, when other types were also in development, employee levels at Hawker rose from 2,366 at the start of 1938 to 13,207 in August 1942. Around the time of Dunkirk in June 1940, at the height of the crisis, everyone worked 12-hour shifts, with food breaks only, for seven days, or seven nights, per week. War damage was surprisingly light: despite the vulnerability of the factories, the only bombs to drop at principal Hawker sites were on 21 September 1940 at Brooklands, one of which damaged the dope shop, and at Langley, where a bomb went through the roof of the wing shop before production had been established and damaged some stored vehicles. One person was killed.

At its maximum output, the Langley production line was fed by five lines of fuselage and centre section assemblies, mounted on wheeled trolleys for ease of movement down the line. One unit was removed in turn from the front of each track to the fabric and dope shop before joining the final erection line, then moved to the flight shed. The sequence would start again with the next five fuselages. This move was timed to occur at the end of each day and night shift. Average production time from the initial laydown of the fuselage primary structure to being ready for delivery was then 45 days.

However, the bulk of the total build cycle was occupied by material supply and manufacture of parts ahead of the start of assembly, which made the time taken to construct the aircraft more like 40 or 50 weeks. Air Ministry planning in early 1940 estimated an average of 10,300 man hours for an airframe structure weight of 2,468 lb, the equivalent figures for the Spitfire being 15,200 man hours for a structural weight of 2,055 lb. There were therefore definite advantages in producing the simpler Hurricane in time for the vital Battle of Britain, until it was superseded by later versions of the higher-performance Spitfire.

Peak quarterly production from Langley was 725 aircraft, the equivalent of eight per day, every day, by the second quarter of 1942. At the start of the war, 497 Hurricanes had been delivered from the Hawker factories, but by the second phase of the Battle of Britain, which began on 7 August 1940, 2,309 had been delivered, equipping 32 RAF squadrons. By comparison, only 1,400 Spitfires had been delivered and 19 squadrons were in operation.

Delivery records indicate that 9,920 Hurricanes left the factory in total, in addition to four which were lost on pre-delivery test, plus the prototype. The highest annual output achieved by all factories was 2,741 Hurricanes during 1943, with a monthly average of 228.5 aircraft, a magnificent achievement by Hawker and its sub-contractors and a triumph of wartime planning.

Canadian built Hurricane Mk X AG122 used by Rolls-Royce for engine development. (*BAe*)

Canadian built RCAF Hurricane XII at Rockcliffe on 16 September 1942 without a spinner fitted over the hub of the Hamilton Hydromatic three-blade propeller, and with an exhaust shield on the fuselage to reduce glare when flying at night. (*Public Archives of Canada*)

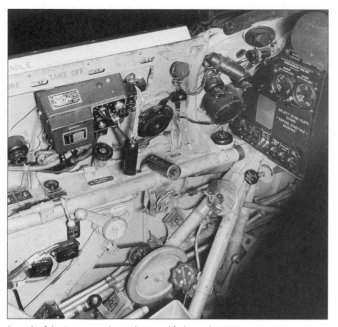

Port side of the Hurricane cockpit with trim and fuel controls. (*HSA*)

Starboard side of the Hurricane cockpit with flap controls. (*HSA*)

The second Mk IV conversion to a Hurricane Mk V was KZ193, seen armed with a pair of Vickers 40 mm anti-armour guns in November 1943. (*IWM*)

Removable panels on the top wing surface gave access for rearming the .303 in machine guns in a Hurricane Mk IIb. (*Author's Collection*)

The 20 mm cannons in the Hurricane Mk IIc packed quite a punch and were very effective against hostile aircraft and soft skinned ground targets. (*Author's Collection*)

Hurricane fuselage assembly at Langley.

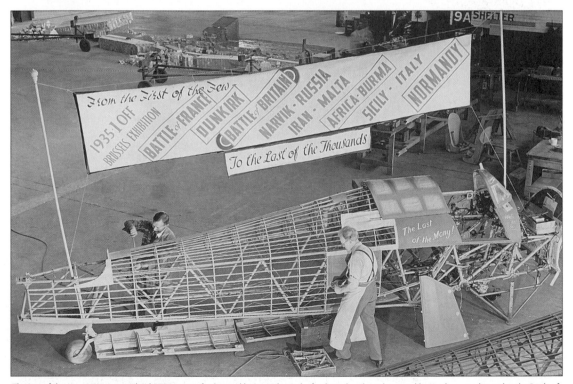

'The Last of the Many'. Hurricane Mk IId PZ865 starts final assembly at Langley and, after being bought and operated by Hawker, was donated to the Battle of Britain Memorial Flight. (*Author's Collection*)

Hurricane Mk IIc PZ865 'The Last of the Many', bought back by Hawker Aircraft, being flown by veteran PWS George Bulman, who made the maiden flight of the Hurricane Prototype. (*Author's Collection*)

*

In July 1944 'The Last of the Many', PZ865, was the centrepiece of a ceremony held at Langley. Flown by George Bulman, it was now nearly nine years since he had first tested its prototype. And what adventurous years they had been! This Hurricane, the last off the production line, was bought back by Hawker after the war, and registered G-AMAU for a number of air races in the 1950s. Refurbished and returned to its military markings in the late 1960s, it became part of the Hawker collection of historic aircraft based at Dunsfold, until it was donated to the Battle of Britain Memorial Flight in the early 1970s. It is still in service with the Flight, based at Coningsby, sharing air shows with another Hurricane, a number of Spitfires and a Lancaster, the full-throated howl of its Merlin engine providing an unforgettable experience for a new generation of admiring youngsters.

CHAPTER 3

SERVICE ENTRY AND EARLY COMBAT

111 Squadron at Northolt was the first RAF unit to receive Hurricanes. By the middle of December 1937, nine Hurricanes had flown and four were ready for delivery. Commanded by Sqn Ldr John Gillan, the squadron was flying Gauntlets, and expected the first Hurricanes on 1 January. However, four were delivered from Brooklands to Northolt without delay, and arrived before Christmas, although they did not appear on RAF charge until the New Year. Four more aircraft were delivered in January and the full establishment of 16 Hurricanes had been delivered by the end of February. The squadron was split into two flights with six aircraft each, and the remaining four in reserve, usually on routine maintenance.

The squadron pilots were faced with the daunting task of converting from 230 mph biplanes with open cockpit and fixed undercarriage, to a 330 mph monoplane with wing flaps, enclosed cockpit and retractable undercarriage. These early Hurricane Mk Is were not up to the full production standard and still had a hand pump for retracting the main wheels. Even Sqn Ldr Gillan and his flight commanders were novices on the new aircraft, but they were tasked with bringing the squadron up to operational standards and to undertake what were in effect service trials while further Hurricanes were issued to other units. Inevitably there were accidents, including one fatality.

To help build confidence in the Hurricane, Sqn Ldr Gillan planned a dramatic high speed flight to Edinburgh. However, he encountered strong headwinds when flying to Turnhouse on 10 February, so decided to refuel immediately after arrival and take advantage of the tail winds for the return. It was beginning to get dark as he climbed to 17,000 ft above cloud, without oxygen, for the return. Identifying Bedford through a gap in the clouds, he commenced his dive and arrived over Northolt, covering the distance of 327 miles in 48 minutes, at an average speed of 408.75 mph. The Merlin had been run at full power for the entire flight with an 80mph tailwind and behaved perfectly. As a result of this flight, not only was squadron confidence maintained, but the pilot gained the nickname of 'Downwind Gillan' and was later awarded the AFC.

The next Hurricane unit was 3 Squadron, based at Kenley and commanded by Sqn Ldr H.L.P Lester, a 40 year-old RFC veteran. The first Hurricanes began to arrive in March 1938 to replace Gladiators, but owing to the small size of the airfield at the time, the pilots had difficulty operating the new aircraft, resulting in a number of accidents, including two aircraft written off with one pilot killed. The squadron reverted to Gladiators until Kenley could be enlarged, and the squadron was not re-equipped with Hurricanes until July 1939, by which time they were based at Biggin Hill.

The first Hurricane unit was 111 Squadron, whose first aircraft arrived at Northolt before Christmas 1937. The initial production aircraft featured a retractable tailwheel as seen with the formation, and did not have the later lower rudder extension. (*Author's Collection*)

At North Weald, 56 Squadron became the third unit to equip with the new monoplane fighters, replacing Gladiators, with 20 aircraft being delivered during May and June. The CO, Sqn Ldr Charles Lea-Cox, was an RFC veteran. Nine aircraft were allocated to each flight, of which three were to be used for conversion training. The facilities at North Weald allowed the squadron to become fully operational by day and night by August.

All Hurricanes delivered to the first three squadrons were to the early production standard without the ventral fairing and increased rudder area which were later introduced to improve recovery from a spin.

The latter modification was incorporated on the 61st aircraft delivered.

During September 1938, the Munich Crisis made war with Germany inevitable, and there was an urgency to deliver further Hurricanes and Spitfires to the RAF and train pilots to fly them. Instead of the dozen or so fighter squadrons expected to be equipped by this time with the new monoplane fighters, only 111 and 56 Squadrons were operational with Hurricanes and only a small number of Spitfires had been delivered to 19 Squadron at Duxford in August. While Spitfire production was still becoming established, the rate of Hurricane production was accelerated sufficiently to re-equip a new squadron every month. By the end of the year more than 30 aircraft were being delivered monthly from Brooklands, allowing replacement of early standard Mk Is and attrition replacements.

In July and August, 87 Squadron at Debden, flying Gladiators, was split into two flights, 'A' Flight to become the nucleus of a new 85 Squadron, and both flights to re-equip with Hurricanes. 85 Squadron became operational in November with the arrival of Sqn Ldr David Atcherley as commanding officer. In August, 73 Squadron, commanded by Sqn Ldr Eric Finch, re-equipped at Digby, followed by 32 Squadron at Biggin Hill. The three Tangmere based units then received Hurricanes, starting with 1 Squadron in October, followed by 43 and 79 Squadrons in November. Only two squadrons were flying Spitfires and neither was yet operational.

With Hurricane production continuing to increase, further units were re-equipped in early 1939, 213 Squadron at Wittering in January, 46 Squadron at Digby in February and the first of the RAuxAF units, 501 Squadron at Filton in March and 504 Squadron at Hucknall in April. The re-equipping of these two auxiliary squadrons before other regular units was rather surprising, as the 'weekend warriors' had normally been issued with obsolete aircraft types. However, it was calculated that the pilots had been in the reserve for some years and were generally more experienced flyers. They were also tasked in particular with the defence of two vital engine factories, respectively Bristol and Rolls-Royce, requiring more effective aircraft.

The number of units receiving both Hurricanes and Spitfires rose rapidly, and Hurricane production soon increased beyond the rate needed to equip the regular combat squadrons, creating the capacity to supply training units such as 11 Advanced Training

Pool at Andover. Station flights also were supplied with enough Hurricanes to help with conversion of new pilots.

When war was formally declared on 1 September 1939, deliveries of Hurricanes were well on target, and sixteen squadrons were fully operational, with 601 Squadron RAuxAF still working up to operational standards. 610 Squadron RAuxAF received Hurricanes at the outbreak of war, but changed to Spitfires before becoming operational. There were a total of 280 operational Hurricanes, all with fabric covered wings and powered by Merlin II engines, with 133 at maintenance units, training units and test establishments. A further 169 had either been exported, written off, were being repaired, or were awaiting delivery from Brooklands. Only 28 of the original order remained to be completed.

Following the declaration of war by Britain and France, as part of an established agreement, a British Expeditionary Force (BEF) was sent across the Channel in the area of the Franco-Belgian border. The contribution by the RAF was the air component of the BEF and the Advanced Air Striking Force (AASF). The former was tasked with the support and protection of the BEF and included 85 and 87 Squadrons, equipped with Hurricanes. In addition to light bomber units with the AASF, there were also 1 and 73 Squadrons, equipped with Hurricanes. Their duties included the protection of the vulnerable Blenheim and Battle bombers, both in the air and on the ground, as well as air defence over British occupied areas of northern France.

At the outbreak of war, 111 Squadron was based at Acklington, flying the improved Hurricanes powered by Merlin III engines driving a DH or Rotol three-blade propeller. The squadron commanding officer, Sqn Ldr Harry Broadhurst, later to become Air Chief Marshal, gained the first victory of the war

The full establishment for 111 Squadron was 16 Hurricane Mk Is, all of which had been delivered by the end of February 1938. The squadron was split into two flights of six aircraft each, with four held in reserve for routine maintenance. Ground crew are learning to maintain the new aircraft type. (*RAF Museum*)

The initial Mk I Hurricanes with 111 Squadron were to the early production standard with a hand start Merlin II driving a Watts fixed pitch wooden propeller. (*RAF Museum*)

The 111 Squadron pilots in effect performed service trials with early Hurricanes at Northolt and were supported by Hawker Aircraft at nearby Kingston and Brooklands. (*Author's Collection*)

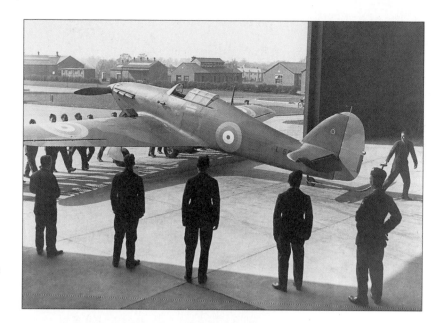

To help build confidence in the new aircraft, Sqn Ldr Gillan, CO of 111 Squadron, made a record flight in Hurricane I L1555 from Edinburgh to Northolt on 10 February 1938. He covered the 327 miles in 48 minutes with a tail wind, giving an average speed of 408.75 mph. (*Flight*)

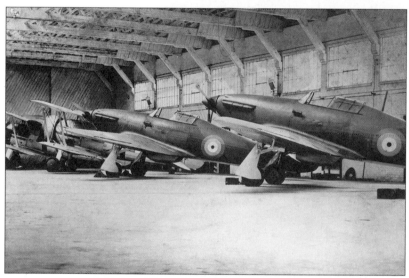

The second unit to equip with Hurricanes was 3 Squadron at Kenley in March 1938, replacing Gladiators. (*RAF Museum*)

Hurricanes issued to 3 Squadron were early Mk I standard, but were withdrawn owing to the limited size of Kenley aerodrome. They did not return to the squadron until July 1939, by which time a move had been made to Biggin Hill. (*Author's Collection*)

At North Weald, 56 Squadron began to replace their Gladiators in May 1938, by which time the retractable tail wheel had been abandoned, but the ventral fairing and extended rudder had still not been incorporated. (*RAF Museum*)

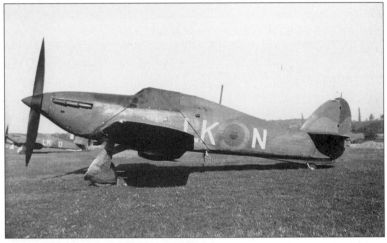

In July 1938 'B' Flight of 87 Squadron at Debden began to receive Hurricane Mk Is to replace Gladiators. (*Author's Collection*)

July 1938, 'A' Flight of 87 Squadron was split off to form the nucleus of a new 85 Squadron, and became operational with Hurricane Mk Is by November. Both 85 and 87 Squadrons were based at Lille-Seclin in France by December. (*IWM*)

when he shot down a He111H on 29 November into the sea off Newcastle.

The priority was to re-equip with newer models, those units in France which still operated the early Hurricanes using Merlin IIs to drive the Watts propeller. Then, there were demands from the French for more fighters, since their aircraft were inadequate to match the far superior German aircraft. The demands were strongly resisted by Air Chief Marshall Dowding, Commander in Chief of Fighter Command, who was concerned about sending more fighters and pilots to a lost cause. However, he did eventually agree to send 607 and 615 Squadrons RAuxAF, which were still equipped with Gladiators. Two other RAF squadrons were also expected to cross the Channel but 46 Squadron was diverted instead to Norway and only 501 arrived in France; however, 3 and 79 Squadrons were put on standby if required. During this period of 'phoney war', when activity was quiet, Dowding did not see the need to risk further squadrons in France. It was therefore expected that, should an additional requirement exist, this would be fulfilled initially by adding aircraft and pilots to the existing four squadrons.

Denmark was overrun by German forces in just one day, 9 April 1940. This collapse was followed rapidly by major advances into Norway, where Narvik was captured, the vital airfield at Stavanger was occupied by airborne forces, and major landings of troops were made at a number of other locations, including Oslo. British reaction was rapid, but inadequate, landings being made between 15 and 18 April with the object of moving north against Narvik, and south to join up with the Norwegian army north of Oslo. The only air cover provided was 263 Squadron, with obsolete Gladiators operating from the frozen Lake Lesjaskog. They remained there only a week before the withdrawal of all British forces from the country.

Britain then reverted to an earlier plan of attack in northern Norway, capturing Narvik. Air cover was provided by replacement Gladiators from 263 Squadron, and 46 Squadron commanded by Sqn Ldr Kenneth Cross with 18 Hurricanes. The Hurricanes were loaded aboard HMS *Glorious* at Greenock on 10 May, and were flown off a carrier deck for the first time on 25 May, landing at Skaanland and Bardufoss, 46 Squadron making the latter airfield its base. Hurricanes first went into action on 28 May when a Ju88 was shot down, followed by a pair of Do26 flying boats loaded with German alpine troops.

During the first week in June, with advances by German forces, both squadrons were regularly in action claiming some 20 enemy aircraft destroyed. Two Hurricanes were shot down, and two were damaged in accidents, with one pilot wounded.

From 3 June the position of the Allied forces around Narvik was becoming difficult, with the overwhelming German advance preventing any chance of recapturing the port. The decision was made to commence a withdrawal, overshadowed in the news of the day by the major débacle going on at Dunkirk, supported by RAF and FAA aircraft. On 7 June, 46 Squadron were in action against He111s over Narvik and, that evening, RAF personnel were ordered to destroy the surviving ten Hurricanes and board a ship bound for Britain. Next day, although he and his pilots had never landed on a carrier before, rather than destroy his aircraft Cross obtained authority instead to take the Hurricanes to the nearby HMS *Glorious*, where all ten landed safely. The remaining four Hurricanes in Norway were destroyed, and the remainder of the RAF personnel boarded the MV *Andorra Star*, sailing for home.

Glorious sailed westward with her escort to avoid attack from German shore based

At Tangmere, 1 Squadron was followed by 43 Squadron in November 1938 with Hurricane Is, this example having the camouflage toned down during the lead-up to the outbreak of war. (*RAF Museum*)

The third and final unit at Tangmere to be re-equipped with Hurricanes was 79 Squadron in November 1938. By this time the Merlins were started electrically using a battery trolley known as a 'trolley-ack'. (*Author's Collection*)

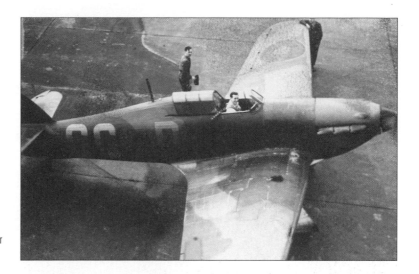

The second unit to equip with Hurricanes at North Weald was 151 Squadron in December 1938. (*RAF Museum*)

At North Weald 17 Squadron began to take delivery of Hurricane Mk Is in June 1939. This aircraft was trestled for undercarriage checks and is having the unit code painted on the fuselage side. (*RAF Museum*)

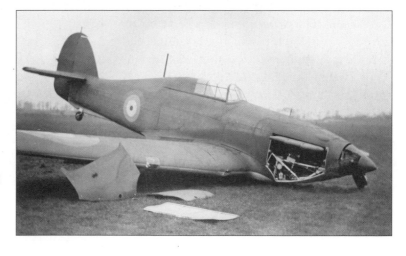

The first RAuxAF unit to receive Hurricanes was 501 Squadron at Filton in March 1939, tasked with the defence of the Bristol Aircraft and Engine works. Hurricane I L1869 suffered a slight accident, with a wheels-up landing damaging the wooden propeller. (*RAF Museum*)

In April 1939, 504 Squadron RAuxAF took delivery of Hurricanes to help defend the important Rolls-Royce factories at Hucknall and nearby Derby against enemy air attack. Most of the pilots were experienced veterans, but without combat experience. (*Author's Collection*)

aircraft, but she was intercepted by two German battle cruisers, *Scharnhorst* and *Gneisenau*. The *Scharnhorst* opened fire at 28,000 yards, far beyond the range of the Royal Navy guns, and the ship was set on fire. Twenty minutes after the order to abandon ship, *Glorious* turned over and sank with the loss of 1,515 men of the RN and RAF. Sixty hours after the loss of the carrier and its escorts, three officers and 35 men were picked up by a Norwegian fishing boat. Among the survivors was the gallant Sqn Ldr Cross.

Meanwhile, with the AASF Hurricane units, 1 Squadron, led by Sqn Ldr P.J.H. Halahan, was based at Vassingcourt, west of Nancy, and 73 Squadron, led by Sqn Ldr J.W.C. Moore, was based at Rouvres. Flt Lt P.P. Hanks of 1 Squadron was credited with the first RAF victory in France, on 30 October 1939, and a total of 26 'kills' were eventually claimed by the squadron during the 'phoney war'. 73 Squadron claimed 30 victories by May 1940, and Flg Off E.J. 'Cobber' Kain was awarded the DFC for becoming the first 'ace' of the war when he racked up his fifth kill.

The Air Component Hurricane units, 85 and 87 Squadrons, were based at Lille/Seclin close to the Belgian border. Commanded by

When war was declared on 1 September 1939, 601 Squadron RAuxAF was in the process of receiving Hurricanes, a Mk I being seen with Flg Off Whitney and his ground crew. The aircraft is connected to the trolley-ack ready for starting. (*RAF Museum*)

Part of the British Expeditionary Force sent to defend France on the outbreak of war were Hurricanes of 85 and 87 Squadrons. The pilots of 87 Squadron run to their Hurricanes for a 'scramble' in March 1940 on one of the rudimentary French airfields. (*Author's Collection*)

RAF squadrons in France were based at primitive airfields with accommodation under canvas. The pilot climbs aboard YV-G of 85 Squadron ready for another sortie. (*RAF Museum*)

The RAF contribution also included the Advanced Air Striking Force with Hurricanes of 1 and 73 Squadrons. Hurricanes of 1 Squadron are seen during a practice attack in France in 1940, but this was soon replaced by the real thing. (*IWM*)

Hurricane Mk I of 73 Squadron, flown by Sgt P.V. Ayerst on finals to land at an advanced French airfield in May 1940. This aircraft is fitted with a Watts fixed pitch wooden propeller. (*IWM*)

In Britain at the declaration of war, 111 Squadron was based at Acklington, and gained the first claim of the war when CO Sqn Ldr Harry Broadhurst shot down a He111 into the sea off Newcastle. (*Author's Collection*)

Sqn Ldr J.O.W. Oliver, 85 Squadron opened their account with a victory on 21 November 1939. 87 Squadron was split between Lille/Seclin, co-operating with the Lysanders of 2 Squadron at Senon, the commanding officer being Sqn Ldr J.S. Dewar. Although they did not see much action, nevertheless they claimed a 'kill' on 2 November.

607 and 615 Squadrons were based at Vitry-en-Artois and Abbeville respectively, 607 exchanging its Gladiators for Hurricanes from 8 April, 1939. Their only conversion training had been on a Miles Master low wing monoplane with flaps and retractable undercarriage and their only previous victory had been claimed while flying Gladiators in Britain. After four weeks of the phoney war, the pilots were hardly prepared for the

intense ten days of action which preceded the Dunkirk withdrawal. The commanding officer was Sqn Ldr L.E. Smith. 615 Squadron, commanded by Sqn Ldr J.R. Kayll, had been in the process of replacing its Gladiators with Hurricanes when the German Blitzkrieg on France commenced.

Many of the commanding officers of these units were experienced veterans of the First World War and often led their squadrons into battle although, owing to their age, they were sometimes unsuited to modern combat flying. Also, at that time there was no co-ordination of the fighter operations. Squadrons operated independently and were rarely used to escort the vulnerable bombers. While the pilots were well trained in flying skills, they were not prepared for modern warfare. The French air support was totally inadequate and, at the start, both Belgium and Holland were neutral, until invaded by the Germans. When it did finally go into action, the Belgian Air Force was equipped with a collection of mainly obsolete biplanes; however, they did have 11 Hurricanes with Escadrille 2/I/2, being the survivors of the original 20 supplied by the RAF in 1939. These insignificant forces faced a massive onslaught from the modern, combat experienced Luftwaffe, who had seen action during the Spanish Civil War.

The German offensive started on Friday 10 May with an air and ground attack on Holland, protecting the northern flank for the advances into Belgium and Northern France. The sweep through the Ardennes and Luxembourg would bypass the Maginot Line of defences, opening up the whole of Northern France.

Most of the Belgian Hurricanes were destroyed or damaged in the German attack on Schaffen-Diest on the first day of the invasion. In the air operations over Northern France, German bombers hit 47 airfields, although some escaped with only light damage. The defending RAF fighters were in action from first light, the targets being mainly unescorted He111s and Do17s. Both 1 and 73 Squadron were in action early, both sustaining and inflicting damage.

Despite RAF Blenheims going into action over Holland, the end of the first day saw large areas under German control. The first line of Belgian defence had been penetrated and Luxembourg had been occupied. RAF Hurricanes had put up an excellent defence, but there were too few to cope, and advance intelligence of attacks was non-existent. On the first day, the Hurricane squadrons claimed 60 confirmed victories, with 16 probables, and 22 damaged – mainly against light bombers and reconnaissance aircraft. The RAF had lost 15 Hurricanes with no pilots killed.

On the next day, 11 May, Bf109s and Bf110s were encountered over Holland and a dozen Hurricanes of 32 Squadron from Biggin Hill were sent to Ypenburg. 56 Squadron patrolled off the coast without sighting the enemy, but 17 Squadron flying from Martlesham Heath met with stiff opposition from Bf109s, suffering losses to both aircraft and pilots. The Northern France based Hurricane units of the AASF and Air Component meanwhile were busy defending against a number of enemy bomber attacks. A total of 55 victories were claimed for the day, although these were thought to be exaggerated, with a further five probables and six 'damaged'. The Luftwaffe losses for the day were more in the region of 34 aircraft. Losses to 11 Group Hurricane squadrons flying from bases in Britain were five aircraft, with two pilots killed and two taken prisoner. Ten of the French based Hurricanes were destroyed, but all the pilots survived, some suffering injuries.

By Sunday 12 May, German surface forces were rapidly advancing from Holland into Belgium. Hurricanes of 1 Squadron were tasked with providing defence of the vulnerable Battles, which were ordered to attack bridges vital to the German advance. Hurricanes flew to the target area beforehand and were engaged by Bf109s, while the Battles were wiped out by intense ground fire. When the German bombers went into action, the AASF and Air Component Hurricanes continued to fight back, but were too heavily outnumbered for the defence of such widespread attacks on selected targets. Overall claimed victories for the French based Hurricanes were 52 destroyed, with the Luftwaffe acknowledging about half that number. Hurricane losses were 15 aircraft, including five from 1 Squadron and four from 501 Squadron. Five pilots were killed, including one from 4(C) Flt who was involved in a flying accident.

When Germany invaded Norway in early April 1940, 46 Squadron Hurricanes joined 263 Squadron Gladiators against the German advance. The 46 Squadron Hurricanes were loaded by crane aboard HMS *Glorious* at Greenock on 10 May. (*RAF Museum*)

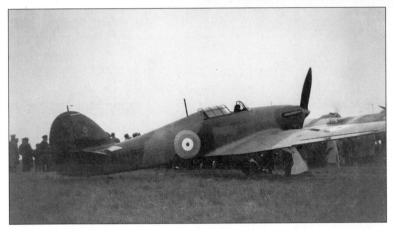

The first victory claimed in France was by Flt Lt P.P. Hanks of 1 Squadron on 30 October 1939. Hurricane I L1681 of 1 Squadron was lost in France in May 1940. (*Author's Collection*)

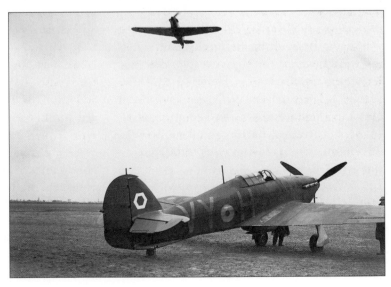

85 Squadron with the characteristic hexagon tail marking on Hurricane VY-H ready to depart from Lille with another aircraft overhead. (*IWM*)

The Air Component Hurricane units were initially based at Lille-Seclin near the Belgian border. 87 Squadron Hurricane I L1628 had to make a forced landing in Belgium and became the first Hurricane to be interned, but the pilot was returned. (*AELR Air Museum, Brussels*)

On Monday 13 May, the Germans broke through the defences at Sedan on the Belgians' southern flank and 504 Squadron moved to Lille/Marcq. All Allied resistance was being overrun in Holland, resulting in the withdrawal of the supporting British and French forces, leaving the Dutch forces to be defeated. The situation in Belgium was little better. 56 Squadron was tasked to provide cover for another Battle bombing attack, which on this occasion was reported as successful.

67 Wing AASF was very active, with both 1 and 73 Squadrons sharing the destruction of a number of He111Ps with the French. Within 60 Wing, only 85 Squadron succeeded in claiming enemy victories, with three He111Ps shot down in the Antwerp area.

Out of a patrol of three 607 Squadron Hurricanes in 61 Wing, one was shot down by Bf109s and another slightly damaged. 615 Squadron were tasked with the escort of Blenheims, one of the pilots being lost. Newcomers to the Wing were 504 Squadron, who saw little action. In 63 Wing, 3 Squadron were in combat, but 79 Squadron did not see any action. With eleven more Hurricanes lost during the day, two in accidents, and four pilots killed, a further 32 Hurricanes and pilots were allocated as replacements to the squadrons as required, nine being delivered to 73 Squadron at Rheims-Champagne.

By Tuesday 14 May, Holland was in the final stages of occupation. Rotterdam surrendered. The Belgian Air Force had ceased to exist in all but name, yet Hurricanes continued to arrive as reinforcements for the units in France. Five were flown into Merville for 615 Squadron and 607 Squadron at Vitry added seven new aircraft together with their inexperienced combat pilots. Four Canadian pilots were attached to 607 Squadron from 242 Squadron in Britain. At Merville, 3 Squadron received nine replacement pilots and aircraft, although this was rapidly reduced to eight when one was damaged during a forced landing. Six new pilots flew their Hurricanes to Lille/Seclin for 85 Squadron, but despite the new additions it was still not enough to provide protection of the airfields, and some of the discarded Gladiators were used for local defence.

The day's operations began with 504 Squadron shooting down a Ju88, and continued with 3 Squadron, which claimed one Do17 for the loss of one Hurricane with the pilot wounded in the leg. There were greater numbers of Bf109s escorting the bombers on this day and 607 Squadron, as well as 85 and 87 Squadrons, were ordered to attack a large formation of He111s escorted by many Bf109s. Three He111Hs were claimed, but four Hurricane pilots were killed. 73 Squadron was tasked with the defence of 103 Squadron Battles over Nouvion and Douzy bridges. Six Ju87Bs were shot down by Hurricanes, with a further Stuka hit by AA fire, and four Bf109s destroyed. 73 Squadron then destroyed two Stukas, and damaged two more, but two pilots were killed. 3 Squadron pilots claimed 11 Stukas, although German figures account for only eight losses. By the end of the day, 27 Hurricanes had been shot down with the death of 15 pilots and four wounded. A further two pilots had been killed in combat with bombers or by ground fire.

By Wednesday 15 May, Holland had been mostly overrun by the Germans, although there was some resistance still in Zeeland, and Antwerp was threatened, with the AASF beginning to fall back in a southerly direction. The French Prime Minister stated that the battle had been lost, but he appealed anyway for another ten Hurricane squadrons. Although the War Cabinet considered supplying them, Dowding managed to persuade them not to send any further squadrons to France, since it would leave Britain undefended in the event of the expected attack and invasion which would surely follow the fall of Northern Europe.

Meanwhile, the 67 Wing AASF Hurricane squadrons in France were mainly engaged in the protection of their own airfields. Two Bf110Cs were shot down by 73 and 1 Squadrons, with two more damaged in crash landings, but bombs fell on the 1 Squadron base at Berry-au-Bac. 61 Wing destroyed three He111Hs and 63 Wing were again in action. By the end of the day, 21 more Hurricanes had been lost, half to the Bf110 crews, and three shot down by Bf109s. Five pilots were killed and two captured, with four wounded.

Although there was still resistance in Zeeland, the main Dutch forces surrendered on 16 May. Pressure came from the British forces in France for more Hurricane units and the War Cabinet agreed that four more Hurricane squadrons should be sent immediately with two more kept at readiness. In addition, 20 experienced pilots were to be sent to France to replace tired or wounded pilots who had been in action. Quite naturally, Dowding did not welcome these new reinforcements and wrote to the Air Ministry. Following a tour of the battle area by Wg Cdr The Duke of Hamilton three days later, the decision was made to send no further Hurricanes and pilots to almost certain defeat in France.

The three 67 Wing squadrons were busy moving to other airfields, but flew some

615 Squadron converted from Gladiators to Hurricanes at Abbeville just as the German Blitzkrieg started. (*RAF Museum*)

The Belgian Air Force had 11 Hurricanes left out of the original 20 supplied from Britain when the Germans invaded on 10 May 1940. Most of the Hurricanes of 2-eme Escadrille were neatly lined up on Schaffen-Diest airfield when the enemy aircraft attacked from over the woods in the background. (*AELR Air Museum, Brussels*)

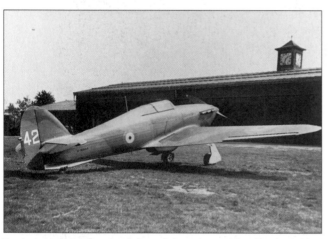

The plan had been for Hurricanes to be licence built in Belgium to follow those supplied from Britain. It appears that only a few were flight tested and one delivered to a squadron before the German invasion. H-10042 was one of these locally built Hurricanes with a Watts wooden propeller. (*AELR Air Museum, Brussels*)

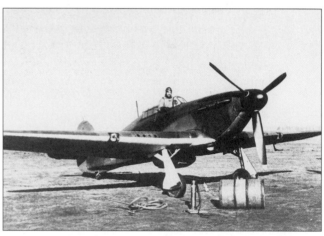

Licence built Belgian Hurricane H-10039 was the only one to be fitted with a Rotol three-blade variable pitch propeller. (*AELR Air Museum, Brussels*)

patrols. Some of the unserviceable Hurricanes had to be destroyed. 87 squadron in 60 Wing received six pilot reinforcements who were ferrying replacement Hurricanes and, as no transport was available, they joined the unit. Although a few were squadron pilots, others were straight out of training, while some had no Hurricane experience. Only two survived to return to Britain. Six 56 Squadron Hurricane reinforcements arrived at Vitry, followed by six from each of 229, 253 and 245 Squadrons. Six from 601 Squadron were attached to 3 Squadron at Merville and six more from 242 Squadron joined 85 Squadron at Lille/Seclin.

Although there were plenty of Hurricanes flowing off the production lines

On 13 May 504 Squadron moved to Lille/Marcq to escape the German advance. Aircraft operated in primitive conditions, rearming in the field. (*RAF Museum*)

in Britain, the loss of experienced pilots was becoming critical. 16 May was quieter for air combat; nevertheless, 13 Hurricanes were lost, mainly to Bf109s, with five pilots killed and one taken prisoner. Over the previous three days, 52 Hurricanes had been lost, with the deaths of 25 pilots and three taken prisoner, a rate which could not be sustained without jeopardising the defence of Britain itself.

Parts of Holland and Belgium were still resisting the German advances, but the enemy armies broke through on 17 May, separating the Allied Northern and Southern Armies. 11 Group Fighter Command had units deployed in France during the day to support the locally based units, but returned to Britain in the evening. Six Hurricanes each from 'A' Flight of 601 Squadron and 'B' Flight 213 Squadron were attached to 3 Squadron at

Merville. Abbéville was the temporary base for Hurricanes from 32 and 151 Squadrons, and flights from 111, 213 and 601 Squadrons. With the fall of Rheims, 73 and 501 Squadrons with 67 Wing evacuated Anglure, and flew to the 61 Wing airfield at Villeneuve.

1 Squadron was called into action following a report that retreating Allied troops were being attacked near Sedan. Hurricane pilots achieved three victories against Bf110Cs with one Hurricane lost, another damaged beyond repair and no loss of pilots. Most of the squadrons were by now involved in replacing exhausted pilots who needed leave, as well as lost aircraft. Hurricanes of 56 and 229 Squadrons shot down two Do17Zs near Cambrai, followed by three He111Ps by 56 Squadron near Valenciennes.

Conditions in France caused accidents to RAF Hurricanes. Hurricane I L2047, from the first production batch but with a three blade variable pitch propeller, was in operation with 87 Squadron. (*Author's Collection*)

By 14 May the Belgian Air Force had ceased to exist, the Hurricanes reduced to wreckage by the Luftwaffe. (*AELR Air Museum, Brussels*)

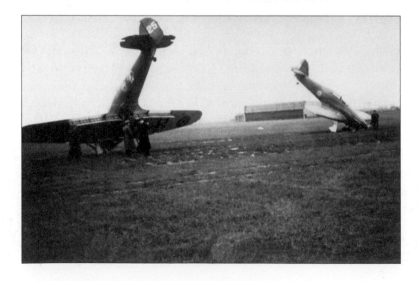

Where Belgian Air Force Hurricanes had not been destroyed by enemy action, the poor airfield conditions caused mishaps, examples being these two Hurricanes nosed over at Wevelghem. (*AELR Air Museum, Brussels*)

At the start of the Battle of Britain one of the tactics deployed by 32 Squadron was the head-on attack, which was effective in breaking up enemy formations. Hurricane I P3522 of 32 Squadron is seen at Hawkinge in July 1940 ready for the start of the Battle. (*Author's Collection*)

From their temporary base at Abbeville, 151 Squadron attacked some Ju87s, claiming four destroyed and two probables for the loss of no Hurricanes, although records later confirmed that seven Stukas were destroyed. 17 Squadron also destroyed three Ju87Bs. By the end of the day at least 16 Hurricanes had been lost, three through accidents, but no pilots were killed though one was taken prisoner. Three of the Hurricane losses had been 11 Group aircraft, one from 151 Squadron, the others from 17 Squadron.

With the main German advances on 18 May, Hurricane units withdrew from their bases. 1 Squadron went to Anglure; 73 Squadron to Gaye; 79 Squadron to Merville, where they were joined for the day by aircraft from 145 and 601 Squadron; and 253 Squadron B Flight to Lille/Marcq. In addition, 17 Squadron and flights from 111 and 213 Squadrons were also based at Lille/Marcq for the day, while 'A' Flight of 56 Squadron went to Lille/Seclin. Flights from 111 and 253 Squadrons, followed by 151 Squadron, were sent to Vitry, but following a raid the base was evacuated and most of the surviving Hurricanes returned to Britain, leaving 607 Squadron and part of 56 Squadron to fly from Norrent-Fontes. Any Hurricanes damaged beyond repair were destroyed on the ground.

Hurricane pilots claimed 57 confirmed victories, with 20 probables, although the true figure was closer to 39 German aircraft destroyed. The majority of the claims were against bombers. The Hurricanes were totally outnumbered; at least 33 were destroyed or crash landed, with seven pilots killed and a further five taken prisoner.

With the rapid German advance any unserviceable Hurricanes were destroyed and abandoned. (*AELR Air Museum Brussels*)

RAF cover of the Dunkirk evacuation included air defence patrols by Hurricanes. On the second day four Hurricanes and four Spitfires were lost, but some of the pilots were able to return by ship. Here a Hurricane has crash landed on the beach close to abandoned transports. (*AELR Air Museum, Brussels*)

Some 100 Spitfires and Hurricanes were lost during the evacuation of Dunkirk, a number crashing on the beaches. (*Author's Collection*)

On Sunday 19 May, the Germans reached Peronne with a clear run to the coast. The airfields at Lille were abandoned later in the day, and Merville now became the base for 85 and 87 Squadrons, as well as 17 and 32 Squadrons from 11 Group. 504 Squadron moved to Norrent-Fontes, where a flight of 607 Squadron was still based, and 'B' Flight of 56 Squadron returned to the UK. A composite of 111 and 253 Squadrons operated from Britain.

1 Squadron was still operating at full strength from Anglure and destroyed five He111Ps, while 73 Squadron, also at full strength, destroyed three Ju88As and damaged another. 3 Squadron took off from Merville to patrol the Lille area and during the day 14 He111Ps were shot down, with the loss of many of the crews. The Hurricane pilots had claimed 74 victories, with 25 probables, although German losses recorded were around 47. There were a total of 22

Hurricanes shot down and 13 damaged in forced landings, with eight pilots killed, three taken prisoner and seven wounded. During the fierce fighting, Hurricanes had been engaged in almost continual defence of airfields and the town of Lille.

The next day, the Germans reached the coast between Arras and the Somme, further separating the Allied Northern and Southern Armies, and Merville was evacuated, the squadrons returning to Britain. Moorsele was evacuated by 615 Squadron, which moved to Norrent-Fontes; but, by the end of the day, that also had to be abandoned, and all the serviceable Hurricanes were flown back to Britain. The only three AASF units to remain in France were 1, 73 and 501 Squadrons, who were not in action that day. At Merville, the combined 60/63 Wing had some 50 Hurricanes dispersed around the airfield following the arrival of 85 and 87 Squadrons. The Merville units saw plenty of action before returning to Britain. Within 61 Wing, 615 Squadron were very active from Norrent-Fontes with 13 Hurricanes on ground attack duties against German transport, occasioning at least seven losses to Hurricanes. At the end of the day, the serviceable aircraft were mostly flown back to Kenley. With eight Hurricanes lost, three pilots had been killed and one taken prisoner.

By Tuesday 21 May, the German armies had reached the coast in force and the British and French armies launched an armoured counterattack from the southern flank. With 67 Wing, seven new pilots arrived for 73 Squadron at Gaye. Support was also provided by 11 Group, with an uneventful patrol over France by 151 Squadron from Manston, with 17 and 32 Squadrons. 253 and 229 Squadrons were operating from Hawkinge, but encountered few enemy aircraft. Nonetheless, four more victories were confirmed for the loss of three Hurricanes, one pilot being killed and another taken prisoner.

With all the flyable aircraft evacuated from Merville, transport aircraft flew in to pick up the remaining personnel, and a couple of damaged Hurricanes were made serviceable enough to be ferried back to Britain, but much equipment had to be abandoned as the RAF presence in northern France finally came to an end.

*

A total of 452 Hurricanes had been sent to France, but only 66 returned to Britain after the withdrawal of the Air Component. 386 aircraft had been lost in all, a high rate of attrition, of which 178 were abandoned as unserviceable and destroyed by the retreating Allied forces. During the eleven days of combat between 10 and 20 May, the Air Component lost 203 Hurricanes, about half of them in combat. It is estimated that 499

victories were claimed by Hurricane pilots, with 123 probables, as against the Luftwaffe's own figures, which estimated losses at 299 with a further 65 seriously damaged. A total of 56 RAF and FAA pilots had been killed, with 18 taken prisoner and 36 wounded. As a result of this campaign, almost every one of the established Hurricane squadrons saw action in northern France, apart from 46 Squadron, which was active in Norway.

The surviving pilots had therefore gained much valuable combat experience in preparation for the ensuing Battle of Britain. Lessons had been learned about combat tactics as, to begin with, Hurricanes were being sent up in small numbers and were usually hopelessly outnumbered. The rudimentary conditions in France, with often incompetent command and lack of proper overall control, made fighting conditions difficult. The grass airfields were without proper air traffic control and lacked any form of defence against attack from the air, or ground forces. As a result, the Hurricanes were often defending their own bases against attack, instead of supporting the Allied armies or attempting to destroy enemy bombers over their targets. Although the Hurricane was later adapted with cannon to become a very effective ground attack aircraft, even against tanks, the eight Browning machine guns fitted to the earlier models were largely ineffective against ground targets, and the aircraft was vulnerable to ground fire.

The three Hurricane units with the AASF, 1, 73 and 501 Squadrons, remained with the westward retreating French army until mid-June, with new pilots being sent to replace the battle weary ones, but made little significant contribution. A gap of 30 miles separated the Northern and Southern Armies, with no hope of closing it. The Germans had control of the coastline from Gravelines to

With the fall of Reims, 73 and 501 Squadrons moved from Anglure to Villeneuve. Hurricane I L2124 from the first production batch, but with a three-blade propeller, of 501 Squadron, is being prepared for the next sortie. (*RAF Museum*)

the mouth of the Somme, and the remains of the BEF, Belgian and northern French armies were completely encircled. All air cover had to come from airfields in southern England, where there was now a growing number of Spitfire squadrons.

On 22 May, 151 Squadron claimed a Ju88 while on coastal patrol and 605 Squadron was in action near Arras, losing four Hurricanes for the destruction of three He111s. Later in the day, 32 Squadron claimed four Bf109s for the loss of one Hurricane. Near Merville, Ju87s were engaged, with the destruction of six aircraft and no loss of Hurricanes.

The next day, the RAF was able to mount better coordinated patrols, and Spitfires were in action for the first time against Bf109s and

Bf110s. Seven Hurricane units were in action, but were at a distinct disadvantage against the German fighters, losing ten aircraft, but claiming only six. The German forces were close to controlling the ports of Calais and Boulogne, while the Allied Northern Army had retreated into a perimeter around Dunkirk. Apparently, evacuation was not being given serious consideration at this stage.

Spitfires began to claim more enemy aircraft on Friday 24 May, and the Hurricanes had a quiet day, with one claim by 111 Squadron and another by 73 Squadron operating from Gaye, east of Paris. However, 73 Squadron lost two aircraft, one pilot being seriously injured, and Boulogne fell to the Germans.

The rudimentary grass airfields in France were without air traffic control and lacked any form of defence against air or ground attack. A 501 Squadron Hurricane stands out on an exposed airfield during the Battle of France, 1940. (*RAF Museum*)

The next day, 605 Squadron claimed four Ju87s over Calais, with one pilot killed, and 73 Squadron in France claimed a Do17 with one pilot taken prisoner. On Saturday 26 May, just over two weeks from the initial German advances into Holland and Belgium, the decision was taken to evacuate the Allied armies from Dunkirk. The squadrons of Fighter Command were tasked with providing air cover for this difficult operation, when 338,226 Allied troops were brought to safety across the Channel by an armada of ships of all sizes.

On the first day of the evacuation, 11 Group had seven Hurricane squadrons together with nine Spitfire units as support, initially with one squadron at a time patrolling over Dunkirk. In case of a large-scale attack by the Germans, one Hurricane and one Spitfire squadron were kept at readiness.

On 27 May the Germans attacked from the air in increasing strength and the RAF was able to claim around 16 bombers, losing four each of the Hurricanes and Spitfires. Although the bombers were able to score hits, only two ships were sunk in Dunkirk harbour. On 28 May, RAF fighter patrols were doubled in strength, but there were fewer bombers, with more Bf109s. On that day only four bombers were claimed, but so were 19 German fighters, the RAF losing 13 aircraft with five pilots saved. Owing to the RAF fighters being outnumbered, often by more than ten to one, patrols of up to four squadrons commenced on 29 May with a fresh 111 Squadron joining the battle. Operations were not generally in wings, but were in squadron pairs flying independently. On one occasion, three Hurricane squadrons, together with a squadron of Defiants, clashed with about 80 Bf109s covering a dive bombing attack by Ju87s. About 22 enemy aircraft were claimed as destroyed, for the loss of four Hurricanes, but the remaining Ju87s got through to Dunkirk, sinking five ships.

Bad weather reduced air activity on 30 and 31 May, but an attack by Ju87s on 1 June resulted in the loss of three RN destroyers loaded with troops. As an added precaution,

A Hurricane IIa with eight .303 in machine guns was kept at readiness for the defence of Langley airfield, but is reported to have seen no action. (*HSA*)

the withdrawal was confined to the hours of darkness on 2 and 3 June, but early on 2 June a raid by some 120 German aircraft was met by five Hurricane and Spitfire squadrons over Dunkirk. As a result, no serious damage was done to the shipping and this proved to be the last major raid on Dunkirk, all further attacks being by smaller numbers of Ju87s and Ju88s.

The troop withdrawal took six days, lasting until Saturday 1 June, during which time Fighter Command units claimed 258 destroyed and 119 probable enemy aircraft destroyed for the loss of some 100 Hurricanes and Spitfires. Pilot losses exceeded 50 per cent, including 12 Hurricane veterans from the fighting in France and Belgium.

The three Hurricane squadrons of the AASF were reinforced in June by 17 and 242 Squadrons. They progressively retreated from airfield to airfield providing defensive cover for evacuations from Le Havre, Cherbourg, Brest and La Rochelle until they themselves were withdrawn to Britain via the Channel Islands, ready to join the defences in the Battle of Britain. 1 Squadron was evacuated without its aircraft by sea from St Nazaire on 18 June, while 73 Squadron destroyed their surviving Hurricanes and escaped through St Malo on 17 June. 501 Squadron covered the evacuation of BEF troops from Cherbourg on 19 June, operating from Jersey, and then returned to England with eight surviving Hurricanes.

During the Battle of France some 386 Hurricanes had been lost, out of a total of 949 aircraft. Although the aircraft were being replaced, the loss of over 200 pilots, including twenty-nine squadron and flight commanders, was critical. It would take time to train their replacements.

71 (Eagle) Squadron was formed with American volunteers at Church Fenton in November 1940, Flg Off 'Red' Tobin being one of the pilots. (*Author's Collection*)

CHAPTER 4

THE BATTLE OF BRITAIN

After the First World War Britain's air defences had been largely neglected, and the Government were slow to appreciate the hostile intentions of Germany. Rearmament did not come until it was almost too late. The target strength of the RAF had included 52 fighter squadrons, but the calculations had not anticipated the fall of France, with the loss of so many pilots and aircraft, let alone the need to defend Britain subsequently. The experience of air combat in France had forced RAF commanders to improvise a more flexible form of attack, replacing the set-piece, 'follow-my-leader' approach that was a survival of the previous war. From the evacuation of Dunkirk on 3 June, however, there was a pause of about a month in the German advances, while sporadic French and Allied resistance continued in Europe. This gave the RAF a breathing space in which to evolve new tactics and training throughout Fighter Command.

On 1 July, British home territory was invaded for the first and only time by the Germans, when the Channel Islands were occupied. By this time, Fighter Command Order of Battle was 30 squadrons in 11 Group in the south of Britain, of which 17 were equipped with Hurricanes and eight with Spitfires; 12 Group north of London with 11 squadrons, three equipped with Hurricanes and five with Spitfires; and 13 Group in the north of Britain. 13 Group had a total of 17 squadrons spread from Yorkshire to Scotland, nine with Hurricanes and six with Spitfires.

At the commencement of the Battle of Britain on 8 August 1940 the balance had changed very little, with 13 Hurricane and six Spitfire squadrons in 11 Group; five Hurricane and six Spitfire squadrons in 12 Group; and nine Hurricane and three Spitfire squadrons in 13 Group. The west of Britain was defended by 10 Group with three Hurricane and four Spitfire squadrons. Many of the units in more remote locations were recent veterans of the fighting in France, taking the opportunity to bring in new replacement pilots and train them for combat. However 1, 32, 79, 85, 501, 615 Squadrons and a number of other combat experienced units were in 11 Group, ready to use their skills to defend London and the South-East from attack. The experienced pilots were distributed amongst the key Sector airfields of Biggin Hill, North Weald, Kenley and Northolt to help develop and try new tactics amongst the less experienced pilots.

The majority of the Fighter Command squadrons were equipped with Hurricanes, which outnumbered all the other aircraft types combined. This was also true of the strategically placed 11 Group, led by Air Vice-Marshal Keith Park, which was deployed in the front line across the south of England, facing the anticipated German onslaught. It was not just the strength on paper that was critical, but also the state of readiness. The serviceability rate for Hurricane units was around 75 per cent, even though about 100 of the aircraft had seen combat in France. The Spitfires had only been in operation over Dunkirk but had an availability rate of just 72 per cent.

In July 1940, 85 Squadron based at Castle Camps was active in the Battle. A group of pilots relax by a Hurricane fitted with a deflector to avoid glare from the exhaust when flying at night. (*RAF Museum*)

Although the Spitfire was more advanced than the Hurricane, it did require special maintenance support, whereas the rugged Hurricane was more readily available for combat. The Hurricane could absorb battle damage, land at primitive forward airfields, and be ready to return to operations quickly after rudimentary repairs. Although it was slower than the Spitfire, and soon to be outperformed by the enemy, it was a well established, tried and tested fighter with good manoeuvrability.

Amongst new tactics developed by Sqn Ldr John Worrall, CO of 32 Squadron, was to open the attack with a head-on charge, which had the effect of breaking up the enemy bomber formations. A less gung-ho approach was generally adopted towards the end of the Battle of Britain, of a paired aircraft combat unit, with the number two covering the leader's tail.

The RAF had a total of 905 fighter aircraft available for the defence of Britain, including Hurricanes, Spitfires, Blenheims and Defiants, the latter two types being largely outperformed by the enemy. Amongst the immediate reserves held at MUs were 92 Hurricanes and, if needed desperately, a further 38 single seater fighters, including Gladiators, were with Group fighter pools and station flights for local air defence.

Pilot numbers were critical following the loss of so many experienced aircrew in France. Although a total of 1,103 were listed with the squadrons, only about 820 were combat ready, the remainder being brought up to the required standard with the squadrons. Operational training units (OTUs) were producing about 20 new Hurricane pilots each week, but because newer versions were being issued to the combat units, the training organization was using the early production batch with Merlin II engines, wooden propeller, fabric covered wings and ring-and-bead gun sights. As a result, when the new pilots joined the squadron they had to be converted to the later standard of Hurricane with variable pitch propeller and reflector gun sight, as well as learning how to operate the aircraft in combat.

Normally a squadron would have a minimum strength of 18 operational pilots, but during the Battle it was often less. The situation reached crisis levels during early September when pilot losses reached the equivalent of two squadrons every day. By this stage, training courses at OTUs had been so shortened that pilots were arriving on squadrons with less than 20 hours on Hurricanes or Spitfires, learning to fly their aircraft operationally from the first sortie.

The Luftwaffe commenced hostilities against Britain at the beginning of July, with a small number of probing sorties along the east coast of England to test the defences. Goering had given them the task of denying the Channel to Allied shipping, and of discouraging the Royal Navy from using the bases from Dover round to Plymouth. Ju87 Stukas and Do17 bombers were used to attack shipping in the Channel. This gave the Luftwaffe crews the opportunity to train on over-water flying, and hopefully, from the German point of view, tied up RAF pilots on defensive convoy patrols.

The first actual attack on a convoy in the Channel came on 7 July approaching the Isle of Wight, where 145 Squadron were on standing patrol. They shot down one Do17P. Soon afterwards, 43 Squadron took over and accounted for a further Do17P, followed by another 'kill' for 601 Squadron. A total of seven German bombers were claimed during the day for the loss of one Hurricane and five Spitfires, mainly to Bf109Es. While the German bombers were threatening the approaching convoys, free-ranging Bf109s were able to pick off Hurricanes and Spitfires at their most vulnerable, when they were either returning short of fuel or getting airborne for the next patrol.

On the second day, Park tried to ensure that the RAF fighters were not sent to defend convoys when there was a chance of German free rangers being encountered. However, with Luftwaffe units based just across the Channel, even if no attackers were detected on radar, they could very quickly appear. Hurricanes claimed two bombers, one each over the coasts of Sussex and Yorkshire, but two Hurricanes and two Spitfires were lost with their pilots. During the first ten days of combat the Hurricane pilots claimed 13 bombers, seven fighters and one reconnaissance aircraft, with the loss of eight aircraft and five pilots, one of whom was Sqn Ldr Joslin, CO of 79 Squadron.

On 10 July, the RAF was involved in the heaviest dogfight to date when 22 Hurricanes of 32, 56 and 111 Squadrons, plus eight Spitfires of 74 Squadron, did battle against a force of Do17s, Bf110s and Bf109s over a convoy off the Kent coast. This was the first time 111 Squadron used the head-on attack to break up a bomber formation.

Channel convoys continued to be attacked throughout July, with Hurricane pilots gaining some victories. Eight He111s and three Bf110s were claimed on 11 July by 145, 238 and 601 Squadrons with the loss of two Hurricanes, both pilots being rescued. On 13 July, the Hurricanes of 43, 56 and 238 Squadrons claimed two Do17s, a Ju88, Bf110 and a Bf109, for the loss of three aircraft and pilots during an attack on a convoy in the Channel. On 19 July, Hurricanes of 111 Squadron went to the aid of 141 Squadron Defiants which were being attacked by Bf109Es, allowing the surviving four Defiants to escape. On 29 July, Dover harbour became the object of attack by nearly 50 Ju87s,

601 Squadron claimed a third Do17 during convoy air defence over the Channel. Hurricanes of 601 Squadron are refuelling at Tangmere with the pilots ready to go. (*C.E. Brown*)

Even early in the Battle active units had to be withdrawn to less hectic areas to allow replacement pilots to be trained while defending against attacks from northern Europe. One of these units was 111 Squadron, with Hurricane Mk Is at Wick, early 1940. (*Author's Collection*)

escorted by about 80 Bf109s. Spitfires of 41 Squadron were ordered into the air from Manston, joined by the Hurricanes from 501 Squadron at Hawkinge, resulting in four Stukas being shot down.

Since June it had been realized that the fast and heavily armed Bf110 could be tackled successfully by Hurricanes. When threatened, the Bf110 formations would form a defensive circle, so that each aircraft covered the tail of the one in front, while they gradually orbited towards home or into cloud. The Hurricane pilots could use their greater manoeuvrability to advantage and make attacks from various angles, avoiding the forward firing guns of the Bf110s. During the first month of combat over Britain, Hurricane pilots claimed 87 enemy aircraft shot down, out of a total of 187, with a loss of 40 Hurricanes and 16 pilots killed.

Because of the pressure of combat, heavy losses and pilot fatigue, a number of active squadrons had had to be withdrawn to less hectic airfields in the northern part of Britain, where replacement pilots could be trained while defending against possible attacks from northern Europe. The German units meanwhile were operating over hostile territory and, while their aircraft losses were only about half those of the RAF, aircrew losses were up to seven times those of the Allies. While Spitfire squadrons were struggling to maintain pilot strength, Hurricane units were managing better. The numbers were further boosted by volunteers from the FAA, and the arrival of Czech, Polish, Canadian and American volunteer pilots, as well as the formation of the first RCAF squadron, all of whom were flying Hurricanes. However, overall strength of Fighter Command was only about 75 per cent of the numbers that appeared on paper, while the main battle was still to be fought and won.

303 Squadron was the second unit to be formed with Polish volunteers, at Northolt on 2 August 1940. (*J.B. Cynk*)

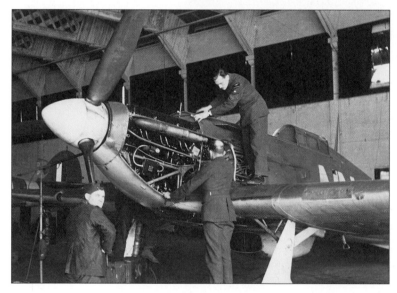

After the first month of combat in the Battle, additional Hurricane units were manned by Allied volunteers. Among the Czech units was 310 Squadron, which became operational at Duxford on 10 July 1940. (*Author's Collection*)

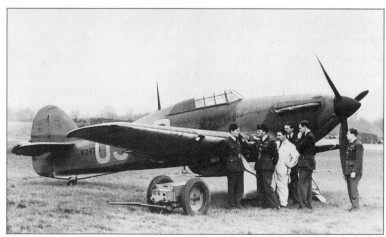

56 Squadron were again involved in combat over the Channel on 13 July claiming some victories. Hawker built Hurricane I N2479 is seen during 1940. (*Author's Collection*)

The first RCAF unit, 401 Squadron, was formed from 1 Squadron RCAF at Middle Wallop on 20 June 1940 with Hurricane Mk Is. A group of pilots 'scramble' for the photographer, to their Hurricanes. (*Air Ministry*)

During the first week in August the German forces consolidated, preparing as it seemed for the expected assault on Britain. And, with the diversion of the convoys from the Channel to the western ports, and the consequent removal of the escorting RN ships away from the southern ports, some pressure was taken off the RAF fighters. This lull in the fighting allowed some further Hurricane units to be formed, including the second Polish squadron, No 303, at Northolt. Because 11 Group was becoming too large to maintain control, two sectors were allocated to the new 10 Group covering the South-West of Britain.

On 8 August, the Luftwaffe recommenced attacks with orders to destroy the RAF in the air and on the ground in preparation for an air and sea invasion to be launched within the month. Goering was convinced that Fighter Command had been fatally weakened during July and sent bombers over to attack the southern airfields and radar installations. He was not expecting heavy losses. The aircraft most often allocated to this task was the vulnerable, though accurate, Ju87, covered by a fighter escort. The designated fighters were the Bf110s, but in turn they required the support of the shorter endurance Bf109s, which were unable to stay over the targets long enough to be effective.

In early August an attempt was made to take a convoy of 20 unladen merchant ships from the Thames estuary to load in western ports. The convoy was detected by German radar near Calais on 7 August and attacked by Ju87s covered by Bf110s and Bf109s. The RAF shield consisted of 18 Hurricanes of 145, 238 and 257 Squadrons, with 609 Squadron Spitfires. The RAF fighters dived through the German escort and shot down two of the Stukas before being engaged. A further Ju87, a BF110 and three Bf109s were claimed for the loss of three Hurricanes. Four ships were sunk, however, and seven damaged. A second enemy attack was mounted when, as before, the Hurricanes of 43 and 145 Squadrons were in good position above and attacked out of the sun. Total losses to the enemy were 10 Ju87s, four Bf110s, 11 Bf109s and one He59, but 12 Hurricane pilots were killed, with 14 aircraft lost. Only four of the ships escaped damage by that evening.

On 11 August, German tactics changed to fly sweeps from the Thames estuary to the Dorset coast, hoping to catch RAF fighters in transit to or from a patrol. Park's controllers provided support to these vulnerable formations, with additional Spitfire squadrons carrying plenty of fuel and ammunition. A major raid was directed at Portland on 11 August and more than 70 fighters were put in the air from 10 and 11 Groups to cover Portland harbour and the airfields at Tangmere and Warmwell. Hurricanes of 1, 87, 145, 213, 238 and 601 Squadrons were joined by Spitfires of 152 and 609 Squadrons over Weymouth Bay, meeting the German fighters ahead of the bombers. The enemy tactics worked well: 16 Hurricanes were shot down with the loss of 13 pilots, 145 Squadron losing four further aircraft. Enemy losses to Hurricanes totalled 18 aircraft, casualties including three senior officers of the German bomber force. This loss resulted in an order for German fighters in future to stay as close escort to the bombers, limiting their freedom to pursue the attacking fighters.

Allied radar was having increasing success at predicting the build-up of enemy raids over the French coast, enabling the RAF fighters to scramble early and so gain a height advantage. The coastal radar stations now became priority German targets. On 12 August four Bf110s attacked the radar stations at Dover, Rye, Pevensey and the English Dunkirk and damaged three of the installations. Although they were operational again by the same afternoon, it was just long enough for the Germans. With the RAF relatively blind, a large fleet of bombers was assembled over France, while an advance raid severely damaged the airfields at both Lympne and Hawkinge. The major bombing raid was picked up late by Ventnor radar as it approached the Isle of Wight. The bomber group split into two at the last minute, one formation heading for Portsmouth, the other for Ventnor radar itself.

Brand and Park ordered 48 Hurricanes of 145, 213 and 257 Squadrons into the air, together with ten Spitfires of 266 Squadron. RAF squadrons were ordered to attack in waves to spread the risk and were able to combat the circling Bf110s, with the Ju88s being fired on by the AA guns at Portsmouth. The Bf109s were still too far away to offer protection, and Hurricanes shot down 10 Ju88s over Portsmouth, while 615 Squadron Hurricanes were able to shoot down two of the approaching Bf109s before they could come to the aid of the departing enemy bombers. German losses totalled 11 Ju88s, five Bf110s and four Bf109s, but Portsmouth dockyard was severely damaged and Ventnor radar was out of operation for three days. 145 squadron lost three more pilots and Hurricanes, bringing the squadron's casualties since the beginning of the month to 11 pilots killed and 13 Hurricanes lost. There was no alternative for 145 squadron but to withdraw to Drem for rest and training of replacements.

Although Ju87s had suffered heavy losses earlier in August, they were to return in strength for the start of the 'softening up'

With a change of German tactics on 11 August, a major raid was directed at Portland, Tangmere and Warmwell. Among the defenders was 1 Squadron, a tidy formation of Mk IIcs being seen after the Battle. (*RAF Museum*)

phase in preparation for the planned invasion. To have the greatest effect, the Stukas were to attack in three separate *Luftflotten* from bases as far apart as Norway and the Brest peninsula, in an attempt to overwhelm Fighter Command defences. For this attack the weather needed to be perfect, and 13 August was the chosen day, although the main raid had to be postponed until the afternoon. Some bombers, however, had taken off unescorted in the morning and could not be recalled. Instead of a coordinated attack, a number of isolated raids developed, including one which severely damaged Eastchurch airfield. Five Do17s were shot down, all by Hurricanes, one of them an experimentally armed 151 Squadron aircraft with two 20 mm cannons under the wings.

In the afternoon the main force of over 300 enemy aircraft crossed the Channel along a front about 40 miles wide, flying over the English coast to the west of the Isle of Wight. At the same time, Bf109s were sent on free chases to attempt to draw away the RAF fighters. Fortunately, the Bf109s were at their extreme range and departed before interception, but they had alerted the defending controllers. The OC of 10 Group, Brand was able to scramble seven squadrons deploying over 90 fighters from Warmwell, Exeter, Middle Wallop and Tangmere to meet the incoming attack. On arrival at the coast the enemy formation split into three, one group flying up the Solent towards Southampton. Several Ju88s attempted a raid on Portland, but 213 and 601 Squadron Hurricanes shot down three of the Bf110 escort and the Ju88s jettisoned their bombs and headed for home. The third element made for the airfields at Warmwell and Middle Wallop but, with the escorts already departed, the damage they did was negligible.

When an empty convoy of ships attempted to escape from the Thames Estuary in early August 1940, 43 Squadron were involved in defence against German raiders. Hurricane IIcs are seen at Tangmere after the Battle in August 1942. (*RAF Museum*)

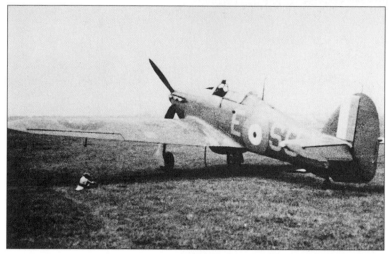

145 Squadron Hurricanes were also involved in attempting to defend the convoy from the Thames Estuary in August. One of their Mk Is is seen in mid-1940. Only four of the original 20 ships escaped damage. (*RAF Museum*)

A Hurricane of 213 Squadron being rearmed earlier in the Battle at Biggin Hill, June 1940. This unit was also part of the air defence force protecting the south coast and RAF airfields. (*IWM*)

Pilots of 601 RAuxAF Hurricanes relax between sorties on one of the often muddy airfields during the Battle of Britain. (*Author's Collection*)

However, in the late afternoon, 40 Ju87s escorted by free chasing Bf109s struck at RAF Detling, causing extensive damage and killing 67 personnel, including the station commander. It was fortunate that Detling was not part of the fighter defences, as 22 aircraft were destroyed, as well as three messes, hangars and the operations block.

Despite, or perhaps because of, the lack of coordination of this, the first all-out Luftwaffe attack on Britain, losses on both sides were fairly heavy. 15 German bombers were shot down by 12 Hurricanes and three Spitfires, six Ju87s were shot down by Spitfires, 15 Bf110s were claimed by 12 Hurricanes, a Spitfire and ground defences, and nine Bf109s were destroyed by two Hurricanes and seven Spitfires. Fighter Command lost 12 Hurricanes, with three

pilots killed and three badly injured, and one Spitfire.

The next day, Hurricanes shot down two He111s, two Ju87s and four Bf109s for the loss of four aircraft. An opportunity was taken to rearrange the defences of Fighter Command, with 238 Squadron Hurricanes moved from Middle Wallop to St Eval to help cover the western approaches. Their place was taken at Middle Wallop by 249 Squadron, which flew in Hurricanes from Church Fenton.

*

If the deadline for the planned invasion was to arrive before the unpredictable Autumn weather set in, the main assault had to follow immediately. Dowding and his squadrons were as ready as they could be to meet the onslaught. There was unease among the aircrew of the Luftwaffe, however. Their bomber formations were still vulnerable to British fighters, and were not being adequately protected by the short-range Bf109s and Bf110s. German fighter pilots felt unnecessarily restricted by the order to fly close escort, and their endurance was not sufficient to give full protection. The Ju87 Stukas had already sustained heavy losses and were proving vulnerable for the first time, as never before had they been faced with such an effective air defence

Thursday 15 August was codenamed by the Germans *Adler Tag* – Eagle Day, and it was to involve the Scandinavian based German bombers, as well as French based squadrons. Hawkinge in Kent was the first target, around midday, when a force of about 50 Ju87s supported by Bf109s attacked. Initial defence was by 501 Squadron Hurricanes, which shot down two Ju87s, but lost two aircraft to the Bf109s. Then, three more Ju87s were destroyed by Spitfires. The Ju87s also caused considerable damage at Lympne, but no aircraft were caught on the ground at either airfield.

Up to this time, 10 and 11 Groups had borne the brunt of the defence, but now the squadrons further north would play a role, even though they were supposedly on 'rest'. A force of some 63 He111s with an escort of 21 Bf110s was detected crossing the North Sea approaching the Firth of Forth, turning south when 50 miles out towards Newcastle and Sunderland. They were successfully intercepted by 18 Hurricanes from 79 and 605 Squadrons and Spitfires from 72 Squadron based at Drem and Acklington. The Luftwaffe lost eight He111s, of which four were shot down by Hurricanes, and seven Bf110s, three destroyed by Hurricanes.

Another incoming raid was detected approaching the Humber, and a dozen each of Hurricanes and Spitfires of 73 and 616 Squadrons were scrambled from Leconfield and Church Fenton. The enemy force proved to be about 50 unescorted Ju88s from Aalborg in Denmark, their target the bomber base at Driffield, where ten Whitleys were destroyed on the ground. As the Ju88s departed, they were bounced by the fighters, with five claimed by Hurricanes and another two by Spitfires, two other Ju88s being so badly damaged that they later crashed. Neither of these northern raids resulted in losses to Fighter Command.

The emphasis then returned to the South, where a major attack put Martlesham Heath out of action for two days. Hurricanes of 1 and 17 Squadrons provided the defences, but three were shot down by escorting Bf109s.

A further raid started building in the South-East, with nearly 90 Do17s escorted by some 130 Bf109s detected approaching Deal, supported by 60 Bf109s on free chases over Kent. 24 Hurricanes and 12 Spitfires were already airborne and directed towards the enemy, with another 40 or so Hurricanes scrambled from Croydon and Biggin Hill as additional support. The bomber formation was so well protected that only two Do17s were shot down, and the formation split into two, one group seriously damaging the Short Bros aircraft factory at Rochester and the other attacking the airfield at Eastchurch.

Meanwhile, two more raids were in progress over southern Britain. Some 60 Ju88s escorted by 40 Bf110s attacked Middle Wallop and Worthy Down at about 1800 hrs and, again, Portland was the target for 40 Ju87s, escorted by 20 Bf110s and 60 Bf109s. The raiders were driven off by around 56 Hurricanes of 43, 87, 213, 249 and 601 Squadrons, as well as 24 Spitfires of 234 and 609 Squadrons.

A final raid worth mentioning was on Croydon Aerodrome by 15 Bf110s and eight

During August 257 'Burma' Squadron was active in the Battle operating from Debden, Martlesham Heath and North Weald. The unit's Hurricanes are on approach after returning from another raid. (*Author's Collection*)

Sqd Ldr Bob Stanford-Tuck was CO of 257 'Burma' Squadron when the unit took part in the great battle for the defence of London on 15 September 1940. (*Air Ministry*)

87 Squadron Hurricanes led by Sqn Ldr Ian Gleed were also directed into attack enemy raiders approaching Portland on 11 August. (*Author's Collection*)

On 'Eagle Day', 15 August, 601 Squadron Hurricanes provided the initial defence of Hawkinge, which was attacked by Ju87s escorted by Bf109s. 601 Squadron pilots run to their aircraft for another scramble while the ground crew start engines. (*IWM*)

In an effort to saturate RAF defences, the Luftwaffe attacked from a number of directions on 'Eagle Day'. Hurricanes of 79 and 605 Squadrons intercepted a raid across the North Sea towards Newcastle. A flight of Hurricane IIbs of 79 Squadron is seen here after the Battle of Britain. (*IWM*)

Hawker built Hurricane Mk I N2358 of 17 Squadron at Debden in August 1940 with Plt Off Stevens and his ground crew before the pilot climbs aboard. (*Author's Collection*)

Although of poor quality this is a rare photo of 249 Squadron Hurricane Mk Is taking off from North Weald in September 1940. The squadron also participated in actions on 'Eagle Day'. (*Author's Collection*)

On 24 August RAF fighter airfields became prime Luftwaffe targets with 151 Squadron scrambling from North Weald to claim four He111s. In 1941 the unit moved to Wittering equipped with Hurricane Mk IIcs. (*Author's Collection*)

Duxford was the main sector airfield for 12 Group. Sqn Ldr Douglas Bader, CO of 242 Squadron, believed the best method of attack was with large fighter wings, which often took too long to form up ready for attack. He is flying the lead aircraft in this distant shot. (*IWM*)

On 18 August Hurricanes of 43 Squadron 'The Fighting Cocks' were engaged in the defence of Poling radar. Some of the pilots position the insignia on a Hurricane Mk II after the Battle. (*IWM*)

An unsuccessful attempt was made by the Luftwaffe to overwhelm the RAF fighter defences on 13 August. 601 RAuxAF Squadron was among the defending units scoring victories and helping to minimize damage to airfields. (*HSA*)

Bf109s, just as 111 Squadron was taking off. 32 Squadron Hurricanes were quickly on the scene from Biggin Hill, attacking the enemy, despite considerable damage and casualties on and around the airfield. The Bf109s had to break off owing to shortage of fuel and the Bf110s formed a defensive circle, breaking away individually and becoming prey to Hurricanes.

In this important day for the German air attack, when around 70 per cent of Allied Fighter Command pilots were in action at least once and some units flew up to four combat sorties, German losses were 64 aircraft. Hurricanes claimed 41 victories, Spitfires 16 and other defences the remainder. RAF losses in the air amounted to 17 Hurricanes, with seven pilots killed and two

taken prisoner in France, plus 11 Spitfires. For the first time, however, the German High Command was aware that it had not, and now probably could not, shatter the Allied air defence of Britain. *Adler Tag* was to prove a decisive turning point in the Battle.

*

Although serious damage had been inflicted by enemy bombers on ports, airfields and aircraft factories, Fighter Command had been able to meet all the threats from one end of Britain to the other. The Luftwaffe belief that the entire RAF fighter defence was concentrated in southern England was to prove a costly mistake, with many experienced German aircrew killed that day.

Luftwaffe pressure continued the next day, but a further 50 German aircraft were shot down, 19 by Hurricanes, 20 by Spitfires and 11 to other defences, on widespread raids against a number of airfields. RAF losses amounted to 11 Hurricanes with four pilots killed, one of whom was the first American volunteer to be lost from 601 Squadron, plus ten Spitfires with the loss of another four pilots.

One noteworthy engagement on this day involved three Hurricanes of 249 Squadron, led by Flt Lt James Nicholson, who approached a raid building up over Gosport. As they were about to attack the Bf110s, they were bounced by Bf109s from behind and two of the Hurricanes were set ablaze. One pilot baled out, but Nicholson pressed his attack on a Bf110 before baling out with extensive burns to his face and hands. Both pilots were fired on and hit by local land forces as they descended by parachute. The other pilot was shot dead but Nicholson survived and, after a long stay in hospital, was awarded the Victoria Cross. This was the only Fighter Command VC award but, sadly, Nicholson was later to die in the war in Asia.

After a relatively quiet day on 17 August, more major raids were detected on the 18th, with heavy attacks along the south coast to overwhelm the RAF defences. Once again, airfields were the prime targets, with Biggin Hill and Kenley singled out for attention by a large force of He111s, Ju88s and Do17s, supported by free ranging Bf109s. Ten Hurricanes were destroyed on the ground at Kenley, and a further five which managed to take off were intercepted by Bf109s.

Despite standing patrols being ordered to cover the airfields while hostile raiders were over Britain, Croydon was hit again, and West Malling, which was not yet operational. A formation detected approaching the Isle of Wight had the Poling radar site and the airfields at Thorney Island, Gosport and Ford as targets. Hurricanes of 43 and 601 Squadrons were well placed to cover the attack on the radar station, although it was put out of action for a week, and succeeded in destroying five Ju87s, while the Spitfires of 234 Squadron kept the Bf109s busy. A further 13 Ju87s were shot down by Spitfires of 152 and 602 Squadrons. Total German losses that day were 66 aircraft, 32 to Hurricanes, 29 to Spitfires and the remainder to other defences. Fighter Command lost 36 Hurricanes, including those destroyed on the ground, with eight pilots killed, and six Spitfires, with one pilot lost. Fortunately, it was not too difficult to replace the destroyed Hurricanes from RAF stocks, and seven of the damaged Hurricanes were repaired and later returned to service. It was becoming harder, though, to replace the pilots.

For the Luftwaffe, the losses were causing even greater concern. The Ju87 was proving too vulnerable, with nearly 25 per cent destroyed and 136 aircrew killed, a rate of attrition which meant that the Stuka force would have ceased to exist by mid-September. As a result, they were withdrawn from operations where fighter opposition would be encountered. The slow-flying BF110s, too, were suffering unacceptable losses. In a period of ten days in August, 86 BF110s, with many experienced aircrew, had been shot down. The aircraft's operational role therefore changed from vulnerable escort to fighter-bomber, leaving more of their protective shield of Bf109s for free ranging sorties.

Despite the ferocious air battles between 8 and 18 August, amid exaggerated claims of RAF losses, the Luftwaffe still could not detect any weakening in the Fighter Command defences. Allied fighter aircraft stocks were constantly being replenished by the factories working round the clock. Pilot numbers were swelled by volunteers from the FAA, and some of the surviving Battle pilots

On the day after 'Eagle Day', Flt Lt James Nicholson became the only Fighter Command pilot to be awarded the Victoria Cross. (*Author's Collection*)

On 'Eagle Day' Martlesham Heath was put out of action for two days with Hurricanes of 1 and 17 Squadrons providing defence. Hawker built Hurricane Mk I P3395 of 1 Squadron is seen in a typical dispersal at Wittering, after the Battle in November 1940. (*IWM*)

were retrained to operate Hurricanes. Dowding's view was that, if losses did not exceed the average rate for July to the middle of August, it should be possible to hold the Luftwaffe at bay until the poorer Autumn weather set in.

Coincidentally, due to a period of bad weather there was relatively little air combat from 19 to 23 August, allowing redeployment of some RAF squadrons. Meanwhile, the Luftwaffe was also taking advantage of the opportunity to replace lost aircrew and take stock, with operational priority still being given to the destruction of the fighter airfields and aircraft factories. Bf109s were taken off close escort duties and allocated to offensive sweeps in greater strength to destroy Fighter Command in the air and on the ground. This

was the move most feared by Dowding and his Group and Sector commanders.

The new pattern of attacks started on 24 August with the key Spitfire airfield at Hornchurch one of the day's main targets. Manston was attacked by Ju88s and overall losses to the vulnerable Defiants was so great that they were withdrawn from day fighting. North Weald was also hit, but 151 Squadron Hurricanes were able to scramble in time to claim four He111s. The enemy lost 18 aircraft during the day, with ten Hurricanes shot down and two pilots killed. Spitfires claimed four Bf109s for the loss of six aircraft, and no pilot losses.

The next day, the Luftwaffe tactic of flying free rangers along the south coast did not attract RAF fighters as usual. They were

56 Squadron was also in action against an unescorted formation of He111 bombers on 29 August. Squadron aircraft operated from North Weald in July 1940. (*IWM*)

253 Squadron was in fighter-to-fighter combat with about 90 Bf109s on 29 August, led by Sqn Ldr Tom Gleave. (*RAF Museum*)

The climax of the Battle came on 7 September when German attacks were aimed at London in an effort to lure into the air and destroy as many RAF fighters as possible. Among 21 RAF fighter Squadrons scrambled was 253 Squadron, their Mk IIs including Hawker built Z3971. (*Author's Collection*)

Hurricanes of 257 'Burma' Squadron based at North Weald, led by Sqn Ldr Tuck, were in action against Luftwaffe bombers on 7 September. The Docks were well alight before it was realised that London was the target. (*Author's Collection*)

Hurricanes of 303 Polish Squadron based at Northolt in early September 1940 were scrambled to meet the enemy bombers over the Capital on 7 September. Hawker built Mk I P3700 at Northolt. (*J.B. Cynk*)

Among the 14 Hurricane and seven Spitfire squadrons defending London on 7 September was 310 (Czech) Squadron. This Hurricane crash landed after a mid-air collision near Duxford on 29 October. (*Author's Collection*)

being held on the ground in readiness for later attacks, the major one that eventually came being on Warmwell. During the day 14 enemy aircraft were shot down by Hurricanes for the loss of eight aircraft and five pilots, while Spitfires accounted for seven enemy aircraft. 32 Squadron was now so reduced in strength that it was ordered north to rest and re-equip. With the deaths of ten pilots, nine others wounded and one taken prisoner, Fighter Command had lost the equivalent of two squadrons in two days.

On 26 August, although damage to ground installations was reduced, Fighter Command losses continued to rise. 15 Hurricanes were shot down with the death of one pilot, as well as nine Spitfires with three pilots lost. Nine RAF pilots had also been wounded. German losses amounted to 34 aircraft. And, as their operations were over hostile territory, the aircrew were all invariably lost to the Luftwaffe through either being killed or taken prisoner.

There had also been conflict between Park in 11 Group and his immediate neighbour to the north, Leigh-Mallory, who headed 12 Group from his main sector station at Duxford. Whenever Park's airfields to the north of London were being attacked, 11 Group called for support from 12 Group. However, Leigh-Mallory believed the best method of attack was in large numbers with the squadrons formed as wings. It took so long to get these airborne and formed up that by the time the wing was ready to counter-attack, the enemy aircraft were usually on their way home, having done their damage. It was also difficult to coordinate a wing formation made up of a mix of Hurricane and Spitfire squadrons. If 11 Group had attempted to form defensive wings, it would have left the airfields vulnerable, while the

504 Squadron was also in action over London on 7 September. Gloster built Hurricane Mk I P3174 is ready for engine start. (*Author's Collection*)

The Italian Air Force was involved only once in a direct attack on Britain and was met by Hurricanes of 17, 46 and 257 Squadrons. During the Battle 17 Squadron were based at Debden and one of the aircraft used by the unit was Hurricane Mk I P3878, seen ready for action. (*RAF Museum*)

Front line units of 10, 11 and 12 Groups were sent 'on rest' for retraining and defence of northern Britain. 245 squadron operated Hurricane Mk Is from Belfast Aldergrove, one of the aircraft being Gloster built W9200. (*RAF Museum*)

257 'Burma' Squadron were the first RAF unit to be in action against the Italian Air Force at the end of the Battle of Britain, and also took part in the culmination of the Battle on 15 September when 185 enemy aircraft were destroyed. (*Air Ministry*)

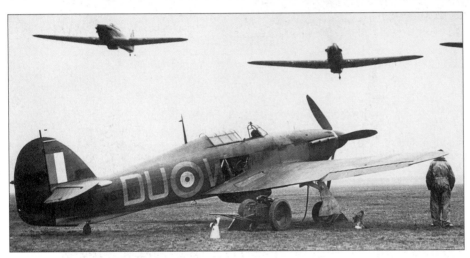

312 (Czech) Squadron formed at Duxford on 29 August 1940 in time to participate in the final stages of the Battle. Gloster built Mk I V6935 is seen here at Speke in late 1940. (*Author's Collection*)

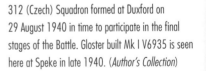

The first of three American volunteer units, 71 'Eagle' Squadron was formed at Kirton-in-Lindsey on 19 September 1940, just as the Battle was coming to a close. The unit was ready to commence operations in February 1941. (*IWM*)

Sqn Ldr Peter Townsend was CO of 85 Squadron and leads this squadron formation in late 1940, after the Battle. (*IWM*)

87 Squadron based at Colerne in February 1941 was allocated to night fighter duties using black painted Hurricanes but without the assistance of AI radar. (*Author's Collection*)

After the Battle of Britain, the Luftwaffe commenced night bombing raids on London and other major industrial centres. 85 Squadron was faced with locating targets without the aid of AI radar. One of their matt black painted Hurricane Mk Is is ready for the next operation. (*IWM*)

After the Battle of Britain, Hurricanes continued to operate from Britain increasingly on fighter ground attack duties with the faster Spitfires used for air defence. 615 Squadron were based at Kenley in the early part of 1941 and Hurricane II Z2703 carries the presentation markings of nearby Croydon. (*IWM*)

In addition to two Polish squadrons formed during the Battle of Britain, two more Polish units were equipped with Hurricanes, including 306 Squadron with Hurricane Mk Is at Church Fenton on 28 August 1941. Gloster built Mk I V7118:UZ-V is nearest. (*IWM*)

Before entry into service of AI radar equipped Beaufighters, a number of Hurricane units were allotted to night defence. 3 Squadron with cannon armed Hurricane Mk IIcs based at Hunsdon in the Autumn of 1941 for night fighter and ground attack duties, one of the aircraft being Hawker built BD867. (*IWM*)

With RAF air superiority after the Battle of Britain there was time for the formal fighter line-ups. 174 Squadron equipped with Hurricane IIbs at Manston on 3 March 1942, seen in the fighter-bomber role. (*Author's Collection*)

large formation lacked the desired flexibility. As a result the 11 Group airfields often sustained greater damage than necessary, even though Leigh-Mallory claimed to be destroying some of the raiders.

Thanks to poor weather conditions, 27 August was quiet but, on the following day, an attack was detected approaching the Thames Estuary, splitting into two and making Rochford and Eastchurch the targets. Assuming that the Kent based fighters would go after the departing bombers, a series of free ranging Bf109s flew in over Kent with numerous dogfights breaking out. Out of 28 German aircraft shot down, 15 were Bf109s, for the loss of six Hurricanes with one pilot killed, and seven Spitfires with four pilots lost.

There was more heavy fighting on 29 August, mainly involving fighter to fighter combat, with nine Bf109s claimed for the loss of six Hurricanes and three Spitfires. In view of this rate of attrition, attempts were made the next day to avoid engaging the enemy

fighters and concentrate instead on hostile bombers. Hurricanes of 1, 56 and 242 Squadrons intercepted a formation of He111s north of London after the escort had to return home. A section of four Hurricanes of 253 Squadron led by Sqn Ldr Tom Gleave was vectored against what was believed to be a large bomber raid, but on climbing through cloud found the enemy formation consisted of about 90 Bf109s. Gleave managed to destroy at least three of the Bf109s, but his three colleagues were shot down, two being killed. At the end of the day the claims by the fighters were 16 bombers, of which 12 were shot down by Hurricanes, six Bf110s all destroyed by Hurricanes and 16 Bf109s, also by Hurricanes. Fighter Command losses included nine Hurricanes, with six pilots killed.

With the German pressure building again, on 31 August there began a bad week for Fighter Command. The first day was the worst for the Hurricane squadrons, with 24 losses. Reinforcements were brought south from rest and training to help fend off attacks on sector airfields such as Biggin Hill, which was put out of action twice, and Brooklands, where the Vickers factory was badly damaged, with many casualties. Detling was hit again, although it was not a fighter airfield, and the bomb dump was hit at Eastchurch, demolishing many of the surrounding buildings. During this disastrous week, 107 Hurricanes were shot down as well as 71 Spitfires, with the loss of 55 pilots and 78 seriously wounded. This was the equivalent of a squadron of pilots a day, and two squadrons of aircraft. In the face of superior German numbers, fatigue and the inexperience of replacement pilots were beginning to tell.

The climax of the Battle came on 7 September, when Goering switched from attacking airfields to mounting raids on London in an effort to attract every remaining fighter into the air, where they might be destroyed. A total of about 1,000 enemy aircraft were sent against Britain, split between the north Kent coast and across the south coast. Within 14 minutes all Fighter Command squadrons within a 70 miles radius of London were in the air and on the way to intercept. A total of 21 Squadrons, including Hurricanes of 43, 46, 73, 79, 111, 242, 249, 253, 257, 303, 310, 504, 605 and 607, were airborne to protect the airfields, and had to be diverted against the first bombing raid when it was realised that London was the target. By this time, the enemy bombers had unloaded over London Docks and were being chased by the Duxford Wing as they started to head for home. Meanwhile, 11 Group fighters heading for the enemy formation approached from the south, making this one of the biggest air battles of the war, with about 1,250 aircraft in the air. It lasted just 30 minutes. The Duxford Wing with 43, 240 and 310 Hurricane Squadrons and one Spitfire

squadron was just forming up when it was hit by a swarm of Bf109s, losing 15 Hurricanes in less than twenty minutes. With the Docks burning fiercely, the final toll in the air for the day was 29 Hurricanes and 14 Spitfires, with the loss of 17 pilots, including two squadron commanders and three flight commanders. German losses amounted to 52 aircraft, including 26 fighters.

Paradoxically, Goering's change in tactics to bombing London, most often at night, let Fighter Command off the hook. No longer having to defend the airfields, the depleted squadrons could be replaced by the rested units from the north of Britain. If the Germans had not discontinued the raids on the airfields at that point, Fighter Command would almost certainly have been unable to sustain its casualties at the prevailing rate. In the first two months of the Battle of Britain the equivalent of 11 squadrons had been lost, greater than the number of new squadrons brought into action since the beginning of the Battle. Many experienced pilots had been killed or injured, and the new pilots had still to learn the rules of combat if they were to survive. Luftwaffe losses had also been high, but they had had more pilots to start with and could more readily withstand a war of attrition.

However, the German leadership was convinced by this time that Fighter Command was all but destroyed. On 15 September, now known as Battle of Britain Day, there came another massive attack on London. Fighter Command had been spending the week since the last major attack resting and restoring strength, and was able to win a resounding victory. For the loss of 20 Hurricanes, including seven pilots killed, and seven Spitfires with three pilots killed, the Luftwaffe lost 36 bombers and 23 fighters with 163 aircrew either killed or taken prisoner. The RAF was still obviously a potent fighting force, and at this stage Hitler

A number of Hurricanes were sponsored by individuals, organizations, cities and even countries. Hurricane IIb BN795 with 174 Squadron was one of three presented by the mother of Wg Cdr John 'Downwind' Gillan, former CO of 111 Squadron, killed in action on 29 August 1941. Named 'Our John', the aircraft was at Odiham on 1 March 1943 with Flt Lt Sterne. (*Author's Collection*)

abandoned any idea of an invasion of Britain, at least until the following Spring.

With bombing of British cities now confined mainly to night raids against civilian targets, Dowding realised that the Luftwaffe did not have the capacity to launch further attacks by day, although a number were attempted. One was on 27 September, when a formation was intercepted over Surrey and Sussex by 120 Hurricanes and Spitfires. Another large-scale attack on the aircraft factory at Filton was met by five of the 10 Group squadrons. German losses amounted to 54 aircraft for the loss of ten Hurricanes, with five pilots killed, and ten more pilots killed in 18 Spitfire losses. The next day, Luftwaffe fighters shot down 11 Hurricanes and five Spitfires for the loss of only ten German aircraft. German bomber attacks by day decreased further during October, apart from some isolated, high flying Bf109s carrying 550 lb bombs which they released at random over London. These were generally too high to be intercepted in time. An additional raid intercepted by Hurricanes of 17, 46 and 257 Squadrons was the only one against Britain by the Italian Air Force, at the time based in Belgium. The target was Harwich but the inexperienced Italians were easily outperformed, losing ten aircraft with no losses to Fighter Command.

Defeat in the Battle of Britain did not destroy the Luftwaffe, but it did prove sufficiently frustrating to halt the German invasion, whereupon Hitler turned his attentions to Operation Barbarossa, possibly the most disastrous German miscalculation of the war. The Germans still possessed a strong force of medium bombers, which were causing great destruction to the cities and industry of Britain, as at the time Britain's night defences were totally inadequate.

* Birtles: *Mosquito, the Illustrated History*, Sutton Publishing Limited 1998.

Airborne Interception (AI) radar was in its infancy, and the night defences relied upon black painted Hurricanes and Defiants groping about in the dark in the hope of spotting an enemy aircraft held long enough in the glare of searchlights to shoot it down. It was the AI-equipped Beaufighters and, later, Mosquitos, which were able to combat this threat.*

*

Almost half the RAF fighter pilots who had been in the service prior to the war lost their

Part of the interim night fighter defences, 247 (China-British) Squadron was based at Middle Wallop with Hurricane Mk IIbs in early 1943. The aircraft were often painted black and featured a shield on the fuselage to avoid the pilot's night vision being affected by the exhaust glow of the Merlin. (*IWM*)

A 229 Squadron Hurricane being refuelled during the Battle, the guns having been fired in anger during the previous sortie. (*IWM*)

lives in the Battles of France and Britain; along, of course, with many others: overseas volunteers, reservists and raw recruits. The top scoring pilot was a Czech, Sergeant Josef František of 303 Squadron, who shot down 17 enemy aircraft during the Battle of Britain, but sadly was killed in combat on 8 October 1940.

After the Battle, Hurricanes continued to operate in Britain, but less in air defence as their ground attack role was developed. 175 Squadron at Warmwell was equipped with Hurricane IIbs from 3 March 1942 until April 1943. Soon after equipping, the squadron was tasked with a 'firepower' demonstration consisting of an attack on stationary army vehicles and dummy soldiers near the deserted village of Imber on Salisbury Plain. The demonstration on 13 April was staged for an invited audience of military personnel. The weather was dry and sunny, but haze caused reduced visibility for the pilots. Six Hurricanes of 175 Squadron made low-level approaches to the targets, two achieving good results. Tragically, the sixth Hurricane mistook the stand where the spectators were gathered for the target and opened fire, killing 25 Army personnel, including Brigadier Grant Taylor, the most senior officer to lose his life. 71 others were injured to varying degrees. However, the accident did not prevent the Hurricane from adopting valuable new roles in many other theatres of the war, as we shall see.

A loose formation of FAA Hurricane Mk Is, including V6541, AE977 and Z7060. These aircraft are armed with .303 in machine guns and are not fitted with arrester hooks. (*IWM*)

CHAPTER 5

SEA HURRICANES

After the Battle of Britain, the next major challenge for the RAF was protection of the North Atlantic convoys bringing vital supplies to Britain. Hitler had ordered Admiral Raeder to increase air and U-boat attacks on Allied shipping, to starve Britain into submission. Before the German invasion of Norway in April 1940, the trade routes were threatened only by a few U-boats and surface raiders, with any air attacks confined to routes along the east coast of Britain and in the Channel. Even after the occupation of Norway, Atlantic convoys could still approach around southern Ireland into the Irish Sea, but with the fall of France in June 1940, Germany controlled the entire European coastline from north of the Arctic Circle to the Pyrenees.

Although the Germans had not produced any four-engined, long-range heavy bombers, the Focke-Wulf 200 Condor was adapted for maritime patrol and attack. A number were based at Bordeaux. In the first two and a half months of operations from late August 1940, these converted passenger airliners sank nearly 90,000 tons of Allied shipping. Condors were able to fly more than 1,000 miles out into the Atlantic, far beyond the range of Britain's shore based fighters. Normal patrols were flown at 2,000 ft at 190 mph, searching for easy targets such as solitary ships or stragglers from convoys.

Once Germany had selected the Condor as the most suitable aircraft for long-range maritime patrols, ten military versions were ordered, six of them fitted with defensive armament and bomb racks. Preparations started for service introduction on 1 October 1939 with the formation of I/KG 40s flying armed reconnaissance sorties to cover the invasion of Norway. An improved version of the Condor was then produced with a forward firing 20 mm cannon fitted in the forward section of a ventral gondola, complemented by a rearward firing 7.9 mm machine gun in the rear of the gondola. Additional armament included forward and rearward firing 7.9 mm machine gun turrets in the nose and tail. The weapons load consisted of six 250 kg (551 lb) bombs or two externally suspended aerial mines. By attacking ships from abeam at low level, even though there was no bomb sight provided, the Condors could hardly miss. Despite their success, production was not increased significantly, and the ones in operation suffered from serviceability problems, including structural failures when manoeuvring violently.

Director of Fighter operations at the Air Ministry was Air Commodore Donald Stevenson, who was concerned that not enough was being done by the Admiralty to protect Britain's lifeline convoys on the Western Approaches. The Condor was by far the major threat, although it was vulnerable to air attack as it was not a robust military machine, and was being produced in relatively small numbers. Stevenson persuaded Air Chief Marshal Sir Charles Portal, the newly appointed Chief of the Air Staff, to call a conference on 12 November 1940 to discuss fighter protection for the Allied convoys. Invited were Admiral of the

The Camships had a ramp mounted between the bow and foremast with a Hurricane at readiness, and usually a second one below as a replacement. (*Author's Collection*)

The launch of the Hurricane from a Camship was propelled by a bank of 3 in rockets creating a deafening noise and jet of flame. (*IWM*)

Hurricanes were lifted aboard Camships from the dockside. Here, MSFU Gloster built Hurricane I V6756 is being lifted aboard *Empire Tide* with a second aircraft to follow. (*HSA*)

For ground training the MSFU had a ramp built at Speke. The undercarriage was down to allow the wheels to touch the ground as the aircraft dropped after take-off in light wind. Sea Hurricane Ia Z4936 is being lifted into position for another launch. (*Author's Collection*)

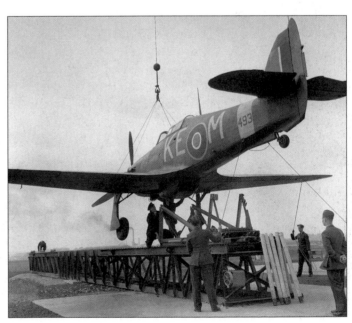

Once located on the catapult, the main undercarriage was retracted ready for launching. (*RAF Museum*)

Fleet Sir Dudley Pound, the First Sea Lord; Admiral Tom Phillips, Chief of Naval Air Services and the commanders-in-chief of Fighter and Coastal Commands.

Two things were immediately obvious: RAF bombing attacks would have to be directed at the Condor factory and main operating base at Bremen, and anti-aircraft defences would have to be improved on the merchant ships. There was a requirement for high performance fighters capable of intercepting the Condors at extreme range. Although aircraft carriers were the logical answer, the losses of *Courageous* and *Glorious* early in the war and the demands of the Mediterranean theatre meant there were none available for convoy duties. During discussions it was suggested that selected ships should be fitted, not only with radar to detect the raiders, but also with a catapult to allow two or three fighters to be carried. The idea of an expendable fighter flown by a pilot on a one-way trip had been born.

With Condors continuing to sink Allied shipping in the Atlantic, the first suggestion was to route convoys from the northwest, where Condors from France and Norway would be at the limit of their range. The convoys could pass through the danger zone under cover of darkness and be protected by land based fighters after dawn. This proved impracticable, though, resulting in new interest being taken in the one-way fighter idea. But what would be the most suitable platform? Although tankers had the deck accommodation, they were too slow for a launch, where at least 10-12 knots forward speed was essential.

While causing considerable damage, the bombing of the Bordeaux Condor base had little effect on attacks on the convoys. As a short notice stopgap, the catapult training ship HMS *Pegasus* sailed on 9 December carrying two Fulmars, which had inadequate speed to be of much use. With pressure from Churchill, the decision was taken in principle on 30 December 1940 to prepare a number of merchant ships for convoy defence. These were known as Catapult Aircraft Merchant Ships, or Camships, which would be an integral part of the convoy while in the danger zone.

While the Camships were being adapted, four auxiliary naval vessels, the *Ariguani*, *Maplin*, *Patia* and *Springbank* were fitted with catapults and known as Fighter Catapult Ships. Each was to carry two expendable fighters, one ready to go on the trolley, the other stored in reserve. The ships were used only in the danger zone, escorting outgoing convoys to the western limit and picking up the incoming convoys, taking on average 17 days of concentrated convoy defence.

After considering a number of aircraft types, the Hurricane was selected as the most robust, and because in the aftermath of the Battle of Britain it was increasingly available from Fighter Command, which had taken delivery of more Spitfires. Three pilots were usually allocated to each ship, and after launch and interception of the raider they would either have to try to reach the nearest land, or ditch the aircraft close to a ship in the hope of being picked up before succumbing to exposure! The ideal launch method, it was decided, was a simple catapult propelled by banks of 3 in rockets.

On 6 March 1941, Churchill proclaimed that the Battle of the Atlantic had begun. Defensive action was to be taken against both U-boat and Condors, the Camships to be available as soon as possible. Within three months of this announcement, four Fighter Catapult Ships and the first of the new Camships, the *Michael E*, were ready for service.

Although there was a vision for some 200 Camships, the problems of supply in terms of pilots, aircraft and Merlin engines from both sides of the Atlantic could be insurmountable with all the other priorities to consider. Effectiveness of the concept had yet to be proven, and the total number of these special ships was reduced to 35, with any expansion to await successful results. The Fighter Catapult Ships (FCS) were to be used on the Britain to Gibraltar route, with the Camships initially allocated to convoys between Britain and the eastern seaboard of Canada. This ensured the quickest turnaround for supplies of Canadian built Hurricanes, and enabled the Camships to operate in the danger zone for as long as possible.

Camships required at least 85 ft from the bow to the foremast to accommodate the catapult, those selected being large freighters of 9,000 tons and over, their freight carrying capacity being equally important. Even with maximum utilization of the Camships the pilots and crews were unlikely to spend more than thirty days annually on convoy duty, owing to the time taken for loading, repairs, maintenance, training and leave.

Catapult trials had been completed on land and, by the end of March, 60 Merlin III powered Hurricane Is had been allocated for convoy protection. The fitting of rocket catapults to ships had started, and the modified Hurricanes, which did not need arrester hooks because they would not be coming back, became known as Hurricats. Local reinforcement of the airframe and catapult spools were fitted. A new organization, known as 9 Group Fighter Command, was formed at Speke, Liverpool, to control the operations of the new Merchant Ship Fighter Unit (MSFU), consisting of 35 ship detachments.

It was very much a combined services operation. The Navy was responsible for manning the FCS in an emergency, and the RAF was responsible for Camship operations.

The Hurricane and crew were often exposed to the elements on Camships. Flt Lt Turley-George and Plt Off Fenwick on board the Empire Tide ready for departure as part of the escort of convoy PQ17 to Russia. (*Author's Collection*)

In addition to the pilot, maintenance was undertaken by the RAF sea crew consisting of a fitter, rigger, armourer and radio-telephone operator. The Navy provided the fighter direction officers (FDOs) to guide the pilots to the target and assist in the recovery, together with radar operators and torpedo men for servicing the catapults. The Army however was responsible for manning the anti-aircraft guns, all the combined operations personnel being volunteers. Finally, the crews of the Camships were civilian merchant seamen.

The RAF pilots, all of whom were officers in command of the specialist team, were volunteers. They had to be experienced and capable of operating aggressively after long periods of inactivity. Plus, they had to be good sailors. However, the Fleet Air Arm (FAA) pilots for the FCS did not have the same choice to volunteer for a one-way ride, possibly to a watery grave. A number were simply posted to 804 Squadron at Sydenham, Belfast, together with their FDOs.

The rocket catapult launched the aircraft at close to 3.5 g, creating a deafening noise and flame, and a recoil which required the personnel and ship's structure to be protected during launch. The pilot forced his head back into the padded headrest with the right elbow wedged into the hip to avoid involuntary pullback as the aircraft shot forward. Owing to the rotation of the Merlin engine, the Hurricane had a tendency to slew to the left

98 Squadron RAF was based at Kaldarnes in Iceland with Hurricane Mk Is from June to July 1941 for convoy protection on departure and arrival from Russia. In August 1941, the unit was renumbered 1423 Flight with Hurricane Mk IIas, examples being Z4037, Z4045, Z4048 and Z4049 here preparing for take-off. (*Author's Collection*)

on take-off and was longitudinally unstable at slow speed. The aircraft was therefore prepared for take-off with one-third starboard rudder, one-third flaps and the elevator and trim tabs neutral. The heavy Hurricanes showed a tendency to drop after launch in a light wind, but care had to be taken not to climb until well above the stalling speed, particularly with a fully loaded operational aircraft. This was particularly noticeable in ground based training with the catapult at Speke, where the elevation was only 6 ft and the undercarriage was kept down. At sea the catapults were mounted some 40 ft above the water, giving much more time to recover into the launch headwind.

Then, there was the minor problem of how the pilot would get home. Previous experience of ditching fighters at sea suggested they would go straight down and the Hurricane, with its large air-scoop under the centre section, had the worst reputation of all, tending to flip over on to its back immediately on impact. The drill was to abandon the aircraft at around 2,000 ft, trimming it slightly tail heavy, and to fall out after inverting the aircraft. The aim was to be pointing away from the convoy, but to land as close as possible ahead of the designated pick-up ship.

Once training was complete, individual teams led by the pilot were despatched to the appropriate west coast port where Hurricanes were loaded from the dockside fully assembled. The pilot was in the cockpit for the lift, to retract the undercarriage before the aircraft was lowered on to the catapult. The breakdown of responsibility for these operations, referred to earlier, was a complex issue, with the MSFU crews signing the ship's articles as supernumerary officers or deck-hands, coming under the jurisdiction of the captain and having civilian identities in neutral ports. Although the decision to launch was the captain's responsibility, it was the pilot who decided if the conditions were suitable.

The first launch at sea in the operational trials was made by Plt Off H.J. Davidson, the

The bow of the Camships was sufficiently above sea level to allow a slight drop of the aircraft after launch. MSFU Hurricane I in position for launch. (*Author's Collection*)

During August 1942, FAA carriers were used on Operation Pedestal which was the supply of beleaguered Malta. HMS *Furious* with a Hurricane is positioned for take-off for the long flight to Malta after the ships left Gibraltar. (*Author's Collection*)

Sea Hurricanes also operated off more sophisticated carriers and had a Vee-arrester hook fitted under the rear fuselage. (*Author's Collection*)

Conditions on Russian convoys even during the summer were inhospitable, with life expectancy very short in the event of a ditching in the cold ocean. (*Author's Collection*)

Gloster built Sea Hurricane Mk Ia Z4852 in April 1943 fitted with FAA radio, but without an arrester hook, powered by a Merlin III engine. (*RAF Museum*)

Gloster built Sea Hurricane Mk Ic V6471 in April 1943 armed with four 20 mm cannons and fitted with an arrester hook. (*IWM*)

Sea Hurricane Mk IIc NF717 in April 1943 armed with four 20 mm cannons and powered by a Merlin XX engine. (*IWM*)

first pilot to be posted to MSFU. He had never been launched before. He joined the SS *Empire Rainbow*, the first of the regular Camships, at Greenock on the Clyde on 31 May 1941. She steamed downriver at 10 knots into a two-knot wind, the Hurricane blasted off down the rail and dropped the port wing beneath the bows of the ship, staggering into a turn to the left. When the aircraft was next seen by the observers on the bridge it was 100 yds ahead, low down. The port wing touched the water, but the aircraft recovered and eventually climbed away at right angles to the ship, to the great relief of everyone on board. Davidson landed safely at Abbotsinch. On analysis of the take-off, it appeared that the pilot had omitted to select 30 degrees of flap and the proper rudder correction to prevent the swing to port! Only 11 of the 13 rockets had ignited and a cover plate had blown off, hitting the tail wheel, which may have slowed the take-off. After further checks by a Farnborough test pilot a drill was introduced to ensure that the throttle friction nut was tightened to avoid loss of power at launch. Despite this interesting first take-off, Davidson was not held to blame and on 8 June he sailed for Nova Scotia on the *Empire Rainbow*. By the end of the same month there were six Camships on convoy duty.

Meanwhile, the FAA crews from 804 Squadron on the FCSs had been operating the whole time in the danger zone without the boredom of spending many weeks 'off watch' as their RAF counterparts on the Camships were doing. They returned more frequently to base at Sydenham, getting to know their colleagues better, and they served on ships operated by the Royal Navy with less confusion of responsibility. However, they generally flew individually, and never as a squadron. The FCSs were in operation from early January 1941, *Pegasus* being the first, while three of the four ex-banana boats,

Springbank, *Ariguani* and *Maplin* went into service in May, the first three ships equipped to carry Fulmars and Maplin Hurricanes.

As we have seen, the *Michael E* was the first of the Camships. She had a Sea Hurricane Ia loaded aboard at Belfast for her maiden voyage. Because there was a shortage of RAF pilots for this trip, FAA pilot Sub-Lieutenant Birrell was chosen, having been one of 25 Navy pilots who flew in the Battle of Britain. He had his first ground launched catapult experience from Gosport in a Hurricane, followed by a Fulmar launch from Farnborough, ready for his first proper launch from the ship. This proved something of a challenge when only half the rockets fired. He made a safe landing at Sydenham, however, and the ship sailed to join the convoy on 28 May. As no the Condors came within range, the Hurricat was never launched: the ship was torpedoed by a U-boat outside Condor range after the convoy had dispersed. Birrell and his crew survived to join another Camship.

The Hurricats did prove to be a deterrent to the Condors, even though they had little surplus speed to catch the enemy raiders. A successful attack needed to be made from head-on or abeam to ensure killing the enemy pilot. Any attack from below or from the rear was likely to be unsuccessful owing to the armour plating and heavy defensive armament, while with four engines, hitting one was unlikely to stop the aircraft. Forced to keep a safe distance, rather than leading the attack, the wary Condor crews tended instead to become spotters for the U-boats.

By the beginning of July 25 Sea Hurricane Ias had been delivered to MSFU and 16 Camships had sailed, but without any launches. Of the FCSs, *Maplin* alone was equipped with two Sea Hurricanes and three pilots, ready for the maiden voyage on 9 May. Hurricanes gave better performance than the Fulmars, which could barely catch

By the end of 1941, 885 Squadron was equipped with Sea Hurricane Mk Ibs on board HMS *Victorious* and, by late 1942, 801 Squadron had taken their place, here behind the shelter of wind breaks.

the Condors even under ideal conditions. Unfortunately, the Hurricanes supplied had already been in service with the RAF, and some even dated from the Battle of Britain. Possibly they were considered expendable, but their condition and performance were poor.

*

After an uneventful first trip, on her second voyage the FCS, HMS *Maplin*, saw more action. Sailing for Halifax, Nova Scotia in mid-July with two Hurricanes and Lt R.W.H. Everett and Sub-Lts C.W. Walker and J.E. Scott as pilots, the 8,000 ton ship was filled with empty fuel drums to help with buoyancy and painted a pale pink for camouflage. According to an illicit diary kept by John Scott, on 18 July, when Bob Everett was in

the cockpit, a Condor began to orbit the convoy closer than usual. It then flew off, but suddenly another Condor was seen approaching the convoy at low level and already closing in. Bob was catapulted off and turned into position for a head-on attack. Just as he was about to fire, the Condor lost a section of the starboard wing, shot off by the gunners aboard HMS *Norman Prince*, and crashed into the sea with the loss of all on board. Bob Everett had enough fuel to fly for just under two hours to St Angelo by Lough Erne near Donegal Bay.

Bob rejoined the ship for its next voyage on the Gibraltar run, again with John Scott, but Dickie Mancus replacing Cecil Walker. On the return voyage escorting Convoy SL 81 from Sierra Leone, the RN escorts were *St Albans*, *Campbeltown* and *Wanderer*. At 14.00 hrs on 2 August Bob Everett climbed

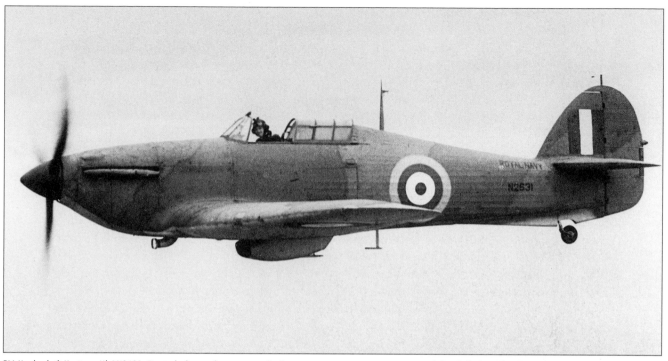

FAA Hawker built Hurricane Mk I N2631. Due to the large radiator scoop under the wing centre-section it was not recommended to ditch, the preferred option being to abandon at 2,000 ft close to the designated escort ship. (*FAA Museum*)

into the Hurricat cockpit for his spell of duty, with the *Maplin* some 450 miles from Land's End and no hope of reaching land if launched. After about ten minutes a suspected U-boat was spotted, followed by a Condor shadowing in the distance as a contact plane. Soon after the first Condor departed back to base, a second one was spotted approaching the convoy. The Hurricat was ready to go and Everett started the engine while the ship turned into the wind. With the engine at full throttle, he gave the signal to launch and roared off over the bow.

A tail chase then started with the Hurricane slowly gaining on the heavily armed Condor from the starboard side. The rear gunner began to fire at Everett, who, at 244 mph, still could not get abeam of the enemy, while by now, shots were also coming from the nose gun. Everett hadn't made up enough ground to turn from abeam with the target head-on, but the problem resolved itself when the Condor pilot instead turned sharply to port, almost losing him, and then returned to his original track, presenting the ideal target. Everett held his fire until 200 yards range, aiming for the cockpit. There appeared to be no effect as he dropped astern and fired the last of his ammunition and, to make matters worse, his windscreen suddenly became obscured by engine oil from where the Condor gunners had scored a hit. Looking out for the Condor, he saw that it was still flying on, but losing oil as well. Then a glow of fire erupted inside and, dropping one wing, the aircraft crashed into the sea.

By this time, Everett was at 200 ft about 40 miles from the escort and having engine problems. He climbed to 2,000 ft to get a bearing and flew back to the convoy where, unknown to him, two of the escorts were busy depth-charging U-boats. On his approach, *Wanderer* put about to recover him and he prepared to bale out half a mile from the ship. He rolled the aircraft over to drop clear, but when he was half way out the nose jerked up instead of down, forcing him back in the seat. After a second unsuccessful attempt, he decided to risk ditching, stalling on to the surface with the tail down but, true to its reputation, the aircraft sank instantly. Struggling out of the cockpit, he fought his way to the surface and was picked up by a boat lowered from the *Wanderer*. For destroying the first Condor by Hurricat, Bob Everett was awarded the DSO; ironically, while ferrying a Hurricane from Belfast to Abingdon on 26 January 1942, he was killed when his aircraft crashed into the sea off Anglesey.

*

Whereas the FCS was under RN control, there were often difficulties between the RAF crews and the Merchant Navy command of the Camships, especially as the threat of the Condors appeared to have diminished, thanks to the protection of the Hurricats. The MSFU crews were subject to the regulations of the Merchant Shipping Act under the captain's direction, but the captain had no powers under the Air Force Act. As time went on, though, relations improved considerably; especially when the pilot and his team adapted to the captain's personality.

Three months after the sailing of the first Camship, 39 pilots and 164 men had completed their training at Speke, with 37 Camship sailings. Although pilots were in short supply no North Atlantic convoy escorted by a Camship had successfully been attacked from the air. The whole Camship scheme was reviewed with the possibility of

withdrawing them and replacing them with FCS under the control of the RN, but it was still believed that they provided an effective deterrent, despite tying up valuable pilot resources. By contrast, the route from Gibraltar was suffering losses from the Condor/U-boat combination and there was too much for the FCS to cover.

A second launch by 804 Squadron was from *Maplin* on 2 September with Walker in the cockpit. He was launched against a Condor, which eventually flew off damaged after jettisoning its bombs. The Condor probably survived only because the Hurricat was too lightly armed with machine guns, instead of cannons, and its performance would undoubtedly have been better had it been a Hurricane II with a Merlin XX engine. Walker successfully abandoned his Hurricat after an hour of combat flying and was soon picked up from the sea.

With the loss of the two surviving Fulmar equipped FCSs to enemy action in September and October, only the better equipped *Maplin* was left, and was adapted to carry a third Hurricat in reserve. On 19 September 1941, a decision was taken to transfer six Camships on to the Gibraltar route. They would be in the danger zone for fourteen days, seven out and seven back. Two pilots were allocated to each ship and a pool was formed at Gibraltar of three Hurricats and three MSFU pilots. The first of the Gibraltar bound Camships, the *Empire Gale*, sailed on 3 October and a week later the last of the 35 Camships went into service, the remainder being allocated to the North Atlantic convoys.

The first operational launching from a Camship on a North Atlantic convoy after nearly five months of escort duties was on 1 November 1941, by George Varley. About 550 miles off the Irish coast, there was a U-boat alert. A Condor was spotted in front of the convoy, flying at 1,000 ft. Varley was fired off from the *Empire Foam* and chased

HMS *Biter* and *Avenger* were part of the escort for convoy PQ18 which left for Russia in September 1942 with 802 Squadron Hurricanes on the exposed deck, but at least they could be landed back. (*IWM*)

after the Condor, which by then was starting a run with bomb doors open. Seeing the Hurricat approaching, the German pilot broke off and made for the nearby cloud layer, where Varley lost it. Thinking that this aircraft might be a decoy, he dropped back out of the cloud, but after nearly two hours in the air no other hostile aircraft was seen. Varley could not jettison the emergency cockpit side panel and after trying a number of times to get out, he climbed over the side and started walking along the wing until he fell off. He was rapidly picked up by the escort ship and dumped in a hot bath fully clothed to recover from the effects of exposure.

Camships were equally as vulnerable to U-boat attack as the other ships, but for three months there were no losses. Then, on 19 September and 2 October, two Camships were torpedoed, but without loss to MSFU personnel. On 3 October the *Empire Wave* was sunk with the loss of two MSFU men and another severely injured, the survivors remaining in an open boat for 14 days before reaching Iceland in poor condition.

Owing to cold and corrosion, it was a difficult task to keep the vulnerable and fragile aircraft serviceable in the winter storms. By the end of 1941, thanks to the Hurricat deterrent, many of the Condors had been transferred to other duties, but to remove the Camships would only invite them back. However, there was pressure for the crews to be returned to more active duties, and there was also a need to protect the Russian convoys. On 3 January 1942, the operation of Camships on the North Atlantic convoys was suspended and some of the ships returned to operating purely as freighters. Convoy protection was continued on the Gibraltar run, however, and the MSFU organisation was retained 'pending developments', which allowed a period of reorganisation and training. On 3 March 1942, sailings of Camships on the North Atlantic convoys were resumed, and on 28 March the decision was made to deploy Camships on the notorious Murmansk run.

The first Camship to join a convoy to Russia was *Empire Morn*, which sailed with PQ15 from Hvalfjord on 26 April. Despite an attack by torpedo carrying Heinkel 111 bombers, which succeeded in sinking three ships in the convoy, conditions were too bad to risk launching the Hurricat. Not only did the pilots not have immersion suits to protect them against exposure in the water, but with temperatures down to minus 25 deg. F, it was too cold even to sit in the aircraft cockpit on readiness.

To help divert the German attacks, the Russian convoys were usually phased in pairs, sailing from both ends – Iceland and Russia – simultaneously. The second pair of convoys were PQ16, sailing eastward from Iceland, and QP12 leaving westward from Murmansk. PQ16 was allocated the single Camship *Empire Laurence*. QP12 consisted of 15 merchant ships with the escort including *Empire Morn*, and sailed on 21 May under the protection of land based Russian fighters. PQ16 was formed up at

Hvalfjord on the same day. Helped by poor weather conditions, the two convoys gradually approached one another.

Out of range of the Russian fighter cover, conditions on 25 May appeared right for a German attack on the westbound QP12, and reconnaissance aircraft were spotted in the distance, bringing the MSFU crews to five minutes' readiness. John Kendal was in the cockpit when two torpedo armed Ju88s appeared, and the decision was made to launch. He initially went after the BV138 floatplane as the easiest target, but Kendal's radio was giving trouble with transmissions, although he could hear directions from the ship. When he lost the BV138 in cloud, he went after one of the Ju88s and managed to put both engines out of action, whereupon it crashed in the sea. Kendal then investigated the other Ju88, BV138 and the Condor, but they had all departed for home. It was time to abandon his Hurricat but, because of low cloud, when he climbed to a safe height he was lost to view. Within a short while, the pilotless Hurricane was seen dropping through the overcast, followed immediately behind by Kendal, whose parachute had apparently failed to open. About 50 ft above the water it began to open, but was only half out before the pilot hit the sea. The badly injured Kendal was picked up quickly, but died soon after, the first MSFU pilot to shoot down an enemy aircraft. He had done his job: QP12 arrived at its destination in Iceland without losing any ships.

Meanwhile, the eastbound PQ16 was approaching the hostile area with Al Hay at readiness in his Hurricat cockpit. Six Ju88 bombers appeared, too suddenly for a launch, but then the ship's radar picked up approaching torpedo bombers, four Heinkels, and the plane was fired off. Hay went after the last He111, setting the starboard engine on fire. Despite this damage, the straggler caught up with the formation, and Hay went

824 Squadron operated Sea Hurricane Mk IIcs on convoy escort duties from HMS *Striker* on the approaches to Britain. One aircraft suffered a mishap on 13 June 1944. (*FAA Museum*)

after the second aircraft in the group, reckoning that No. 4 was unlikely to last. While shooting to the rear of the cockpit of the enemy aircraft he was hit by return fire in the glycol tank, which obscured his windscreen, then he himself was hit in the leg. Out of ammunition, and with the engine overheating, it was time to bale out and, after six minutes in the water, he was picked up.

Thanks to the confusion caused by Hay, the attack became disjointed, and although there were a number of near-misses, no ship in the convoy was hit. The Germans were determined, however, and on 27 May the *Empire Laurence* was struck by two bombs, causing serious damage, and the order was given to abandon ship. In the next wave of attacks by Ju88s the magazine was hit, and

the ship sank rapidly. Al Hay was among the survivors. Three other ships in the convoy were also lost in this action. The remaining 28 out of the original 35 ships entered Kola Inlet on 30 May with just over a quarter of the original cargo lost.

Although it was Summer, the conditions from Iceland to Russia were still far from pleasant. Not only did both sides often have to contend with the worst possible weather, but at that time of year and latitude there was almost continuous daylight, making the convoy vulnerable round the clock to U-boats, bombers and torpedo aircraft. Although the Germans often inflicted heavy losses on the convoys, their own resources were stretched to the limit by the harsh operating conditions, especially when they suffered damage. For a crew ditching in the sea there was no chance of survival, since rescue was not possible. Despite this, attacks on the convoys were often pressed home without any regard to the defences, although the Hurricats were a major deterrent.

During August 1942, the Russian convoys were scaled down as British naval forces were preoccupied with Operation Pedestal, which involved taking vital supplies to Malta. Camships also continued to take part in convoy protection duties in the Bay of Biscay. However, in September Churchill ordered the resumption of convoys on the Murmansk run. Leaving Loch Ewe on 2 September 1942, convoy PQ18 joined up with the American contribution off the west coast of Iceland, and the forty merchant ships set out for Russia.

This was the largest convoy to date, and it had the largest escort, including the Camship *Empire Morn* and, for the first time, an American lend-lease escort carrier, the *Avenger*, with a compliment of 12 Sea Hurricane IIbs of 802 Squadron and three Swordfish biplanes on the flight deck. *Avenger* was commissioned on 2 March 1942, but had a short service life, being sunk on 15 November that same year by U-155, west of Gibraltar. Her Swordfish were allocated to reconnaissance, and both they and the Hurricanes had the luxury of being able to land back on board. This ship would stay with the convoy until the main escort took over the defence of the returning eastbound convoy QP14 in the Barents Sea. The protection of the Hurricats would therefore not be needed until after *Avenger* departed. As additional cover, two squadrons of Hampden torpedo bombers were flown to Russia to protect against hostile surface shipping, and a squadron of Catalina flying boats were to carry out long range reconnaissance, also from Russia.

Losses from predatory U-boats soon started, and on 13 September the convoy came within range of the Luftwaffe. *Avenger* was the primary target, the enemy torpedo bombers using what was known as the 'Golden Comb' formation, with a massed attack in line abreast of around forty Heinkel 111s dropping two torpedoes each, straddling the convoy. The only defence was for the ships to turn head-on into the path of some 80 torpedoes, hoping to present less of a target. A number of ships were hit; indeed, a quarter of the convoy was lost in one day, but the *Avenger* survived. In a similar raid the next day, Hurricanes were launched from the *Avenger*, and not only helped to break up the attack but shot down five enemy aircraft over the convoy. A further nine 'damaged' planes were written off on their return. Such was the intensity of flak from the convoy defences that three Hurricanes were shot down by friendly fire. Fortunately, all three pilots survived.

On 16 September the main escort left with *Avenger*, but the next day four Russian destroyers replaced them. The German attacks began again, although the hostile aircraft were now at the extremity of their endurance. The Hurricat was made ready for launch, waiting for the torpedo bombers to follow in the wake of the dive bombing, but conditions were not right for a launch and the torpedoes missed their mark. Jackie Burr was in the cockpit but, before he could get out to change with John Davies, the threat of another attack quickly developed and the aircraft was launched.

As he turned, 15 Heinkels were seen approaching at 50 ft ready to try the 'Golden Comb' again. Burr attacked the approaching aircraft head-on, forcing one of them to fly into the sea. He then used up the remainder of his ammunition on another Heinkel, which flew over the convoy with engines smoking and fell into the icy water. At least two other Heinkels had been damaged and were unlikely to return to base. Burr then flew around the convoy to deter further attack, but although he had the responsibility for the defence of the convoy, without ammunition he could not be greatly effective. He therefore made the decision to save the Hurricane if he could and fly to Archangel, at the extremity of its endurance. With only a rudimentary map for navigation and a distance of 230 miles to fly, with barely 60 gallons in the tanks, he arrived safely with four gallons of fuel remaining, the equivalent of six minutes' flying time! There were no more torpedo attacks on PQ18 and 27 out of the 40 merchant ships arrived safely in Russia with their vital cargoes intact.

Following the introduction of Camships on the Arctic convoys in May 1942, the MSFU reached its operational peak, with a total of 29 in operation on three different routes. At the end of July it was decided to withdraw Camships from the North Atlantic route, and eight were immediately removed from service. By the end of the summer the numbers had been further reduced to 13, eight on the Gibraltar run and the remaining five on the Russian convoys. With the approach of Winter bringing impossible flying conditions, Camships were withdrawn from the Arctic run, but the pilots were trained for deck landing to allow them to operate from the escort carriers. The new organization became eight ship detachments, with a pool of two in reserve at Gibraltar, consisting of 38 pilots, ten FDO and 182 crewmen. A total of 14 Sea Hurricanes were kept for the Camships, with ten more Mk Is at Speke for training.

On 1 November 1942, Flg Off Norman Taylor was aboard the *Empire Heath* on the Gibraltar run when a Condor was sighted approaching the convoy. It singled out the Camship for attack. Taylor was rapidly launched, but had difficulty seeing the hostile aircraft as he was flying straight into the low sun. He gained rapidly on the Condor and fired at the aircraft, despite heavy returning

fire. After a burst of fire from close quarters, the Condor reared up in a climb, apparently towards some clouds, and Taylor was able to fire more shots into the cockpit area. Before reaching the safety of the cloud, the Condor pitched forward into a dive, hitting the sea with the loss of all on board. Taylor then prepared to bale out of the Hurricane, but had some difficulty on entering the water as he could not swim. However, he was safely rescued. For this successful combat, Taylor was awarded the DFC to add to his earlier DFM.

Following the invasion of North Africa in November 1942, the Camships' responsibility was extended to Casablanca and Algiers, and the first Camship escorted convoy to North Africa left Britain on Christmas Eve 1942, arriving at Algiers on 7 January. In early March 1943, it was decided the Camships would no longer escort the Arctic convoys and, soon afterwards, with new escort and merchant aircraft carriers entering service, the decision was taken to disband the MSFU on 15 July. Some met an earlier fate: the *Empire Morn* having been taken off the Arctic convoys, struck a mine off Casablanca in April 1943 and was abandoned. However, she did not sink and was reboarded and towed into port. The *Empire Eve* was torpedoed on 18 May in the Mediterranean and was abandoned before sinking.

The last two Camships in service, the *Empire Tide* and the *Empire Darwin*, left Gibraltar on 23 July 1943 with Convoy SL133. Many of the Condors had been transferred during the Winter to other duties, but they returned in the Spring, their new tactics being to bomb in formation from a minimum altitude of 9,000 ft, making them more difficult to engage. The ships' crews were extra vigilant, despite returning home to an uncertain future. On 28 July, after a number of Condor sightings, one was seen approaching the convoy at 500 ft and 'Jimmy'

The biggest naval action involving Sea Hurricanes was Operation Pedestal in August 1942, the build-up of supplies to Malta ready for the Battle of El Alamein in North Africa. On board HMS *Victorious* was 885 Squadron, followed by HMS *Indomitable* with 880 Squadron and HMS *Eagle* with 801 Squadron. HMS *Eagle* was sunk on 11 August. (*FAA Museum*)

Sea Hurricane Mk IIbs were operated by 804 Squadron from HMS *Furious* in late 1942. Here P2371:S7F is just airborne. (*Author's Collection*)

800 Squadron operated Sea Hurricane Mk IIcs from HMS *Biter* and HMS *Unicorn* in the Mediterranean from October 1942 until November 1943 in support of Operation Torch. (*FAA Museum*)

880 Squadron was a mainly home based Fleet Fighter Squadron with Hurricane Mk Ias in 1941. (*FAA Museum*)

Stewart was fired off in the Hurricat from the *Empire Darwin* to intercept. Meanwhile, two other Condors had begun bombing from high level, just missing the other Camship. Stewart attacked the low level Condor until his guns jammed, but he had dealt it a fatal blow and it plunged into the sea. He then climbed to the other Condors and helped to put them off their attack.

By this time a catapult fault had been repaired on the *Empire Tide* and its Hurricat was ready for launch. Paddy Flynn took off after another low level Condor, which he chased, trying to silence the enemy guns, which were damaging his aircraft. Closing in for the kill he exhausted his ammunition, and the damaged Condor limped away with an engine on fire and losing height. It was later confirmed destroyed. Both pilots returned to

the convoy and baled out, being picked up by the escorts.

The next day the convoy was bombed again from high level but no serious damage was sustained. The value of having more than one Camship in a convoy had been fully demonstrated on the final voyage, but it was not possible to start up MSFU again.

Of the 35 Camships that entered service, a total of 12 were lost to enemy action. Eight operational launchings resulted in six successful interceptions of enemy Condors. The overall deterrent of the Hurricats undoubtedly reduced losses to merchant shipping. The 'one-way trip' concept was by no means suicidal either as, surprisingly, only one pilot was lost on operations.

*

Returning to more conventional naval air operations, at the outbreak of war the Royal Navy had six aircraft carriers in service, HMS *Courageous*, *Glorious*, *Furious*, *Argus*, *Hermes* and *Ark Royal*. As previously mentioned, *Courageous* was lost early in the war and *Glorious* was sunk on 8 June 1940 after embarking the Hurricanes of 46 Squadron during the withdrawal from Norway. However, the fact that 46 Squadron pilots had successfully landed on to the deck of *Glorious* without the benefit of arrester hooks did give an indication of the possible use of the aircraft for carrier based naval operations, in addition to one-way catapult launches from cargo ships; though, aircraft carriers being in such short supply, they could rarely be spared to provide escort to convoys.

With the shortage of pilots in Fighter Command during the Battle of Britain, a number of Fleet Air Arm (FAA) pilots transferred temporarily to the RAF and were trained on the Hurricane at Gosport. The FAA went on to support a number of Allied ground campaigns flying Hurricanes, including Malta and North Africa.

When Italy entered the war on 10 June 1940, German forces were already in control of North Africa, threatening Egypt and the supply route through the Suez Canal. Malta became a strategically vital Allied base (see Chapter 6). The island was suffering badly from enemy attacks, and re-supply was critical. As a break from the Arctic convoys, a major effort was put into the Mediterranean theatre, with HMS *Argus* sailing in on 2 August carrying a dozen Hurricane Is. These were flown off the deck by RAF pilots and arrived at Malta without difficulty. The Hurricane was already demonstrating its superiority over the outdated Sea Gladiator, the cumbersome Fulmar and the ineffective Skua.

It had been fairly straightforward to convert the Hurricane for catapult launching, but for deck landing with an A-frame arrester hook some strengthening was required to avoid tearing the tail off on landing. The first hooked Hurricane was not ready for trails until March 1941, and became the prototype Sea Hurricane Ib, P5187, followed by the conversion of low hours Sea Hurricane Ias and Hurricane Is starting in May 1941. By October, about 120 aircraft had been converted to Sea Hurricane Ibs, including early Hurricane IIas, IIbs and Canadian built Xs, XIs and XIIs. Generally the Sea Hurricane Ib was defined as a hooked Hurricane with armament which did not protrude forward of the wing leading edge, but this was not always the case. The Sea Hurricane Mk Ic was produced by converting some 100 Mk Ibs with 20 mm Oerlikon cannon armed wings fitted, still powered by the 1,030 hp Merlin III engine.

By the end of 1941, the Sea Hurricane Ib was replacing Fulmars with 801 Squadron on HMS *Argus* and *Eagle*, 806 Squadron on *Formidable*, 880 Squadron on *Avenger* and 885 Squadron on *Victorious*. The Sea Hurricane was ready from January 1942 and entered service with 801, 802, 803, 880, 883 and 885 Squadrons. A small number of Sea Hurricane Mk Ibs were fitted with tropical filters and joined 889 Squadron in North Africa. With the increased pressure for the defence of Malta in 1942, 70 Merlin XX powered Hurricane IIcs were fully navalised as Sea Hurricane IIcs.

The biggest Navy action involving Sea Hurricanes took place in August 1942, on Operation Pedestal, which was the supply of Malta as part of the build-up of forces in the Mediterranean ready for the Battle of El Alamein. The powerful escort for just 14 merchant ships from Gibraltar to Malta included four carriers, HMS *Eagle*, *Furious*, *Indomitable* and *Victorious*. The flight decks of *Furious* were blocked with Spitfires destined for Malta and it therefore could not

Convoy escort in Home waters was a duty of 825 Squadron with Sea Hurricane Mk IIcs from HMS *Vindex* from August 1943 until September 1944. (*FAA Museum*)

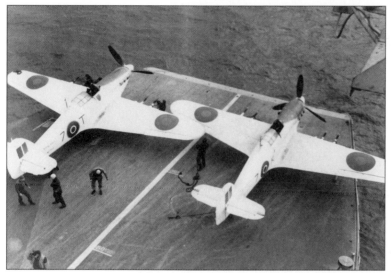

Sea Hurricane Mk IIcs of 835 Squadron were painted with white camouflage for convoy escort duties aboard HMS *Nairana*. (*FAA Museum*)

In addition to combat duties, the FAA used Hurricanes for second line duties. A Sea Hurricane Mk I without arrester hook with TTU at Gosport in early 1939. (*FAA Museum*)

702 Squadron operated Sea Hurricane IIbs from May to July 1942 at Belfast on night fighter defence training. (FAA Museum)

759 Squadron was a Fleet Fighter School based at Eastleigh, Nairobi, one of the Sea Hurricane Ibs being V7438. (FAA Museum)

768 Squadron was a Deck Landing Training School with shore bases at Arbroath and Macrihanish. The unit embarked on HMS *Argus* in August 1943 for practical training. Here, a Sea Hurricane Mk Ib is being refuelled. (*IWM*)

fly off naval fighters. The other carriers had a total of 39 Sea Hurricanes, with 880 Squadron on *Indomitable*, 801 Squadron on *Eagle* and 885 Squadron on *Victorious*, supported by Fulmars and Martlets.

An early loss was HMS *Eagle*, torpedoed by a U-boat on 11 August. The four Sea Hurricanes in the air at the time landed on other carriers, but the rest were lost. The first air attacks began to develop that evening from enemy aircraft based in Sardinia, Sicily and mainland Italy, but the failing light was not suitable for launching Sea Hurricanes. Several bombers were knocked out by the ships' AA guns. The next day, Sea Hurricanes of 885 Squadron were sent up to defend against raiders. As they landed again, *Victorious* was bombed, but flight operations and sailing were not affected. On the third day, *Indomitable* was hit by bombs on the armoured deck, which saved the ship, but a halt was called to flight operations. The Sea Hurricanes in the air at the time landed safely on *Victorious*, the only carrier left fully operational, by now crowded with 47 fighters and nine torpedo bombers. As the convoy neared the Sicilian narrows, where the larger escort ships could not manoeuvre, the Navy had to leave the merchant ships to fend off further Axis attacks for themselves. This resulted in the loss of eight more merchant ships and two cruisers. In the end, despite being escorted by the might of the Royal Navy, only five surviving supply ships reached Malta, included the badly damaged, but still floating, tanker *Ohio*.

Sea Hurricanes of the FAA were involved in one final major operation in the Mediterranean theatre, the support of

Operation Torch, the seaborne landings by the Allies in Morocco and Algeria. The large force of British and American carriers included three British escort carriers, HMS *Biter*, *Dasher* and *Avenger*, with 42 Sea Hurricanes. British naval forces provided support for the Allied landings at Oran and Algiers, where the shipborne fighters carried the American white star to avoid confusing the American gunners. Sea Hurricanes were allocated to the support of the American landings at Oran on 8 November, operating against Vichy French forces, who had shot down eight Albacores previously in a raid on the airfield. Twelve Sea Hurricanes from *Dasher* and *Biter* fought off the French Dewoitine D520 fighters and continued to patrol until the French surrendered on 10 November. The major loss in this operation was *Avenger*, torpedoed by U-155 on 15 November. The ship blew up and sank immediately with the loss of almost all the crew and its compliment of Sea Hurricanes.

Despite these successes, the Operation Torch landings marked the start of a gradual phasing out of the Sea Hurricanes. Their place was taken by Martlets, Hellcats, Corsairs and Seafires. These aircraft were better suited to landing support operations in confined waters, and the elderly Hurricane was being outperformed by the German fighters coming into service by early 1943.

766 Squadron was a Naval Operations Training Unit normally based at Inskip. Incidents during deck operations were not unusual, this Sea Hurricane was damaged landing on HMS *Revenger*, September/October 1944. (*FAA Museum*)

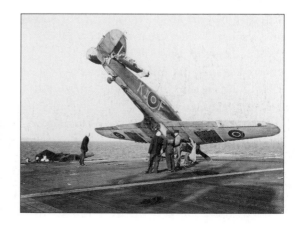

CHAPTER 6

THE MEDITERRANEAN THEATRE

The Mediterranean Theatre covered a vast area from Gibraltar to the Middle East, and from Greece in the north to the desert warfare raging in North Africa. This meant major logistical problems both for the Axis forces, and for the increasingly overstretched Allies. Strategically vital to the region, the fortress island of Malta lay at the centre, dominating the Axis supply lines from Italy to Rommel's desert army in the south. The German intention was to occupy all of North Africa, including the vital Allied supply route through the Suez Canal from the oilfields in the Middle East. Only the small Maltese garrison stood in their way.

Britain meanwhile was facing the imminent threat of invasion from France, only twenty miles across the Channel; the Luftwaffe was continuing its ultimately unsuccessful efforts to destroy the RAF on the ground. While Britain was thus heavily preoccupied with defending her own home territory, keeping the supply lines open to Alexandria and, hence, to Suez had become an equally essential war aim. With the Franco-German armistice in June 1940, Italy entered the war on Germany's side, creating a new threat in the Mediterranean that would shortly be directed against the Allies' key staging post.

To counter the threat, three airfields had been prepared on Malta at Hal Far, Luqa and Takali, but no combat aircraft were based on them until mid-1940. The island did at least have two early warning radar systems in operation, with anti-aircraft guns and searchlights. By the time Mussolini declared war on 10 June 1940, the Italian Air Force in

Sicily had three squadrons of antiquated fighters and some 12 squadrons of obsolete bombers, together with a number of transport aircraft, with additional combat aircraft based in Sardinia. Wasting little time after the declaration, since preparations had already been made, the first bombing raid was launched on the dockyard at Valetta on 11 June, with Hal Far airfield as the secondary target. The raiders were met by the legendary, but obsolete, Gladiators of the Hal Far Fighter Flight, flown by volunteers, who were unable to destroy any of the enemy aircraft on this, the first day of an historic battle that was to last nearly two and a half years.

On 20 June, 830 Squadron FAA at Hal Far, with 12 Swordfish torpedo reconnaissance aircraft, attempted to defend against the first Italian night bombing attack. Two of the Gladiators were damaged in accidents the next day, but the engineering officer was able to rebuild one good aircraft out of the wreckage. On 22 June, a pair of patrolling Gladiators claimed the first victim, an unescorted reconnaissance SM79, which was hit over Valetta and, watched by cheering bystanders, crashed into the sea.

Until now, Alexandria had been the priority for reinforcements, with Hurricanes arriving there even before Italy entered the war. With the increased threat to Malta, a request was made for some Hurricanes on delivery to Alexandria to be retained for the initial defence of the island. The first three arrived on 13 June, the ferry pilots departing the same day, followed by two more on 21

June, the pilots remaining this time with the aircraft. On 20 June, six more Hurricanes arrived at Luqa, just half the number that had set out to fly across Europe from Britain. Two of these were damaged on landing. Because Malta by then had more Hurricanes than Alexandria, three were refuelled and serviced and sent on to Egypt with a Blenheim escort. The five remaining Hurricanes had five additional pilots available. The Hurricanes saw their first combat on 3 July, when Flg Off John Waters shot down a bomber over the island. Hit by Italian escort fighters, he crashed on landing, wrecking the aircraft, but was himself unhurt.

During the early part of July, the Italians continued to bomb Malta, as well as attacking the British Mediterranean Fleet, which had sailed from Alexandria to meet and protect two convoys on their way through the battle zone. On 10 July, Italian bombers arrived late over the island, so that their fighter escort, running low on fuel, was forced to return early. Two bombers were shot down by Hurricanes with no losses to the RAF. On 13 July, Flt Lt Peter Keeble was in a dogfight with three CR42 fighters, but as he shot one down he was hit himself and crashed, becoming the first RAF pilot to lose his life in the defence of Malta. By the end of the month, however, the ground crews were having difficulty keeping the Hurricanes in the air, and the three remaining Gladiators, known as Faith, Hope and Charity, heroically maintained the air defence of the island. One was shot down on 29 July, the pilot being badly burned.

Once Italy entered the war it became clear that Malta needed to be defended more effectively, and would require something more formidable than a few Hurricanes divided between the island and Egypt. With the fall of France, the most practical route for reinforcements was to fly them off an aircraft carrier out of Gibraltar at maximum range,

direct to Malta. In July 1940, 418 Flight was formed at Uxbridge, consisting of one officer and seven sergeant pilots. All had previous experience with the FAA, but preferred to remain with the RAF. They collected Hurricanes from the MU at Hullavington and flew them to Abbotsinch, near Glasgow, where more Hurricanes had been gathered, to be loaded on to HMS *Argus*. Here, they were joined by additional officers, including Flt Lt D.W. Balden, officer in command, who advised the unit that their destination was Malta.

HMS *Argus* sailed from Greenock on 23 July with 12 Hurricanes and two Skuas on board, heading for Gibraltar, where the aircraft were reassembled on deck and the spares loaded aboard a Sunderland. On 31 July *Argus* set sail from Gibraltar, escorted by HMS *Ark Royal* and a number of other capital ships. The Hurricanes were finally in a position to take off for Malta at dawn on 2 August, with a pair of Skuas to navigate. All the aircraft arrived at Malta, covering the 380 miles in 2 hrs 20 mins, but one Hurricane and one Skua were written off on landing, although the crews were unhurt. To provide servicing support for the Hurricanes, two Sunderlands flew in 23 airmen, at the same time providing a rescue capability if required. Additional spares were delivered by submarine but, while the Hurricanes were being prepared for combat, two were wrecked on the ground by Italian bombers. The remaining aircraft with the fighter flight were merged with the newcomers and a three flight squadron was put together, with Sqn Ldr Jock Martin in command.

To counter the continuing enemy night raids, an impromptu night fighter section was formed, the first engagement coming on the night of 13 August when Flg Off Barber shot down one S79, the first night fighter victory of the war outside western Europe. On 16 August, the Hurricane compliment officially

With the fall of France and the entry of Italy into the war, the only effective method of delivering Hurricanes to Malta was by launching from an aircraft carrier out of Gibraltar. Tropical Hurricane Mk I V7563 is fitted with long-range fuel tanks under the wing just after lift-off from HMS *Furious*. (*Author's Collection*)

Owing to enemy night raids on Malta, a night fighter section was formed equipped with Hurricanes, later to become the Night Fighter Unit. Hawker built Hurricane Mk IIa is seen here at Ta Kali after a wheels-up landing, July 1941. (*Author's Collection*)

16 August 1940, the semi-formal Hurricane operations on Malta became formalized with 261 Squadron. (*Author's Collection*)

became 261 Squadron, with Flt Lt Balden promoted to take command, and formed into two flights. The rest of August was fairly quiet. One CR42 was claimed on the 24th, and a Hurricane was damaged.

Early in September, the Italian Air Force acquired the first batch of 15 Ju87 Stukas from Germany and based them at Comiso in southern Sicily, where they were a threat not only to Malta, but also to the Allied shipping passing through the Messina strait. The Stukas made their first attack on Malta with five aircraft on 4 September. None were shot down, and six more returned the next day, again without loss. Following another dive-bombing raid on 14 September, when there were no interceptions, the first Stuka was claimed by a Hurricane on 17 September, with damage to a second, and a CR42 fighter was destroyed. The only RAF loss was a Wellington on the ground at Luqa. On 25 September, three Hurricanes and two Gladiators were scrambled to intercept an approaching raid and a MC200 fighter was shot down.

The following month was not much busier. Some MC200s were intercepted on a reconnaissance sortie on 4 October, and one was shot down by a Hurricane. Another night attack was made on 8 October, when a Hurricane of 261 Squadron was able to shoot down an Italian bomber with the aid of searchlights. This brought total losses to 22 confirmed kills by the defending fighters, as against two Hurricanes and a Gladiator lost by the RAF. In another raid on 16 October, one MC200 was claimed as damaged, making it back as far as an Italian airfield, where it subsequently had to be abandoned. To make room at Luqa for Wellington bombers expected from Britain, on 30 October 261 Squadron moved to the former civil airfield at Takali, which then officially became an RAF base.

Early November saw the resumption of Italian air attacks. A single MC200 was claimed by a Hurricane on 2 November. A convoy carrying ground troop reinforcements sailed from Gibraltar on 7 November, arriving three days later. Another supply convoy left Alexandria at the same time, while five more Wellingtons arrived at Luqa on 8 November. With the discovery by Malta based reconnaissance aircraft of the Italian fleet in Taranto harbour, a famously successful attack was made on the night of 11/12 November by Swordfish flying from HMS *Illustrious*, which sank the majority of the Italian warships at anchor.

With the British fleet now out of range of the Italian Air Force, Malta was attacked again on 12 November, one reconnaissance MC200 being shot down by a Hurricane.

In mid-November, HMS *Argus* sailed again from Gibraltar with another 12 Hurricanes and two Skuas on board, plus 13 RAF pilots and two FAA crews. At dawn on 17 November the first wave of six Hurricanes and one Skua started their take-off for the 400 miles journey to Malta. It was anticipated that they should have had about 45 minutes of fuel in reserve, but 15 minutes was wasted while the flight formed up. The aircraft flew at 150 mph at 2,000 ft, which was not the most economical plan.

A second flight left *Argus* an hour later, allowing the Fleet to turn back towards Gibraltar. As the first group of aircraft continued, the weather changed and they ran into headwinds. Despite good navigation and being met by an escorting Sunderland, two of the Hurricanes ran out of fuel, with the loss of one pilot. The four remaining Hurricanes and the Skua landed safely with practically no fuel left.

The second flight was even less fortunate. They became hopelessly lost and, one by one, ran out of fuel, ditching in the sea, where all the pilots drowned. Only the Skua found land at the last minute and, damaged by gunfire, made a forced landing on a beach in Sicily. This was a tragic loss of so many experienced aircrew, many of whom had chalked up victories in the Battle of Britain. The four surviving Hurricanes and new aircrew joined 261 Squadron, allowing a stronger defence of eight aircraft to be put up against a raid on 23 November. There were no decisive results.

On 26 November, Flt Sgt Dennis Ashton shot down a CR42, but was then attacked by another CR42, crashing fatally into the sea. With the arrival of another convoy and the British fleet active in the area, the Italians mounted a further attack on Malta on 27 November. Hurricanes were up and ready for the raiders. Concentrating on the bombers,

Sgt Robertson claimed one S79, with no losses to the Hurricanes. On the night of 18 December, one of a number of night raids by solo bombers, an enemy aircraft was successfully intercepted. By the end of the year, Malta had fended off sporadic attacks by the Italians and remained a significant strike base, providing facilities for RN destroyers and submarines. RAF fighters had claimed 13 bombers, two Stukas and 16 fighters destroyed, with further enemy aircraft shot down by the ground defences.

Although there were days when there was little or no combat, it did not mean that this was a slack time for the RAF. Malta lay across the main supply routes for Axis traffic into North Africa. Many enemy aircraft were being detected in the vicinity, causing Hurricanes to be scrambled, even though they did not engage. Being at a constant state of readiness meant a lot of wear and tear on the planes. By the end of the year, the maintenance of just 16 Hurricanes, with four in reserve, and four Gladiators had become a considerable challenge for the 261 Squadron ground crews.

*

At the start of 1941, the Allies were showing positive progress, with the Battle of Britain won and invasion staved off, as it turned out, permanently; while the British Army in North Africa was advancing against Rommel's forces into Libya. In Malta things were relatively peaceful until, on 8 January, the situation changed dramatically with the arrival in Sicily of the first of a large force of Luftwaffe bombers and supporting Bf109s.

The initial arrival was of some 96 bombers, including He111s, Ju88s and Ju87 Stukas, with battle-hardened German pilots. By the end of the month Luftwaffe numbers had risen to 141 aircraft, giving the Germans a much more formidable offensive capability than the Italian Air Force. To ease the supply of matèriel to the Axis forces in North Africa, their avowed intention was to destroy the garrison on Malta.

The first enemy raid of the year on Malta took place on 9 January, when 261 Squadron shot down two Italian aircraft for no losses. The British Mediterranean Fleet – Force H – was continuously in action between Gibraltar and Egypt, and on 10 January the carrier HMS *Illustrious* was attacked and badly damaged by Ju87 Stukas. Six bombs hit the carrier, causing heavy casualties and putting the flight deck out of action. The captain withdrew and made for Malta for urgent repairs, arriving in Grand Harbour, Valetta on the same day. The ship now presented a very tempting target. The first Italian air attack came on 13 January without any hits being scored, to be followed by another raid three days later, which was mainly deflected by the ground-based AA guns. The Luftwaffe began to take an active interest on 16 January, with Ju88s escorted by Bf110s and Ju87s escorted by the Italians scoring two direct hits on the disabled carrier. By the end of the raid, four Ju88s and one Ju87 had been claimed destroyed by the fighters, and more damaged by the AA defences. The intensity of the German bombing was far greater than any that had been previously experienced on Malta.

The airfields were bombed on 18 January in an attempt to suppress the fighter defences before further attacks could be mounted against *Illustrious*. Hurricanes and Fulmars claimed seven Ju87s shot down, for the loss of one Fulmar. The next day, the carrier was again the primary target for Ju88s and Ju87s, with Hurricanes leading the air defence. It was estimated the defenders accounted for some 40 enemy aircraft, including 16 to the AA guns and, despite the probability of overclaiming in such a confusing situation, *Illustrious* did not receive any further direct

hits, although she was damaged by some near-misses. On 20 January, a short lull in the enemy raids allowed more pilot reinforcements to arrive, a number of them experienced Battle of Britain veterans; six more Hurricanes were delivered on 29 January.

In addition to fighter aircraft flown from carriers out of Gibraltar, further deliveries were made from West Africa across to Egypt, the initial ferry flight of four Blenheims and five Hurricanes departing on 20 September 1940. On 9 January 1941, 40 Hurricanes took off from the decks of *Furious* and *Argus* to Takoradi and flew the old Imperial Airways route across Nigeria and Sudan to Egypt, where the aircraft could be allocated to whatever part of the theatre needed them most. 38 Hurricanes of the January delivery eventually reached Egypt, eight leaving for Malta on 19 January and arriving at Hal Far in the middle of an attack, joining 261 Squadron. This brought the strength of the Squadron up to 28 Hurricanes, of which five were unserviceable. A further six pilots arrived the next day by Sunderland. HMS *Illustrious* was finally patched up sufficiently for departure on 23 January for Alexandria, and eventually underwent extensive repairs in the USA.

On 26 January, a reconnaissance Ju88 was claimed by two Hurricanes, with another Italian fighter claimed during the morning of 1 February and a Ju88 that evening. On 3 February, the airfields were the target for Ju88s, with two claimed shot down by the defending Hurricanes and Fulmars. Night raiders were detected on 8 February, and six Hurricanes were scrambled, splitting up at 16,000 ft, with one He111 shot down.

A greater enemy threat arrived in Sicily on 9 February in the form of Bf109Es of Luftwaffe squadron 7/JG26, flown by highly experienced pilots. Their first appearance over Malta came three days later. 261

In March 1941 seven Hurricanes of 274 Squadron were flown to Malta from North Africa and attached to 261 Squadron. (*Author's Collection*)

Once at Takoradi the Hurricanes were prepared for the long overland delivery flight to Egypt. (*Air Ministry*)

With the arrival of Luftwaffe Bf109s in Sicily, Malta's defences suffered a number of damaging raids. One example was the destruction of 261 Squadron Hurricanes at Takali after Luftwaffe ground attack. (*Author's Collection*)

Of the 40 Hurricanes which set out across Africa from Takoradi to Egypt, 38 arrived safely, while two made forced landings either because of fuel shortage or owing to unserviceability. (*Author's Collection*)

The old Imperial Airways route from West Africa to Egypt was used to supply Hurricanes, both to the Middle East and to Malta. On 9 January 1941, HMS *Furious* and *Argus* launched 40 Hurricanes to Takoradi. These tropical Hurricane Mk Is were fitted with underwing long-range fuel tanks. One is seen here leaving the deck of HMS *Furious*. (*Author's Collection*)

The carriers, HMS *Ark Royal*, *Eagle* and *Furious* left Gibraltar in mid-May 1941 with 48 Hurricanes of 213, 229 and 249 Squadrons. Only 249 Squadron were to remain for the defence of Malta. Hurricanes are being prepared on the deck of HMS *Furious* for the ferry flight. (*Author's Collection*)

On 3 April 1941, a dozen Hurricane Mk IIas were launched off HMS *Ark Royal* for Malta. Another batch of Hurricanes with long-range fuel tanks is lashed down on HMS *Ark Royal* on 27 June 1941, ready for delivery. (*Author's Collection*)

All 249 Squadron Hurricanes launched from *Ark Royal* arrived in Malta safely, replacing 261 Squadron, which was reallocated to the Mid-East. A 249 Squadron Hurricane at readiness at Ta Kali in the summer of 1941. (*P.G. Leggett*)

Squadron was launched against a formation of Ju88s, but were bounced by the Bf109s, with two Hurricanes shot down and another damaged. The sudden appearance of the Bf109Es had a serious effect on the morale of the squadron, many of whose pilots and aircraft were by now suffering from battle fatigue, particularly after recent losses. The Messerschmits were encountered again on 16 February when six attacked 'A' Flight of 261 Squadron, destroying one Hurricane and damaging two others, although the pilots escaped without injury.

On 23 February, Ju87s returned without the usual fighter cover. One was shot down over the island, another so badly damaged that the crew had to bale out over the coast of Sicily. Two days later, one of a formation of four Bf110s was shot down by a Hurricane, but a Hurricane and pilot were lost during a further engagement in the afternoon.

The following day, a heavy bombing raid was launched with Luqa as the main target. Among the escorting fighters were Bf109s. Eight Hurricanes climbed above the Stukas to dive down in attack, with Bf109s following them. Three Ju87s were shot down, but Bf109s destroyed three Hurricanes with the loss of the pilots and a fourth Hurricane was damaged. Aircraft destroyed on the ground included six Wellingtons of 148 Squadron, while many of the airfield buildings were badly damaged. On 5 March another major raid occurred, with one Ju88 and a Bf109 claimed by the defending Hurricanes, followed by a Ju88 and two Ju87s, for the loss of one Hurricane and its pilot. Next day, five very welcome Hurricane reinforcements flew in via the African route from Cairo, although one was lost the next day to a Bf109. On 10 March, a Bf110 was shot down at night by one of the 261 Squadron Hurricanes.

A week later, further reinforcements arrived from North Africa, consisting of seven Hurricanes from 274 Squadron, which were attached to 261 Squadron. On 18 March, the Italians attacked again, losing at least two CR42s claimed shot down. On 22 March, 261 Squadron suffered serious losses when five Hurricanes were shot down with their pilots in a battle with Ju88s escorted by Bf109s. The next day, perhaps in the belief that the fighter defences had been seriously weakened, a major attack developed, with Ju87s escorted by MC200s, on an approaching convoy. Fourteen Hurricanes were scrambled, however, and confirmed three Ju87s shot down, with one Hurricane lost after the pilot baled out. On 28 March, Bf109s shot down one Hurricane, wounding the pilot. At the end of the month, 261 Squadron was recorded as having 34 Hurricanes on strength, although not all were airworthy.

Significant reinforcements were added to the Malta garrison on 3 April 1941, when 12 Hurricane IIas were launched off HMS *Ark Royal* flown by a number of experienced Battle of Britain veterans. One of the remaining Hurricane Is, V7101, was painted blue all over and allocated to 69 Squadron for photo reconnaissance. The armament and armour plating were removed to reduce weight, and larger fuel tanks were fitted. The new reinforcements were in action the following day, and two were shot down into the sea by Bf109s with the loss of both pilots, although later in the day a Bf109 was

claimed. During the night of 11–12 April a Ju87 was claimed by 261 Squadron, and on 13 April Hurricanes were involved in convoy escort when four Bf109s were spotted. One was shot down into the sea by Flt Lt Mason, while the other three Bf109s retaliated, damaging a Hurricane, which was forced to ditch.

On 20 April a raid was detected building up over Sicily and, initially, two Hurricane IIas were scrambled. A CR42 biplane was soon claimed and Bf109s joined the fight from above, diving right through the formations, while another CR42 soon followed the first to destruction. Two days later, 261 Squadron Hurricanes were on patrol when they were alerted to enemy aircraft in the area. These turned out to be two Bf109s, which damaged one Hurricane. The next day, Flg Off Auger was shot down by a Bf109 and, although he parachuted into the sea, he unfortunately drowned before the rescue services could get a boat out.

On 27 April, news was received that *Ark Royal* was on its way again to Malta with 24 Hurricanes and 26 pilots. Each of three waves was led by a Fulmar and was met from Malta by three Marylands and a Sunderland. As the first wave arrived over Malta, the Sunderland was attacked on landing and set ablaze before sinking at its moorings. 23 of the Hurricanes landed safely, however, making Luqa and Hal Far rather overcrowded; Takali now came into use as a permanent fighter base. Many of the new pilots were combat veterans. In addition to Hurricane reinforcements, a detachment of six Blenheims arrived from 21 Squadron, replacing the remaining seven Wellingtons from 148 Squadron, which were flown to Egypt. Malta was now moving up from a purely defensive footing to having an active strike capability.

Perhaps sensing this, the German assault continued unabated. Bf109s returned in full

Ta Kali after a Bf109 attack destroyed a number of 249 Squadron Hurricanes on the ground. (*F.A. Etchells*)

force on 1 May, claiming two 261 Squadron Hurricane IIs and wounding both pilots. The modified photo reconnaissance Hurricane with 69 Squadron made its first sortie on 4 May, the reduction in weight allowing it to operate regularly up to 30,000 ft, although on one occasion it did reach 36,000 ft, where it was found to be unstable. On 5 May, Hurricanes damaged a Ju88 badly enough for it to crash on landing at its base, killing the crew.

*

By early May, the situation in the Mediterranean Theatre was not so promising. British forces had been driven back by Rommel's army as far as Egypt. The Balkans, including Yugoslavia and Greece, were under German occupation, and the invasion of Crete was imminent. To allow British forces in Egypt to return to the offensive, a fast convoy left Gibraltar on 6 May. Escorted by Force H, it carried tanks, motor transport and 53 crated Hurricanes, the aim being to meet up with the Mediterranean Fleet out of Alexandria at a rendezvous point south of Malta. At the appointed time, however, the island was under attack from He111 bombers escorted by Bf109s, one of which was shot down by a Hurricane. Meanwhile, the rest of the Hurricanes had been attacked by Bf109s. Three aircraft were shot down and a fourth damaged. Just after darkness fell, Hurricanes claimed a Ju88 and He111 destroyed.

As the convoy sailed into Grand Harbour on 9 May, Ju87s were waiting to pounce. Two enemy aircraft were claimed by the defending Hurricanes as they departed. The convoy eventually reached Alexandria on 12 May, having battled its way through the Mediterranean with 238 tanks and 43 crated Hurricanes remaining for the offensive against the Axis forces in North Africa. By this time, Malta had some 50 Hurricanes, mainly Mk IIa and IIbs, and 185 Squadron was formed alongside 261 Squadron to share the defence of the island. The new unit was formed from a nucleus of 'C' Flight of 261 Squadron, with Sqn Ldr Mould as the commanding officer.

The new squadron was in action on 13 May, with aircraft from 261 Squadron, when they were attacked by Bf109s. Two Hurricanes were shot down, killing one of the pilots. This was the first time that the Bf109s had operated in the fighter-bomber role over Malta. On the next afternoon, 185 and 261 Squadrons were again attacked by Bf109s and Pilot Officer Hamilton, who had been successful in shooting down at least five enemy aircraft to date, was himself shot down, dying later from his wounds. Two 185 Squadron Hurricanes took off to provide top cover for 261 Squadron on 15 May, but were bounced by Bf109s, Sgt Wynne crashing at high speed to his death. Meanwhile, a S79 was claimed by Plt Off John Pain and a Wellington was destroyed on the ground at Luqa, with three Beaufighters damaged. RAF losses between 12 and 15 May included five Hurricanes, with four damaged. Then, as German units were having to be withdrawn from Sicily for the offensive against Russia, the Italian Air Force returned to the fray.

The Allied assault on Crete was about to begin. Further reinforcements were on the way from Gibraltar, sailing on the carriers *Ark Royal*, *Eagle* and *Furious*, escorted by a strong force of two battleships, with cruisers and destroyers. Not all the 48 Hurricanes carried were for the defence of the island but, for the first time, there were established RAF

units on board. These were 213, 229 and 249 Squadrons, which had been ordered to prepare for service in the Middle East. As the new convoy approached, Luqa came under attack. A Beaufighter was burnt out on the ground and a 261 Squadron Hurricane shot down, the pilot baling out safely.

The next day, 21 May, Operation Splice, to reinforce the assault on Crete, began, with 213 Squadron taking off from *Furious* for Malta, led by a Fulmar, accompanied by six Hurricanes from 229 Squadron. One Hurricane of 213 Squadron hit the sea while taking off, and crashed. Arriving in Malta, the Hurricanes were turned around quickly and set off for Mersa Matruh, led by 252 Squadron Beaufighters. Soon afterwards, however, seven of 213 Squadron returned, having lost contact with the escort. Meanwhile, 249 Squadron had been launched from *Ark Royal* and, despite being short of fuel, arrived safely on the island just as a bombing raid got under way. It was then that they were told the squadron was to stay on Malta, even though they had no kit. They replaced 261 Squadron, which was being relocated to the Middle East, taking the new Hurricanes with them. This left only the battle-worn aircraft for the new arrivals.

249 Squadron were based at Takali, where they were joined by 185 Squadron with their Hurricane Mk Is, leaving Luqa and Hal Far as bases for bombers and reconnaissance aircraft. These were also staging posts for aircraft en route to the Middle East. Many of the new pilots had combat experience. Their CO was Sqn Ldr Barton, with 8.5 victories already to his credit. Nevertheless, their luck was out. During their first readiness on 25 May, before 249 Squadron could be ordered into the air, an attack by Bf109s destroyed two Hurricanes on the ground and damaged three others.

On 27 May, 249 Squadron moved to Hal Far and, on the following night, Hurricanes prevented several aircraft of an attacking force from reaching their targets. By the end of the month, the defenders had regained much of their air superiority – and, with the Luftwaffe being recalled from Sicily for action on the Russian Front, it was now becoming possible to launch offensive operations from Malta against Sicily and German units in North Africa.

*

Meanwhile, defensive fighter actions had lessened, and the first 'kill' by 249 Squadron was not recorded until 3 June when Sqn Ldr Barton shot one S79 down over the sea. With 46 Squadron, commanded by Sqn Ldr 'Sandy' Rabagliati, scheduled to arrive shortly, 185 Squadron was reassigned to night fighter defence. Including 46 Squadron and the aircraft left behind by 229 Squadron from the previous delivery, 43 Hurricanes in all were despatched to the island, led in by 82 Squadron Blenheims. All arrived safely. After exchanging their Hurricane Mk IIs for the remaining Mk Is on the island, 229 Squadron departed the next day for Mersa Matruh.

In the early hours of 8 June, Hurricanes of 249 Squadron claimed two BR20M bombers. Another, badly damaged, succeeded in returning to base. Alerted by a radar warning of an approaching raid, 249 Squadron Hurricanes were scrambled and destroyed two S79s. Malta had now been in active combat for a year, with a total claim of 106 enemy aircraft shot down.

The first action for 46 Squadron came in the early morning of 11 June, with seven Hurricanes scrambled. One S79 was shot down into the sea for one Hurricane lost. The pilot was posted as missing. The next day, 18 Hurricanes from 46 and 249 Squadrons were scrambled in the early morning to intercept the daily reconnaissance flight. Putting up a spirited fight, one Italian MC200 was shot

down; three of the 249 Squadron aircraft were hit, one pilot being killed, another parachuting into the sea, and the third making a forced landing at Safi. During the afternoon, a Cant rescue floatplane and an escorting CR42 were shot down, with one Hurricane and its pilot lost.

On 14 June, a further delivery of Hurricanes was made to Malta, with 28 aircraft of 238 Squadron from *Victorious* and 20 more with 260 Squadron aboard *Ark Royal*. All the Hurricanes were destined for combat in the North African desert campaign, but five failed to arrive at Malta for a variety of reasons, three losses being attributed to faulty navigation by the inexperienced crew of the escorting Hudson. The other two losses were ascribed to lack of fuel. The majority of the aircraft flew on to Egypt over the next few days.

Owing to the success of the 'blue' Hurricane Mk I on reconnaissance duties with 69 Squadron, a second aircraft, a modified long-range Mk II Z3053, was delivered in mid-June. On the 18th, a MC200 was damaged badly enough to crash land at its base, though one of the defending Hurricanes was lost with its pilot. The rest of the month was a busy time for 46 Squadron, with combat on five days out of eight. At dawn on 23 June, Hurricanes went over to the offensive and shot up the seaplane base at Syracuse. 46 Squadron led an attack on a S79 and 36 escorting MC200s, the S79 being damaged, with two MC200s shot down and no Hurricanes lost. During the afternoon, the new Mk II reconmnaissance plane spotted an Italian supply convoy on its way to Libya and called in reinforcements, but the resulting attack was unsuccessful as no ships were sunk. Four days later, 46 Squadron intercepted a S79 with 24 escorting MC200s. Two of the escorts were claimed. Later in the day, 46 Squadron claimed a further three MC200s; while, on the same day, a further

Although many Hurricanes reached Malta from the carriers out of Gibraltar, some were damaged on arrival, often during enemy raids — such as this Hurricane Mk II on arrival at Ta Kali for 249 Squadron, August 1941. (*F.A. Etchells*)

Hurricanes were not just damaged by enemy action in Malta, this one suffering a take-off crash at Ta Kali in August 1941. Despite the aircraft being wrecked, the pilot suffered only two broken ribs. (*F.A. Etchells*)

22 Hurricanes, including some Mk IIcs armed with cannon, were flown off *Ark Royal*. One went missing en route with the pilot taken prisoner, another crashed on landing.

On 28 June, 46 Squadron was renumbered 126 Squadron, as a new 46 Squadron was to be formed in the Middle East. On 30 June, the squadron moved from Hal Far to Takali with some dispersals at the newly constructed Safi, where there was a dangerously narrow runway bordered by anti-invasion devices. During the first four days in July, no fewer than five Hurricanes crashed at this difficult airfield.

The new 126 Squadron was in action on the day of the move, when six Hurricanes, including some of the Mk IIcs, shot down two MC200s. Also on 30 June, a further delivery was made of Hurricanes from HMS *Ark Royal* and *Furious*. Of 15 Hurricanes from HMS *Furious*, the second crashed on take-off, killing the pilot and seriously injuring a number of aircrew. The remaining eight Hurricanes of the first wave took off safely, but the final six could not be launched due to pilot injuries. 35 Hurricanes reached Malta safely.

Early on 4 July, MC200s were detected approaching the island and were attacked by four Hurricanes of 185 Squadron, with claims of two shot down and three damaged. A 126 Squadron Hurricane crashed on take-off from Safi into the sea, killing the pilot. On the night of 8/9 July, a 249 Squadron Hurricane claimed one of six S79s which had destroyed a Wellington on the ground. Next morning, one MC200 was badly damaged by a Hurricane of 185 Squadron, which crash landed on return to base. Returning to the offensive in the afternoon, four Hurricanes of

126 and 185 Squadrons shot up flying boats at Syracuse, claiming six aircraft destroyed and four damaged. The Italians hit back on 11 July, attacking Hal Far with a strong force of fighters. At least 12 Hurricanes were scrambled from 185 Squadron and, among a number of claims from both sides, five Macchis were confirmed damaged and no Hurricanes lost.

On 17 July, a large force of fighters covered a new reconnaissance aircraft, the Z1007bis, and were met by 185 and 249 Squadrons, two MC200s being destroyed for the loss of one Hurricane. 25 July, a lone reconnaissance Z1007bis accompanied by a heavy force of MC200s was met by 185 and 249 Squadrons, the Z1007bis being the victim of 185 Squadron. Meanwhile, 249 Squadron destroyed two of the escorting MC200s.

In the early hours of 26 July, the Italian Navy attacked Valetta with boats packed with explosives, to break through the harbour defences. While a battle raged in the harbour entrance, cannon armed Hurricanes of 185 and 126 Squadrons attacked four motor boats offshore and sank two. Escorting MC200s joined the fight and two were shot down for the loss of one Hurricane, from which Plt Off Denis Winton baled out and climbed aboard one of the abandoned Italian

A further batch of 14 Hurricanes were flown to Malta from HMS *Ark Royal* in early September, followed on the 13th by 45 more, 23 of whcih continued on to Egypt.

motor boats, becoming perhaps the only RAF pilot to capture an enemy warship single handed. By the end of July, the defending Hurricanes had been credited with 21 confirmed victories for the loss of three, and two pilots killed. There were now 15 Hurricane Is and 60 Mk IIs on the island in addition to other offensive aircraft, including Beaufighters and Blenheims.

The Malta Night Fighter Unit (MNFU) was formed at Takali at the end of July, with eight Hurricane IIcs and four Mk IIbs, Sqn Ldr George Powell-Sheddon commanding. The Hurricanes operated with some success in pairs, aided by searchlights, claiming their first victories on the night of 5/6 August when two BR20M bombers were shot down. On 10 August, Sqn Ldr Rabagliati of 126 Squadron shot down a Z506B. After dark on 11 August, a bombing attack developed over Malta, and a Hurricane of the MNFU shot down a BR20M. On 17 August, Hurricanes returned to Syracuse, destroying two Z506B flying boats and damaging four; and, on the same day, a Ca312 floatplane was shot down off Malta by 249 Squadron.

Two days later, MC200s returned to the island for the first time that month and 126 Squadron chased them back to Sicily, claiming four shot down with no Hurricane losses. The last major engagement of the month came on 26 August, when 126 and 185 Squadrons were scrambled to intercept MC200s, one of which was shot down for the loss of one Hurricane. During that month, the fighters were credited with 12 victories for the loss of one Hurricane and pilot.

September began well. On the morning of the 4th, MC200s were attacked by 126 and 185 Squadrons with the destruction of two Italian fighters and no Hurricanes lost. Another Italian attack was mounted in the afternoon, and was met by 249 Squadron. One MC200 was shot down, but two

Hurricanes were lost with their pilots. Although there was a brief respite from the fighters during the day, attacks from night bombers continued, a Z1007bis being shot down just before dawn on 5 September by a pair of Hurricanes of MNFU, followed by another Z1007bis during the night of 8 September.

On 9 September, 14 Hurricanes were flown in from *Ark Royal*. A further 12 remained on board as there were not enough Blenheims available to escort them, but the next day the new delivery left for the Middle East. On 13 September, a further 45 Hurricanes arrived on Malta from both *Ark Royal* and *Furious*. With 23 flying on to Egypt, the rest remained to bring the local squadrons up to strength and give some of the pilots a chance to rest.

On 28 September, another convoy reached Malta. 185 Squadron Hurricanes were fitted with bombs for raids on Comiso airfield, designed to discourage attacks on shipping being unloaded at Valetta. While six Hurricanes dropped over 5,000 lb of bombs, six more aircraft from the squadron provided top cover. Comiso was hit again by fighter-bomber Hurricanes on 30 September, one Hurricane being lost. The Malta garrison was now on the offensive, and about one third of all Axis cargo shipped to North Africa was being sunk. The Luftwaffe was forced to divert bombers attacking Egypt to Sicily for convoy protection.

At the beginning of October, the Italians used MC202s for the first time over Malta and were met by 185 Squadron. Sqn Ldr 'Boy' Mould was killed in an action on 1 October, when one of the Macchis was forced to land on the Sicilian coast. On 7 October, 249 Squadron made a fighter-bomber attack on Gela station and Comiso, while MNFU made a night attack on railway installations at Sicili in bright moonlight. On 14 October, low flying Macchis strafed Luqa just before dawn, and Hurricanes of MNFU,

Towards the end of 1941, Malta aircraft were able to move to attacking enemy installations and shipping. The FAA also operated Hurricane IIbs and Gloster built BG766s armed with eight .303 in machine guns and 250 lb bombs under the wings. Here a pilot is racing out for another sortie. (*IWM*)

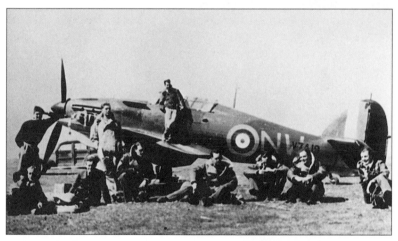

33 Squadron had started to equip with Hurricanes in September 1940, and moved to Eleusis in Greece on 19 February 1941. (*RAF Museum*)

Following the Italian attack on Greece in October 1940, 80 Squadron began to replace Gladiators with Hurricanes on 20 February 1941 at Eleusis. (*Author's Collection*)

213 Squadron provided air defence from Egypt during the evacuation of Crete. (*IWM*)

185 and 249 Squadrons scrambled in defence. Plt Off Barnwell, one of the most successful night fighter pilots, was shot down and killed after destroying one raider.

On 17 October, 249 Squadron provided escort for Blenheims of the newly arrived 18 Squadron for a medium level attack on Syracuse seaplane base. 19 October, two pilots of 249 Squadron went on patrol with long-range ferry tanks fitted, to intercept troop carrying aircraft to North Africa. A single S81 was spotted at low level and shot down. 126 Squadron Hurricanes bombed Comiso during the afternoon. Next morning, another S81 was shot down by two patrolling 185 Squadron Hurricanes. During a strafing attack on Luqa on 22 October by MC202s, one defending 249 Squadron Hurricane was lost, but the pilot was able to bale out. An

attack by MC202 escorted Z1007bis bombers on Grand Harbour on 25 October, defended by 185 Squadron, resulted in one bomber being sent back so badly damaged that it crashed on landing and one MC202 shot down, for the loss of one Hurricane and pilot. On the last night of the month Italian bombers were intercepted by MNFU, which claimed one BR20M destroyed.

*

Offensive efforts involving aircraft based on Malta had caused major losses to Axis shipping over the previous three months, exceeding the rate of new ship construction, but at a heavy cost to the Malta based Blenheim units. Tobruk was still in Allied hands, and both the German and British armies were preparing for an all-out effort to decide control of North Africa. For the Axis powers, crushing Malta had become the main priority if the North African campaign was to succeed.

The island had been used almost entirely as an offensive base during the autumn of 1941, both air and naval resources attacking convoys, air transport and military installations in Italy and North Africa. RAF Blenheim units were supported by the FAA, with torpedo attacks from Swordfish and Albacores, and Hurricanes were being used almost exclusively on ground attack duties over Sicily, with occasional interceptions. Malta now had adequate fighters and pilots with good supplies of fuel, ammunition and food, and the RAF build-up had outnumbered Axis air forces in Africa.

On 8 November, 126 Squadron returned to the defensive against an Italian bombing raid, two MC202s being shot down, and one Hurricane lost, the pilot baling out. The next day, enemy torpedo bombers attacked ships of Force H. Two Hurricanes of 185 Squadron were sent to intercept, one failing to return. A major RAF counteroffensive began on 12 November with a strafing attack by 249 Squadron on Gela airfield, during which Wg Cdr Brown was killed. Later in the morning, 249 and 126 Squadrons carried out a fighter-bomber attack on Comiso, where a Hurricane pilot was shot down and captured.

During these offensive operations, reinforcements were still being flown into Malta. The previous month, 266 Wing had been formed from 242, 605 and the more recently arrived 258 Squadrons. The first two units included Battle of Britain veterans, and although most of the original 1940 pilots had moved on, the pilots did have recent operational experience. 242 and 605 Squadrons were loaded aboard HMS *Argus* and 258's Hurricanes were crated aboard HMS *Athene*, with the ground crew of all three squadrons awaiting disembarkation at Gibraltar. The Hurricanes of 242 and most of 605 were shared out aboard *Argus* and *Ark Royal* and 37 planes took off from the carriers on 12 November, all but three arriving safely. The missing pilots fell into enemy hands.

The carriers were heading back to Gibraltar to pick up the next batch of Hurricanes when *Ark Royal* was hit by torpedoes from U-81 on 13 November and sank with the loss, miraculously, of only one life. The remaining Hurricanes at Gibraltar were redirected to Asia, where hostilities had now spread, and were eventually joined by 605 Squadron and a newly reformed 242 Squadron. The new personnel at Malta were integrated into 185 and 249 Squadrons.

On 21 November, Wg Cdr Downland, the commanding officer of 69 Squadron, was flying the unarmed PR Hurricane II on a reconnaissance sortie over Sicily when he was attacked by MC202s and had to bale out over the sea, later being rescued. A Hurricane of 185 Squadron was lost later in the day on convoy patrol when it was attacked by MC202s. The Italian air offensive continued to build up, and on 22 November 126 Squadron was providing top cover for 249 Squadron during an attack by Ju87s with a strong fighter escort, when one MC202 was shot down for no RAF losses.

November had been a crippling month for the Axis supply convoys. 63 per cent of the cargoes intended for Libya were destroyed, largely thanks to Force H, but also with the help of the Malta based Blenheims, many of whose aircrews were killed in action. The Germans therefore decided to move reinforcements to Sicily and Libya to support their North African campaign, particularly as the atrocious Winter conditions would soon be restricting the Russian offensive and the units could again be spared. At the end of November, fighter strength on Malta consisted of Hurricanes of 126, 185, 249 Squadrons and

During the German occupation of Crete in May 1941 a number of Hurricanes were destroyed on the ground by enemy action. (*Author's Collection*)

MNFU, plus Marylands and Hurricanes, with 69 Squadron for reconnaissance. On the offensive were detachments of 18 and 107 Squadrons with Blenheims and 40, 104 and 221 Squadrons with Wellingtons. From the earliest days of the defence of Malta, the FAA units of 828 and 830 Squadrons provided anti-shipping strike capability with Albacores and Swordfish.

Early in December, MNFU was renamed 1435 (Night Fighter) Flight, command passing to Sqn Ldr Westmacott. After a lull of a few days, Malta based Hurricanes were back in action on the 18th, when 185 Squadron shot down one S84 bomber without loss. Next day, Ju88s were intercepted over an arriving convoy and one was shot down by 126 Squadron.

Just over two weeks later, on 20 December, the Luftwaffe returned in force. Ju88s escorted by Bf109s were met by 249 Squadron over Grand Harbour. One Ju88 was shot down for the loss of two Hurricanes and pilots. On a repeat raid the next day, one MC202 was claimed by Sqn Ldr Rabagliati, for the loss of two Hurricanes, including a pilot. On the 23rd, another 249 Squadron Hurricane and its pilot were lost in an attack by Bf109s on Grand Harbour.

In the week leading up to Christmas 1941 the Luftwaffe completed a total of 25 raids on Malta, the last being an attack by Ju88s escorted by Bf109s. One Ju88 was destroyed for the loss of a Hurricane from 126 Squadron. After a quiet Christmas day, Luqa was strafed and a photo reconnaissance Hurricane of 69 Squadron written off, amongst other aircraft on the ground. To combat regular night attacks by Ju88s, 1435 Flight moved from Takali to Hal Far. There were three more attacks during the daylight hours of 27 December, when 126 Squadron shot down a Ju88, with another destroyed after dark by 1435 Flight.

As the year was coming to an end, a 249 Squadron Hurricane was shot down over the sea, but the pilot was rescued. The following day, came one of the heaviest attacks since the return of the Luftwaffe to Sicily. Five scrambles during the day resulted in three major actions, the first raid being met by 185 and 242 Squadrons. Two Hurricanes collided in mid-air, killing one of the pilots. During the second engagement one Hurricane crashed and one Bf109 was claimed shot down. In the third major raid of the day, two Hurricanes were shot down by Bf109s during ground attacks on Luqa, where about 15 aircraft were destroyed, including nine Wellingtons. The last combat of the year was on the morning of 30 December, when German bombers attacked Luqa, Takali and the docks. They were met by 126 and 249 Squadrons from Takali, two Ju88s being confirmed destroyed.

Since hostilities commenced in June 1940, the fighter pilots on Malta had been credited with a total of 199 Axis aircraft of all types destroyed. In return, the RAF had lost 47 fighter pilots, including one member of the FAA killed in combat, and some 15 had been lost on the ferry flights. At least 90 Hurricanes had been lost in air to air combat, with many more destroyed on the ground. Although Hurricanes were not to vanish entirely from Malta in 1942, it was Spitfires which would now bear the brunt of the defences until Malta finally came through the hardships of the two and a half years' siege.

*

While Hurricanes had played an essential part in the Battle of Malta, they were also in action elsewhere in the Mediterranean

theatre. Following the Italian attack on Greece on 28 October 1940, the major part of British air support was provided by Wellington bombers operating from Malta and Egypt. On 19 November, 80 Squadron, equipped with Gladiators, deployed to Trikkala in Greece, followed on 24 January 1941 by the similarly equipped 112 Squadron, posted to Yannina.

With increased pressure by the Italians and the threat of Germany invading the Balkans, the Hurricanes of 33 Squadron, which had re-equipped the previous September, arrived at Eleusis on 19 February. Primitive airfield conditions and inadequate support made it difficult to keep the Hurricanes serviceable and, in March, 33 Squadron moved to the better airfield at Larissa. 80 Squadron received their first six Hurricane Is on 20 February, replacing Gladiators.

The German invasion of the Balkans started on 6 April with a devastating bombing attack on Belgrade, heralding the push into Greece and Yugoslavia. In defence, the Yugoslav Air Force had 38 Hurricanes, amongst other types, of which about 30 were serviceable, and the Luftwaffe made a partly successful attack on the airfields to destroy this opposition. The 51st Fighter Squadron at Sarajevo had 18 Hurricanes on strength and the 33rd and 34th Fighter Squadrons at Zagreb shared 20 aircraft. Retreating from the rapidly advancing Germans, the Yugoslavs destroyed the Zemun factory, depriving the Hurricane units of replacement aircraft and spares. The surviving aircraft remained in action for only a week, one or two escaping to Greece, to be destroyed soon after by the Luftwaffe's Bf109s.

Meanwhile, the Greek Government had requested all possible reinforcements, but no further Hurricanes could be spared by the RAF. 112 Squadron, with only a handful of Gladiators, withdrew to Crete on 16 April. 208 Squadron was also in the process of

To defend against German air attacks on Allied positions in Syria from the Dodecanese Islands, 213 Squadron arrived in Cyprus in July 1941 with untropicalized Hurricane Mk Is. (*IWM*)

One of 213 Squadron's Hurricane Mk Is is refuelled, rearmed and prepared for the next sortie. (*IWM*)

128 Squadron was formed in Sierra Leone with 15 Hurricane Mk IIbs on 7 October 1941, to discourage Vichy French reconnaissance flights over RAF bases. (*Author's Collection*)

moving to Greece when the Germans invaded, and had one flight of Hurricanes allocated to tactical reconnaissance for Army Co-operation.

By 19 April, German forces had advanced as far as Larrissa, some 20 miles north-west of Athens. 33, 80 and 208 Squadrons were based at Eleusis for the protection of the capital and Piraeus harbour, where British troops were being evacuated. Five Hurricane reinforcements arrived from Egypt on 18 April, bringing the total of serviceable aircraft to 22, with seven more under repair, but on 19 April a hangar was bombed and all seven Hurricanes under repair were destroyed. A further three Hurricanes were lost in combat

during the day, in return for 11 enemy aircraft claimed.

The remaining 15 Hurricanes of 33 and 80 Squadrons were combined on 20 April under the leadership of Sqn Ldr Pattle of 33 Squadron. That evening, while they were waiting to take off, a large formation of Ju88s attacked shipping in Piraeus Harbour. Three RAF pilots shot down five Ju88s for the loss of one Hurricane and pilot, the others destroyed two Bf110s, two Ju88s and three Bf109s for the loss of two aircraft from which the pilots baled out. Meanwhile, Pattle had shot down one Bf110 but, while attacking a second, his aircraft was set on fire and crashed in the harbour, killing the highest scoring pilot of the Second World War. Pattle's remarkable total of victories was eventually determined to be: 40 destroyed in the air, 4 shared kills, 5 destroyed on the ground, with six probables and five damaged, all over a period of just nine months; of which, remarkably, seven victories were claimed while he was flying Gladiators.

The 11 remaining Hurricanes were moved to Argos on 22 April, and were joined by five replacements which arrived from Crete, but a German attack by 40 Bf110s destroyed nine of the Hurricanes on the ground. At first light on 24 April, the seven surviving aircraft left for Crete to provide cover for the arrival of the last evacuation ships from Greece.

The preparations on Crete had been slow and, with German forces occupying all of Greece, the situation had become urgent. The island was occupied by thousands of Allied troops who had been evacuated from Greece and were short of arms and equipment. The only defence was from two airfields and a rudimentary landing strip, while the combined remnants of 33, 80 and 112 Squadrons amounted to 14 Hurricanes and six Gladiators, in addition to a few FAA Fulmars. Against them, the enemy had a force of 430 bombers and 180 fighters plus some 600 transports. The first attacks started in early May with the northern ports as the targets. On 14 May, the Luftwaffe began attacking airfields at Maleme, Heraklion and the strip at Retimo, losing seven Bf109s to the defenders, with four Hurricanes destroyed, among other aircraft. Six more Hurricane replacements were supplied but, by 18 May, only four Hurricanes remained airworthy, and three Gladiators. Permission was given to evacuate the survivors to Egypt the next day.

When the main German assault was made on Crete on 20 May, 12 Hurricanes were sent from Egypt to Heraklion to help cover the Allied evacuation, but two were shot down by 'friendly fire' from the Royal Navy and four more were damaged while landing on the cratered runway. The remaining six Hurricanes, supported by six more from Egypt, fitted with long-range fuel tanks, provided cover until the end of the month when Crete finally fell, with heavy losses on both sides.

Relatively few of the squadrons had converted to Spitfires by the time of the invasion of Sicily on 10 July 1943, and 253 Squadron transferred its Hurricanes temporarily to night fighter duties to provide protection for the airborne forces in transport aircraft and gliders as they neared the coast of Sicily. 127, 213 and 274 Squadrons based in Cyrenaica, Egypt and Cyprus took part in unsuccessful operations against German forces in the Dodecanese Islands in September and November, and a number of offensive sweeps were flown against German occupied airfields in Crete.

A few Hurricane units were available to operate in the Italian campaign, particularly the specialist 6 Squadron, which had fully recovered from the fighting in the Western Desert. Equipped with Hurricane IVs, the squadron arrived at Grottaglie in February 1944. The Hurricanes normally flew with one 40 mm cannon, later discarded, and four 3 in rocket projectiles (RP). The new role of the squadron was to attack Axis shipping and ports on both coasts of the Adriatic, also hitting German headquarters at Durazzo on the Albanian coast, on 29 March. A move was made north-westwards on 4 July to Foggia, to cover the entire Yugoslav coastline. Because of the greater endurance required, Hurricanes were usually fitted with a drop fuel tank under one wing and RP under the other. In five months of operation, the Squadron sank one 5,000 ton ship, 21 schooners, three ferries and 11 other ships in addition to severely damaging 27 further vessels.

Hurricanes returned to parts of Greece later in the war, with a Mk IV armed with RP preparing for take-off. (*IWM*)

A transfer was made to the Balkan Air Force in August, joining 351 and 352 (Yugoslav) Squadrons which had recently been formed with Hurricane Mk IIcs. 6 Squadron remained based in Italy for the time being, sending forward detachments to Niksic, deep in Yugoslavia, for daily anti-armour patrols; while the two Yugoslav units were moved to the island of Vis in the Adriatic in October. For these attacks, the Hurricanes were armed with four 25 lb armour piercing or four 60 lb semi-armour piecing RP, both of which were effective against enemy tanks. 6 Squadron moved to Prkos in Yugoslavia on 9 April 1945, where it remained until the end of the war in Europe. With just a week to go before the final surrender, the Squadron flew a rocket attack against 16 German troopships in the Gulf of Trieste, all of which raised white flags. 6 Squadron was the longest serving Hurricane unit and, in recognition of the skills of its pilots and ruggedness of the aircraft in the anti-armour role, the unit adopted a red 'winged can-opener' in a circle for its insignia, still carried by 6 Squadron Jaguar strike aircraft at Coltishall.

The war in Europe was finally over. Hurricanes had first entered the war in the Mediterranean when German forces invaded Yugoslavia on 6 April 1941. Four years later, the aircraft was back in the same country to witness the appalling devastation caused by the Nazi occupation.

CHAPTER 7

THE NORTH AFRICA CAMPAIGN

Under Rommel, by late 1940 German forces were well established in Libya with the intention of advancing east towards Egypt and the vital strategic route through the Suez Canal. By advancing into the Middle East, Germany would achieve access to the rich oil fields to keep their war machine fuelled for future conquests and deny them to the Allies. The struggle was to last for three years, with both sides experiencing difficulties in moving supplies and reinforcements to the frequently shifting fronts.

The rugged, adaptable Hurricane played a valuable support role in this area of conflict from beginning to end.

The first Hurricanes began to arrive in Egypt in September 1940, equipping 274 Squadron with aircraft coming by sea and from East Africa. 73 Squadron had arrived from Britain, and Hurricanes were supplied to 208 and 3 (RAAF) Squadrons which had been operating Lysanders in the Army Co-operation role. On 9 December 1940, General Wavell launched an attack on Italian ground forces, Hurricanes being allocated to ground attack of troops and soft-skinned vehicles. Hurricanes of 208 Squadron were initially used as escorts for the Lysanders, but with little sign of the Italian Air Force overhead, flew tactical reconnaissance operations up to 50 miles behind enemy lines. On 16 December, the last Italian troops were expelled from Egypt, with 33 Squadron Hurricanes attacking motor transport beyond the port of Bardia.

The pressure to supply Hurricanes to other parts of the Mediterranean, particularly Greece, was resisted, as, although the supply of aircraft was increasing, the conversion of Gladiator pilots was taking time. The formation of new squadrons involved more than just aircraft and pilots. Each required the full logistical support of spheres, equipment, ground crew and supplies. By the date of the capture of Tobruk on 22 January 1941, there were seven units flying Hurricanes in the Mediterranean and Middle East. 208 and 3 (RAAF) Squadrons at Gambut in Libya were both operational, with one flight of Hurricanes and another of Lysanders on tactical reconnaissance duties as already mentioned. From Egypt, 33 Squadron moved to Greece on 19 February, while 73 and 274 Squadrons based at Sidi Haneish were operational in the Western Desert. Further away was 1 Squadron (SAAF) at Khartoum and, fully occupied in the defence of Malta, was 261 Squadron, based on the island.

The poor performance of the Italian forces in December prompted Hitler to offer the services of the Luftwaffe, the first elements of which, as mentioned in the Malta account, arrived in Sicily towards the end of the month. Allied advances continued beyond Tobruk, with Benghazi captured on 7 February, but the advance came to a halt at El Agheila the next day, following which some ground and air components were allocated to the abortive Greek campaign.

As a result, when Rommel's *Afrika Korps* attacked a few weeks later, Wavell had too few troops and the air component was weakened, resulting in a headlong retreat

Commanded by Sqn Ldr P.H. Dunn, 274 Squadron was the first unit in Egypt to equip with Hurricanes when the aircraft arrived from East Africa in September 1940, replacing Gladiators. A Gloster built Mk I P2544 heads a line-up at Amriya, August 1940. (*Author's Collection*)

across the desert. 73 Squadron had been sent back from Gazala West to Bu Amud in Egypt and 274 Squadron had not yet moved forward from Sidi Haneish. The only air support available to cover the withdrawal were two flights of Hurricanes from 208 and 3 (RAAF) Squadrons, and 73 Squadron, still in the process of adding reinforcements. In addition, a flight of 6 Squadron, a short-range tactical reconnaissance unit, was issued with Hurricanes, an event which was to mark a very significant association between Hurricanes and desert warfare.

Hurricanes were operating far from their bases and, with the rapid German advance, often landed at forward airstrips only to find that all fuel and ground crews had departed. Around thirty aircraft had to be abandoned, the pilots seeking lifts back in retreating ground transport. Nevertheless, Hurricanes continued to play a significant part in reducing enemy air superiority. On 5 April, 73 Squadron destroyed twelve Italian aircraft in running battles for the loss of two Hurricanes. A week later, the Squadron set up a detachment at Tobruk with the Hurricane flights of 6 and 3 (RAAF) Squadrons, although German advances had already reached Bardia and Sollum, isolating the Allied forces in the port. The German and Italian air forces made determined efforts to reduce the effectiveness of the port, attacking with Ju87 Stukas supported by Bf109s. The three defending squadrons had 18 Hurricanes and 31 pilots between them. On 21 April, four Ju87s and a Bf109 were claimed shot down, and on the following day the seven surviving Hurricanes of 73 Squadron claimed six enemy aircraft destroyed in an attack by 60 Ju87s and Bf109s, for the loss of one Hurricane. In the evening, 73 Squadron took off with six surviving aircraft to attack about

40 raiders, losing one more for five enemy aircraft destroyed. On 25 April the survivors withdrew to Sidi Haneish in Egypt, followed by the last four pilots of 6 Squadron, who withdrew to Egypt on 8 May.

By this time, stocks of Hurricanes in the Canal Zone had reached over 100 aircraft. General Auchinleck succeeded Wavell as commander of the British forces in the Western Desert in June, with Air Marshall Arthur Tedder in charge of the air components. Having failed to relieve Tobruk and recapture the airfields in eastern Cyrenaica, preparations were made for a new offensive in the late summer. Special Operational Training Units (OTUs) were formed to train new pilots, the first being 71(ME) OTU at Ismailia on 1 June, equipped with 30 Hurricane Is and IIs. Within three months it was turning out about 40 new pilots every five weeks. In October, 74 OTU was formed at Aqir in Palestine to take over the task of training Army Co-operation pilots, leaving 71 OTU to concentrate on air fighting and ground attack roles.

Auchinleck launched his offensive known as Operation Crusader across the Egyptian border on 11 November, by which time Tedder had a significant force of Hurricanes, now better equipped for desert warfare and with better trained pilots. Tactical

reconnaissance units consisted of 6 and 208 Squadrons, still with one flight each of Hurricanes and Lysanders, and 237 and 451(RAAF) Squadrons, all based in Egypt and operational in the Western Desert. Hurricane Mk Is with some IIas and IIbs were still in use by 33, 73, 94 and 260 Squadrons for air defence, with 335(Greek) Squadron in the process of forming. Hurricane Mk IIb bombers equipped 80 Squadron, while 30, 213, 229, 274 and 1(SAAF) Squadrons were equipped with all versions of the Mk II and used for air defence and ground attack. Number 2 PRU operated a maximum of five Hurricanes, with other aircraft from Heliopolis, on photo reconnaissance (PR) work.

The tactical reconnaissance Hurricane Is were fitted with an additional radio for communications with ground forces and some had a vertical camera fitted aft of the cockpit after one or two Browning guns were removed. The later Tac R Mk IIc had one or two cannons removed to accommodate a camera. All the tactical reconnaissance units had variations of a non-standard desert camouflage. The rare PR Hurricanes, of which there were no more than a dozen Mk 1s with 2 PRU, were modified in great secrecy at Heliopolis, starting in January 1941. The first two aircraft were fitted with a pair of f24 8 in cameras, and the other with one vertical and a pair of oblique f24 14 in cameras in the rear fuselage aft of the radiator intake. All armament was removed and additional fuel tanks were installed in the wings. Five more PR Mk Is were modified in March, in time for the aircraft to be particularly helpful during the Iraqi

73 Squadron were operational with Hurricane Mk Is in Egypt in September 1940. A group of pilots are in front of a tropical Mk I in the following year. (*RAF Museum*)

Operational Training Units were formed in the Middle East to train new pilots, Hurricane Mk I '2' serving with 71 OTU at Ismailia in early 1943. (*R.J. Ryley*)

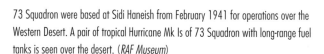

73 Squadron sustained a number of casualties when operating from forward bases in the desert and the five surviving aircraft were withdrawn to Egypt in April 1941. (*RAF Museum*)

73 Squadron were based at Sidi Haneish from February 1941 for operations over the Western Desert. A pair of tropical Hurricane Mk Is of 73 Squadron with long-range fuel tanks is seen over the desert. (*RAF Museum*)

Although Hurricanes did not fly combat missions in Australia, RAAF units played an important part in the war. In September 1940, 3 Squadron RAAF were equipped with Hurricanes. Tropical Mk I P3822 was at Amriya in March 1941. (*Author's Collection*)

208 Squadron operated one flight of Tac R Hurricanes up to 50 miles behind enemy lines, while the other flight flew Lysanders. The films were processed in rather primitive desert conditions. (*Author's Collection*)

and Syrian campaigns. The PR Mk Is were followed by six PR Mk IIs, the first two being delivered to 2 PRU in December after the start of Operation Crusader. They were believed to be capable of 350 mph and reaching an altitude of 38,000 ft. A further batch of about a dozen aircraft was converted between the end of 1942 and early 1943, mainly for the use of 3 PRU in India, but at least three were flown by a detachment of 680(PR) Squadron in Libya as late as July 1944.

Operation Crusader caught the Axis forces by surprise, just as Rommel was preparing to make a final assault on Tobruk. 33 Squadron provided air support against Italian transport behind enemy lines. When it looked possible that Tobruk might be relieved, Rommel ordered two armoured Panzer divisions towards the Egyptian border. This endangered the rear of the Allied forces and threatened the forward landing grounds. Hurricane bombers of 80 Squadron were sent in to attack, although they were less effective at destroying armour than they were against soft-skinned vehicles.

With the pressure off the Tobruk garrison, a breakout was made on 26 November, assisted by four Tac R Hurricanes of 451(RAAF) Squadron, linking up with New

80 Squadron operated Hurricane bombers in support of Operation Crusader, the conditions being somewhat rudimentary. (*IWM*)

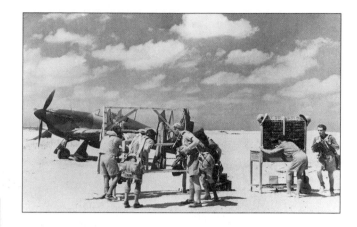

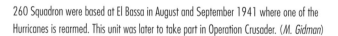

In support of Operation Crusader, November 1941, Hurricanes of 33, 73, 94 and 260 Squadrons were used for air defence. Hurricane Mk Is of 33 Squadron operated from a typical desert airstrip. (*IWM*)

260 Squadron were based at El Bassa in August and September 1941 where one of the Hurricanes is rearmed. This unit was later to take part in Operation Crusader. (*M. Gidman*)

A Hurricane Mk I of 73 Squadron ready for air defence duties in Operation Crusader. (*via R.C.B. Ashworth*)

Additional air defence and ground attacks for Operation Crusader were provided by 30, 213, 229, 274 and 1(SAAF) Squadrons. A Mk II HW798 of 213 Squadron here has the cockpit covered to reduce the heat. (*Author's Collection*)

From January 1941 2 PRU operated about a dozen unarmed photo reconnaissance (PR) Hurricanes out of Heliopolis fitted with cameras in the rear fuselage. (*Author's Collection*)

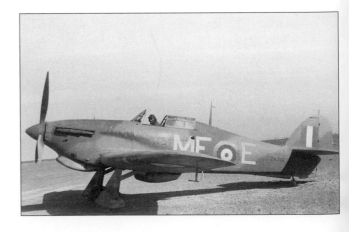

Gloster built Hurricane Mk II of 229 Squadron with some operational damage, mainly to the fabric covering and therefore easily repaired. (*Author's Collection*)

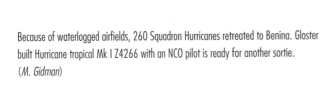

Because of waterlogged airfields, 260 Squadron Hurricanes retreated to Benina. Gloster built Hurricane tropical Mk I Z4266 with an NCO pilot is ready for another sortie. (*M. Gidman*)

Zealand forces approaching from the south-east. Rommel was now threatened with being cut off and started to withdraw under cover of a much strengthened Luftwaffe, which launched dive bomber attacks by Ju87s on the Eighth Army. The Axis fighter defence was provided by hot weather adapted Bf109F-4/Trops of JG27 from Cyrenaica, with a performance of 380 mph at 20,000 ft. Fortunately, the aircraft were poorly armed with only a single 20 mm cannon and two small machine-guns.

Flying immediately ahead of the advancing Commonwealth forces was 208 Squadron, which saw plenty of action. On 29 November, an unarmed Tac R Mk 1 flown by Flg Off P.T. Cotton was attacked by a pair of Bf109Es, and twisted and turned to avoid the enemy gun-fire. After 30 minutes, the enemy ran out of ammunition but, on the way back to base the overstrained Merlin engine failed and the Hurricane landed 15 miles short of the airfield, later to be recovered and repaired. Flg Off Cotton was subsequently awarded the DFC.

The Axis forces fell back to a pre-prepared defensive line at Gazala, from which, after a three-day battle starting on 12 December, Rommel was able to extricate his troops once more. By Christmas, the Eighth Army had advanced to Bengazi and all the Cyrenaican airfields at El Adem, Benina, Berka, Martuba, Gazala, Derna and the numbered (temporary) landing grounds were under Allied occupation. Because the advance had moved so rapidly, Hurricanes were unable to take full advantage of the recaptured airfields and were operating from bases well to the rear. As a result the squadrons were unable to provide the full support required, a situation Tedder corrected rapidly by ensuring that each ground support unit was ready to move in and out of captured airfields at under one hour's notice. In addition, RAF airfield construction units were ordered into captured bases to repair runways without waiting for army engineers, who were also busy supporting the ground advance.

On 9 January 1942, El Agheila was captured and held while supplies attempted to catch up. At this crucial moment, Hurricanes destined for Egypt had to be diverted to South-East Asia to defend against Japanese attacks. Both 17 and 232 Squadrons had sailed from Britain on 12 November, expecting to reach Egypt by December, but the former was sent instead to Burma and the latter to Singapore. 605 Squadron was split between Malta and Palembang in Sumatra.

Axis forces also suffered from a shortage of supplies and aircraft. The support of the German armies on the eastern front against Russia in severe winter conditions required transport aircraft to move supplies effectively. These same aircraft would have been of great value in moving supplies across the Mediterranean to Rommel's army. As has already been mentioned, the forces based on Malta continued to sink enemy supply ships during November and December, and Hitler ordered further Luftwaffe units to Sicily to eliminate Malta as an effective Allied base, and regain air superiority over the supply routes to North Africa. However, despite suffering continuous bombardment, the garrison and people of Malta were not defeated and continued to deprive the *Afrika Korps* of vital supplies.

Despite this lack of supplies, to prevent the Allies consolidating their position at El Agheila, Rommel launched a powerful frontal attack on 21 January, supported by two days of dive bombing against Eighth Army units. The Hurricanes and Tomahawks were grounded by torrential rain at Antelat airfield, 100 miles to the rear, while 238 and 260 Squadrons had managed to move to El Gubba and Benina a few days before. When German armour broke through at El Aghcila, the 100 miles were covered in just over six

'The MacRobert Fighter – Sir Alasdair'; presentation Hurricane IIc HL844 of 94 Squadron, armed with four 20 mm cannons and carrying underwing fuel tanks. (*IWM*)

hours, giving 33, 94 and 229 Squadrons with Hurricanes and 112 Squadron with Tomahawks just 30 minutes to escape. Two unserviceable Hurricanes and four Tomahawks had to be abandoned as German shells began to fall, while the ground crews escaped with RAF armoured car companies.

The squadrons made their way back to Msus, 100 miles to the north-east, where they encountered poor conditions, their stocks of ammunition and fuel soon running out. Despite this, Hurricanes alone destroyed more than 100 Axis vehicles in two days. Within another four days the Hurricanes were withdrawn to Mechili, south of Derna, and Air Marshall Sir Arthur Coningham,

commander of the Western desert air units, ordered all RAF maintenance units to retire behind the Egyptian border to avoid destruction of the vital repair network. The result was that any forward-based aircraft suffering more than superficial damage had to be abandoned.

Sandstorms helped to make the fighting in Cyrenaica very confused during the first week of February, grounding 33 and 238 Squadrons at Gambut. However, the conditions also prevented German air attacks, particularly by Ju87s, while the Eighth Army attempted to consolidate a line of defence between Gazala and Bir Hakim. This was in effect the end of Operation Crusader, in

274 Squadron operated Hurricane Mk IIbs in Greece, Egypt and Libya, including Operation Crusader. This is Hurricane IIb HL795:V with black lightning unit markings through the fuselage roundel. (*RAF Museum*)

A formation of Hurricane IIcs of 94 Squadron based at El Gamil. The furthest three are presentation aircraft from Lady MacRobert, named 'Sir Robert', 'Sir Iain', and 'Sir Alasdair'. (*IWM*)

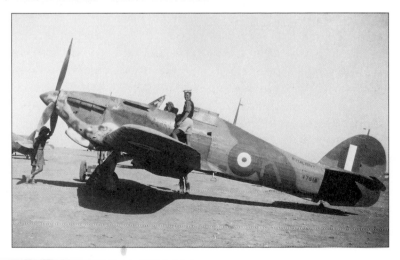

Sea Hurricanes were deployed by the FAA mainly on coastal patrols during the North African campaign. Sea Hurricane Mk I V7816 of 803 Squadron is seen here at Ramat David in 1941. (*Author's Collection*)

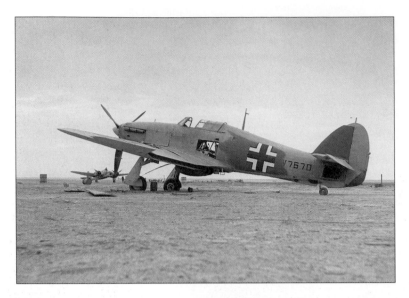

Hawker built Hurricane Mk I V7670 was captured by the German forces at Gambut, but later recaptured by the Allies as they drove back enemy advances. (*IWM*)

As the Allied supply lines became overextended on Operation Crusader, Rommel counterattacked on 21 January 1941. In torrential rain, 238 and 260 Squadrons withdrew to better airfields, the former moving to El Gubba. (*RAF Museum*)

Tactical reconnaissance for the Battle of El Alamein included Hurricanes of 7 and 40 Squadrons SAAF. (*Author's Collection*)

With four wing mounted 20 mm cannons the Hurricane could pack quite a punch, particularly against soft skinned vehicles and troop concentrations. A pilot receives target instructions for the next sortie. (*Author's Collection*)

which harsh lessons had been learned by the combined forces of both sides. All the Hurricane units had been involved in heavy fighting, often with significant success. Pilot losses had been reasonably low, but because it was outperformed in the air by the Bf109F, the Hurricane was felt to be more useful in the ground attack role.

Heavy fighting continued on the ground in Cyrenaica, with the Eighth Army attempting to retire with as much as possible of its organizational capacity still intact, to establish a new defensive line at Gazala.

Meanwhile, Rommel retained his forces against this line, with his supply route from Bengazi and Tripoli now shorter by about 100 miles, and the Allies' supply line stretched correspondingly further.

Axis armour still created a threat which could not be effectively countered by air attack, although maintenance units in the Canal Zone had started modifying some Hurricanes to carry 250 lb bombs. The army commanders requested, with some urgency, American M3 Grant and M4 Sherman tanks; while the RAF urged the rapid clearance of

After maintenance at RAF Kasfaret in Egypt, Gloster built Hurricane Mk I Z4421 is ready for issue to a squadron. (*Aviation Heritage Museum of WA*)

the Hurricane II to carry more effective 500 lb bombs. Although for a number of reasons it was not possible to clear aircraft operating in tropical conditions until later, an early batch of Hurricane IId anti-tank ground attack fighters was in the process of being shipped to the Middle East. These were armed with a pair of 40 mm Vickers S guns, and with the increased effectiveness of these guns against armour, 6 Squadron was designated in May 1942 to prepare for a change to the anti-tank role.

Rommel launched his attack on the Gazala defensive line on 26 May, but the Allies had already been alerted to Italian armour moving forward by a Tac R Hurricane II of 40(SAAF) Squadron and were ready. However, this proved to be a feint, as

Rommel then brought forward two Panzer and one motorised divisions, outflanking the Eighth Army south of Bir Hakim. By the next day these ground units were well to the rear of the Gazala line and had reached 'Knightsbridge' and El Adem. While the Free French Brigade continued to hold Bir Hakim there was no danger of encirclement, and in turn the rear of the Panzer divisions became vulnerable. The Axis forces concentrated their attention on the destruction of Bir Hakim by attacking with the 90th Light Division from the east, and on 3 June Coningham switched the Hurricane IIds from fighting at 'Knightsbridge' to attack the enemy ground forces at Bir Hakim. They were supported by Kittyhawk bombers and Tomahawks in ground attack, while other

Hurricanes dropped supplies in canisters to the defenders.

This fierce battle continued for nine days, with Allied fighters combating Axis air and ground forces. German Ju87s suffered badly and escorting Bf109F pilots found themselves up against tougher opposition when Spitfire Vcs of 145 Squadron joined their first desert battle. Anti-tank Hurricanes were able to destroy about a score of German tanks, but needed more time and practice to evolve the best tactics for dealing with the armoured threat. By 10 June it was obvious that, without strong Allied artillery support, the Free French would no longer be able to hold out at Bir Hakim, and about 2,000 men were ordered to retire and escaped to the east overnight.

Rommel's victory, however, had not been as clear-cut as it seemed. The Axis campaign was based on gaining adequate fuel supplies, with the capture of Tobruk expected by 1 June, but the objective was not achieved until 21 June. The nine days during which the defenders held Bir Hakim avoided an Allied rout and permitted a costly fighting withdrawal by the Eighth Army, supported by Hurricanes providing top cover for the anti-tank Hurricanes in action against ground forces.

73 Squadron continued with the interception of Bf109Fs in June, claiming seven victories for the loss of five pilots, including the CO, Sqn Ldr D.H. Ward. The following month, operating from Burg-el-Arab in Egypt, the squadron destroyed a further 23 enemy aircraft for the loss of another six pilots. It was then withdrawn from the battle and allocated to the night defence of the Suez Canal flying Hurricane NF Mk IIcs.

By early July, Commonwealth forces were withdrawn far into Egypt, behind a line running from a small place called El Alamein, just over 60 miles west of Alexandria. General Montgomery was now in command of the Eighth Army, assisted by Tedder, who began to strengthen the desert forces by creating new units, and re-equipping and retraining the men. The RAF constructed 33 more desert airstrips on which, together with the already established airfields, were based a total of 84 squadrons. The single-engine fighter units amounted to 16 squadrons of Hurricanes, seven Kittyhawks, six Spitfires, one Tomahawk and three USAAF P-40 Warhawks.

For the opening of the Battle of El Alamein on 19 October, Tedder fielded the established squadrons, together with new additions, all now equipped with various versions of the Hurricane Mk II. Tactical reconnaissance was the responsibility of 208, 451(RAAF), 7(SAAF) and 40(SAAF) Squadrons, all based in Egypt and operational over the Western Desert. 274 and 335(Greek) Squadrons were both equipped with Mk IIc and Mk IIb bombers respectively for ground attack duties, while 6 Squadron with Mk IIds specialized in anti-armour attacks. The air defence over the Eighth Army was provided by Hurricanes of 33, 80, 127, 1(SAAF) Squadrons, and offensive sweeps were carried out by 213 Squadron. Patrols along the Mediterranean coast were flown by 889(FAA) Squadron Sea Hurricane Mk 1cs and Mk IIbs, while air defence of the Canal Zone was allocated to 94 and 417(RCAF) Squadrons. No 2 PRU continued to operate an assortment of types, including Hurricane PR MkIs and IIs.

Against them, the Luftwaffe had introduced the new Bf109G 'Gustav', which still suffered from a number of teething troubles, but when fully serviceable was more than a match for the Spitfire Vc, let alone the poorer performing, but more rugged Hurricanes.

On the night of 23/24 October, Montgomery directed his artillery to open up a devastating bombardment of the Axis lines.

Air defence of the Eighth Army at the Battle of Alemein was allocated to 33, 80, 127 and 1 (SAAF) Squadrons. An 80 Squadron tropical Hurricane Mk II being bombed-up for the next sortie. (*Author's Collection*)

During the initial softening-up period, the Desert Air Force flew hundreds of sorties against enemy airfields, destroying as many as possible of the enemy air force on the ground and reducing air cover for the Axis armies. On 27 October, the Luftwaffe put up 20 Ju87Ds with an escort of Bf109Fs to support a counterattack by the 90th Light Division. These were met by 24 Hurricanes and 16 P-40Fs of the USAAF 57th Fighter Group, which claimed 27 Bf109s for the loss of three Hurricanes.

The Hurricane IIds of 6 Squadron were in action from the start, attacking enemy tanks at low level from the rear and breaking away by turning, rather than climbing, avoiding the anti-aircraft guns to which they were vulnerable at higher altitude. On 24 October, 6 Squadron destroyed 18 Axis tanks, supported by 80 Squadron, who provided top cover and attracted most of the hostile fire. By the end of the month, 6 Squadron had claimed 43 tanks and over 100 other vehicles destroyed, but had lost nine aircraft with six pilots, almost all from ground fire.

On 2 November, Operation Supercharger was launched by Montgomery as the major breakthrough thrust. In a dawn attack, 24

For the opening of the Battle of El Alamein, Hurricane IIds of 6 Squadron were allotted the tank-busting role. Hawker built tropical Hurricane Mk IId BP188:JV-Z is nearest the camera. (*IWM*)

Hurricane IIds of 6 Squadron were in action from the start of the Battle of El Alamein attacking enemy armour from low level. Hurricane IId BP188 looks well worn from desert warfare. (*RAF Museum*)

With the British and US landings in North Africa, the first Hurricanes arrived at Maison Blanche without anyone knowing whether or not it was under Allied control. Hurricane operations were then able to commence from a second front over the North African desert. (*IWM*)

In support of the Western Desert Allied thrust, 241 Squadron were deployed with Tac R Mk IIcs from 19 November 1942. Hurricane Mk IIc HW421 at Euston strip in May 1943 was fitted with underwing fuel tanks. (*RAF Museum*)

During the Battle of El Alamein Hurricanes of 889 Squadron FAA maintained coastal defence patrols with Hurricane Mk IIcs. (*FAA Museum*)

32 Squadron landed at Philippeville on 7 December 1942 in support of the Allied landings in North Africa. The desert is not always dry and these Mk IIcs of 32 Squadron at Maison Blanche in March 1944 had to fly from metal plated runways. (*Air Ministry*)

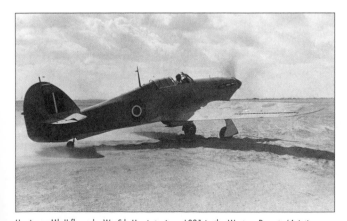

Hurricane Mk II flown by Wg Cdr Morris taxis on LG91 in the Western Desert. (*Aviation Heritage Museum of WA*)

Hurricane Mk IIb 86 707 with the Free French Air Force, used for desert operations with the Allies. (*P. Ward Hunt*)

Hurricanes and Spitfires engaged about 20 Ju87s and escorting Bf109Fs. Later in the day, Hurricanes of 80 and 127 Squadrons intercepted a similar force. Allied claims were the destruction of four Ju87s and two Bf109s for the loss of four Hurricanes and four Spitfires. By 4 November, Rommel's army was in full retreat and the Bf109s were withdrawn, giving the Desert Air Force unrivalled air supremacy. So poor was the Axis air defence that, during the advance on Benghazi, Coningham daringly ordered Hurricanes of 213 and 238 Squadrons to the forward airstrip at Martuba, well to the *rear* of the retreating enemy ground forces. Photo reconnaissance had shown the airfield to have been abandoned by the Luftwaffe, and the two squadrons took the enemy completely by surprise, destroying about 300 vehicles over a period of five days.

With Operation Torch, the Allied landings in Algeria and French Morocco on 8 November, German forces were facing defeat from both the east and west. More aircraft were flown in from Gibraltar, the first arrivals being Hurricane IIcs at Maison Blanche, on the day of the landings. No one could be sure that the airfield was not still in enemy hands, but thankfully, it wasn't. In action the next day, one He111 and a Ju88 were claimed destroyed. These units were followed on 13 November by Hurricane Tac R IIcs of 225 Squadron, and Mk IIcs of 253 Squadron, based at Maison Blanche. On 19 November, 241 Squadron arrived with more Tac R IIcs, and were followed by 32 Squadron with Mk IIcs which landed at Philippeville on 7 December, and the similarly equipped 87 Squadron on 19 December.

Meanwhile, owing to the loss of 14 Hurricane IIds and seven pilots during some 300 sorties over Libya, the tank-busting 6 Squadron was temporarily withdrawn for defensive patrols over Cairo and the Canal Zone in Hurricane Mk IIcs. During this time, replacement anti-armour aircraft were supplied and modified for action, which included re-rating the Merlin XX engines to give more power, equivalent to an additional 40 mph at low level. The engine and radiator too were given some armour protection, allowing 6 Squadron to return to the Libyan Desert on 2 March 1943.

As the campaign in Tunisia approached its climax, more Spitfires were becoming available, allowing a number of the established Hurricane units to re-equip with Spitfire Vcs. However, Tedder, who had been appointed Air Commander in Chief, Mediterranean Air Command, still had 23 Hurricane squadrons at his disposal, in addition to 34 Spitfire squadrons, and six USAAF units. Additional Hurricane units deployed since the start of Operation Supercharger were 32, 73, 87, 123, 134, 237, 238, 241, 253, 336(Greek), 3(SAAF), and 41(SAAF) Squadrons, many of which were involved in operations in the Western Desert.

*

Other, minor actions involving Hurricanes in the Middle East and East Africa theatres spread even thinner, the already scarce resources of the Allied air forces in the Mediterranean region. In January 1941, the Italians had succeeded in taking British Somaliland in East Africa and were threatening the borders of both the Sudan and Kenya, as well as the Allied supply route through the Red Sea. A counter-offensive was drawn up, including 1 Squadron SAAF, which was receiving Hurricanes at Khartoum. Six had arrived in time for the start of the offensive on 17 January. The unit strength increased at the rate of about one aircraft a week, mostly ex-RAF Hurricanes from battles in Europe. The work of overhauling these was completed by the unit's engineers. The Hurricanes provided air support for ground forces as advances were made, destroying at

Battle damaged Hurricanes were often salvaged and delivered to Mid-East MUs for repair and return to combat. A convoy carries three damaged Hurricanes including Z4967 of 229 Squadron to a MU south of Cairo, pyramids in the background. (*Air Ministry*)

As part of the Balkan Air Force, 6 Squadron equipped with Hurricane Mk IVs carried bombs and RP. Hurricane Mk IV LF498 of 6 Squadron destroyed a bridge at Spuz in November 1944 during the Balkan campaign. (*IWM*)

Hurricane of the Central Gunnery School at El Ballah in the Middle East in 1942. (*Author's Collection*)

Landing incident to Gloster built Hurricane Mk I Z4428 of the Air Firing and Fighting School at Bilbies, Egypt, February 1942. (*Author's Collection*)

For Operation Supercharger, tropical Hurricane Mk IIbs were operational with 237 Squadron operating from desert strips. (*IWM*)

213 Squadron took part in some unsuccessful operations against German forces in the Dodecanese Islands in September and November 1943, in addition to offensive patrols against enemy occupied airfields in Crete. 213 Squadron Hurricane IIc HL887, here on a Libyan airfield with a Hudson during the North African campaign. (*IWM*)

In some cases when Hurricanes were badly damaged, they were stripped of useful parts at rudimentary sites in the desert. (*IWM*)

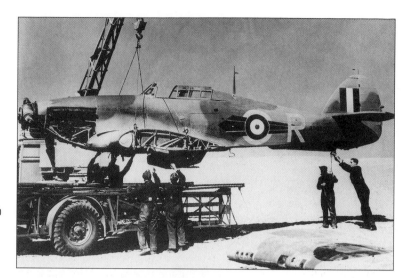

At the climax of the Tunisian campaign, additional Hurricane units became available. Among them was 73 Squadron, whose Mk IIb BD930 is being loaded on a Queen Mary trailer for repairs and return to combat. (*RAF Museum*)

After an engine change and propeller refit a Hurricane is prepared for return to combat from Kasfareet in 1941. (*M. Gidman*)

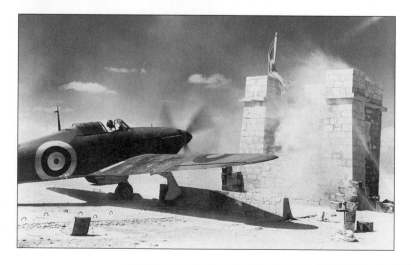

Repairs completed, guns are tested before reissue to a squadron. (*IWM*)

Despite successes against Axis armour, 6 Squadron suffered a high casualty rate and the remnant was withdrawn to Cairo for air defence patrols over Suez to recover and retrain. (*Author's Collection*)

least ten enemy aircraft for no losses to the Hurricanes. On 5 April, Addis Ababa fell to the Allies, and three days later Mussolini's colonial armies were defeated at Massawa. Six very 'tired' Hurricane Mk I s were handed over to 94 Squadron in the Canal Zone.

As the Italian army was being defeated in East Africa, an Iraqi politician, Rashid Ali, seized power in Baghdad. Britain already had a number of treaties with Iraq as well as access to considerable oil resources in Kirkuk and Mosul, with pipelines running to the Mediterranean. As a result, there were substantial, well-established British garrisons

to protect these interests. One of the bases was Habbaniya, 50 miles to the west of Baghdad, which was attacked by Iraqi artillery on the night of 28/29 April 1941. The only RAF aircraft available for the defence were training machines of 4 FTS, fitted with bombs. It was enough. Lacking their own air support, the Iraqis withdrew on the night of 5/6 May.

On 13 May, however, the Iraqis obtained air support by courtesy of the Luftwaffe, units of which had staged through Syria, despite the country at that time being occupied by British forces. Attacks were mounted by Bf110s and He111s against the Gladiators of 94 Squadron, which were soon reinforced by the six Hurricanes from the Canal Zone. The Allies gained their first victory on 20 May, shooting down a He111 over the airfield. The Iraqi rebellion was finally crushed at the end of May.

It was realised however that, if the Luftwaffe could stage through Damascus on the way to Iraq, the same location would bring the enemy within range of the Suez Canal. It was therefore deemed necessary to fortify Syria, using ground forces and tanks of the Australian, Free French and Indian Armies. Air support included the re-equipped 80 Squadron with Hurricane Is and the Hurricane flight of 208 Squadron. The advance into Syria started on 8 June against stiff resistance from about 100 Vichy French combat aircraft. With losses of half the FAA Fulmars, Hurricanes took over the protection of RN ships off the coast and the newly arrived 260 Squadron Hurricanes were brought in to assist.

While the Vichy French scored some successes against RAF Blenheims and ground troops, because of air attacks on their bases they had to withdraw further north out of range of RAF aircraft. With Allied advances, and using aircraft fitted with long-range tanks, all the French airfields now came within range, and the Hurricanes destroyed any French aircraft they could find. In addition, defensive patrols were flown along the Syrian coast to guard against German reinforcements arriving from the Dodecanese Islands. The forces were aided in this task by the Hurricanes of 213 Squadron, which arrived at Nicosia, Cyprus on 19 July with Hurricane Is, which had not been adapted to fly in hot climates. These were replaced by Hurricane IIas the following month. The campaign finally ended when, by the middle of July, the Australians broke through French defences south of Beirut.

At the same time as French forces were being defeated in Syria, some aircraft in the

Hawker built Hurricane MkI N2629 under maintenance at El Ballah in 1941. (*M. Gidman*)

French West African colonies were causing concern. Vichy French Martin 167s were carrying out reconnaissance flights over RAF Sunderland bases in Sierra Leone. To counter these, a Fighter Defence Flight was formed with six Hurricane Is in early August, but the old aircraft were unable to catch the French aircraft. On 7 October, the Flight was expanded into 128 Squadron equipped with 15 Hurricane Ibs. Now, the French flights were discouraged by the improved performance of the RAF aircraft. Following action in Operation Torch, the squadron was disbanded on 8 March 1943 and some of the aircraft passed on to 1432 Army Co-operation Flight in Nigeria.

Versatile and adapted to a wide range of conditions, the reliable Hurricanes saw action in many parts of Africa and the Middle East, although many squadrons and part-squadrons dotted about the region often had to make do with elderly aircraft nearing the end of their service life. Supply lines south and east of the Med were stretched to their limit, both for the Allies and for the Axis forces; and, had it not been for the gallant defence of Malta, it is doubtful whether the Alexandria route could have been kept open, allowing the delivery of aircraft reinforcements to the North Africa campaign, let alone those other far-flung corners of the war outside Europe.

CHAPTER 8

THE ASIA CAMPAIGN

Following their dramatic declaration of war at Pearl Harbor, Japanese land forces attacked Kota Bharu, in northern Malaya, on 8 December 1941. Just over a month later, Hurricanes were in action in Asia.

The first Hurricanes to arrive in Singapore were a collection of crated Mk Is and IIbs aboard a ship which docked on 3 January. Also on board were 24 pilots, including some of the spare crews of 605 Squadron which had been diverted from the Middle East. Pilots and ground crews of 17, 135 and 136 Squadrons arrived in Singapore via the Cape with more Hurricanes on 13 January 1942, and together were formed into 232 Squadron. 258 Squadron was also diverted for the defence of Singapore. After unloading and assembling the initial batch of Hurricanes, it was found that the guns were choked with grease as protection from the sea voyage, and it took several more days to prepare the aircraft for combat.

The first success was on 20 January when, out of a formation of 27 Japanese bombers without escort, eight were claimed shot down. However, when the bombers returned the next day with an escort of Mitsubishi Zeros, five Hurricanes were lost without any enemy casualties. Though better armed, the Hurricanes had been shipped from Middle East stocks and were fitted with tropical filters, which reduced performance, and the larger numbers of Zeros had air superiority. By the middle of January, the pilots and ground crews of 232, 242, 258 and 605 Squadrons had arrived in Singapore, and HMS *Indomitable* was on the way with 48

Hurricane IIas and IIbs taken from Middle East stocks. Vulnerable to enemy air attack, the units were dispersed, 242 and 258 Squadrons remaining at Seletar and 232 and 605 Squadrons to Batavia in Java and Palembang in Sumatra, respectively. Hurricanes were launched from the carrier on 26 January, 15 flying to Seletar and the balance split between two airfields, PI and PII near Palembang.

Advancing rapidly down the Malay Peninsula, the Japanese Army was approaching Singapore. There was little warning, as the radar stations had either been overrun or dismantled to prevent them falling into enemy hands. With only a few minutes' warning of an attack, Hurricanes were often engaged when still vulnerable in the climb. By 28 January, only 21 out of 51 Hurricanes remained operational, and, by the end of the month, 232 Squadron had just eight Hurricanes left, half the normal complement, to defend Singapore. All other units were ordered to withdraw by General Wavell, who had moved from the Middle East on 15 January to become Supreme Allied Commander in the Far East.

During the first ten days of February, Hurricane pilots of 232 Squadron continued to provide what air defence they could, even when, on 8 February, Japanese forces had landed on Singapore and were shelling the airfields. The next day, six enemy bombers were claimed destroyed, with 14 damaged, for the loss of one Hurricane and its pilot. The defence continued until the remaining Hurricanes of 232 Squadron withdrew to

Where possible, defending Hurricanes were camouflaged on the ground against air attack. (*R.F. Donahue*)

Sumatra on 10 February, having had to operate from a crude airstrip only 750 yds long. Five days later, the garrison of Singapore finally surrendered.

Meanwhile, airfields near Palembang were under threat, PI being raided from the air on 23 January. A paratroop attack on 14 February ended with the destruction of a number of Hurricanes on the ground, and all British and Dutch operations were transferred to PII. The next day, Hurricanes escorted a force of Hudsons and Blenheims on a successful attack on Japanese invasion forces off the coast, and later in the day Hurricanes destroyed a number of Zekes on the ground at Banka Island. Although these attacks were successful in slowing the invasion, there were inadequate resources to consolidate the gains and the Japanese response was rapid and violent. Following another airborne attack, this time on PII, there was a hurried and confused withdrawal to Java via Oesthaven, leaving behind all the spare Merlin engines. The airfield had still not been occupied two days later when a party of 50 volunteers from 605 Squadron, led by Grp Capt Gilbert Nicholetts, returned to recover all the spares and equipment.

By 18 February, 18 Hurricanes out of 25 remained serviceable and were based in Java, 232 Squadron at Tjililitan, 242 Squadron at Bandung, 258 Squadron at Kemojoran and 605 Squadron at Andir. The majority of the bomber force was located at Semplak, but was almost completely destroyed by Japanese air attacks on 19 and 22 February. By 28 February, both 242 and 258 Squadrons had virtually ceased to exist and the survivors were absorbed into the remaining two units. The next day, with only 12 Hurricanes remaining operational, all aircraft and personnel were amalgamated into 605 Squadron. On the same day, a combined force of Hurricanes with ten Dutch P-40s and six Buffaloes caused many casualties among an enemy invasion force landing at Eretanwetan, but were unable to stop the advance. On 2 March, the pilots were unable to continue operations from Tjililitan owing to constant enemy attacks, which damaged the airstrip, and the last two Hurricanes were destroyed on 7 March.

These British and Dutch fighters and bombers had continued to attack the Japanese invasion forces but, faced with overwhelming odds, the Dutch Army surrendered on 8 March. During this short campaign the RAF lost an overall total of 435 aircraft with the destruction of 192 enemy aircraft claimed: grim testament to the intensity of the fighting. Over Singapore, Hurricanes had gained some 100 victories but lost 45 of their own aircraft. With the loss of Java and Sumatra, fewer than 500 survivors of the four Hurricane squadrons made what escape they could, many reaching the shores of Australia, while others died at sea or were taken prisoner by the Japanese.

With Singapore and Malaya occupied, the Japanese began the conquest of Burma. The country was strategically important on the path to India and commanded the major supply route to China along the Burma Road via Rangoon. The Japanese were experienced in jungle warfare and continued advancing through the Malayan jungle and the Mergui Archipelago, running along the western coast of the Malay Peninsula. Rangoon had already been heavily bombed on 23 December 1941 and the main attack on Burma followed across the border from Thailand in mid-January. The only air defence was 67 Squadron, with 16 Buffaloes at Mingaladon

near Rangoon; while, 650 miles to the north-east, in China, equipped with 21 P-40s, an American Volunteer Group was defending the supply route along the Burma Road.

India was also vulnerable to air attack and was unable to supply aircraft for air defence against the advancing enemy. The first unit to come to their aid was 17 Squadron, which had left Britain on 12 November 1941 with Hurricane IIas bound for the Middle East. Diverted to Burma en route, they arrived at Mingaladon on 16 January, to be joined by 135 Squadron with Hurricanes on 28 January and the personnel of 136 Squadron on 6 February, who were then sent to India to await more aircraft.

When the Japanese in considerable force made a further attack on Rangoon on Christmas Day 1941, there were still no Hurricanes available. Nevertheless, the defending P-40s claimed 36 hostile aircraft, despite their poorer performance, achieving success by diving repeatedly through the enemy formations. Many of the Buffaloes were destroyed on the ground during these attacks.

At last, a batch of 30 Hurricane Is and IIas arrived in Rangoon as deck cargo from the Middle East and were quickly assembled, some to be flown by pilots of 67 Squadron, soon joined by 17 Squadron. Air Vice-Marshall Donald Stevenson, the Air Officer Commanding the RAF in Burma, ordered Hurricanes and Blenheims to advanced airfields in southern Burma to make strikes at Japanese bases in Thailand. Some 58 aircraft were claimed destroyed, mainly on the ground at Bangkok, during January; but, with the enemy invasion commencing during the second half of the month, all the Allies' advanced airfields were soon overrun. Meanwhile, Japanese air attacks continued on Rangoon and the surrounding area in an effort to gain air superiority over the RAF, the airfield at Moulmein to the east of the capital being taken on 30 January.

Hawker built Hurricane Mk II BE163, possibly of 258 Squadron, wrecked in a drainage ditch and abandoned during the Japanese invasion. (*R.F. Donahue*)

On 5 February, Japanese forces crossed the River Salween, 80 miles east of Rangoon, and in another three weeks were threatening the city's large port, vital to the re-supply of Allied forces. The remaining 24 Hurricanes and four Buffaloes were ordered north with the pilots and ground crews of 17, 67 and 135 Squadrons to an airstrip at Zigon, 100 miles away. For three days these fighters provided cover for the evacuation of Mingaladon and the forces around Rangoon, successfully deterring enemy aircraft from attacking the roads to the north.

Enemy advances were now split into three prongs heading northward, the most threatening for Zigon being the one advancing towards Mandalay along the Sittang river. By mid-March, the dozen surviving Hurricane IIs of 17 and 135 Squadrons had withdrawn to Magwe with P-40s and some 45 Squadron Blenheims. Six serviceable Hurricane Is with 67 Squadron moved to the island of Akyab off the Burma coast.

At Magwe, Hurricanes joined up with Blenheims and, on 20 March, 139 Squadron Hudsons flew a reconnaissance of the southern Burma airfields to locate the main concentrations of enemy occupied airfields. Some 50 Mitsubishi Sally heavy bombers were found at Migaladon and were attacked the next day by ten Hurricanes and nine Blenheims, 16 of the bombers being destroyed on the ground and 11 Oscars in the air. Two Hurricanes and two Blenheims were lost, but shortly afterwards 16 Hurricane IIbs and ten Blenheims arrived at Magwe from the Middle East as replacements.

In retaliation, over the following 24 hours the Japanese made a devastating attack on Magwe with a force of some 200 aircraft,

Allocated to the defence of Singapore at Seletar with 242 Squadron, a 258 Squadron Hurricane Mk IIb Z3826:ZT-A waits with the engine running, ready for another sortie. (*RAF Museum*)

An early non-tropicalized Hurricane in Singapore, protected by a brick built blast pen. (*R.F. Donahue*)

605 Squadron Hurricanes at P1 airstrip near Palembang in Sumatra. (*R.F. Donahue*)

Among the units in East Bengal was 79 Squadron with Hurricane Mk IIs, HV845 being an example. (*IWM*)

The first Hurricane unit to arrive in Burma to combat the Japanese advances was 17 Squadron with Hurricane IIas from the Mid-East. (*Author's Collection*)

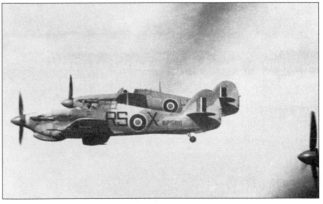

30 Squadron arrived from Egypt at Ratmalana in Ceylon on 6 March 1942 with Hurricane Mk IIs. (*C. Smith*)

146 Squadron re-equipped with Hurricane Mk IIbs in May 1942 at Dum Dum for the defence of Calcutta. (*G.A. Handscombe*)

virtually obliterating the airfield. The surviving dozen Hurricanes were sent to Akyab, where all but one arrived on 26 March, and were back in the fighting the next day against successive waves of Japanese bombers. Three Hurricanes were shot down and four more were destroyed on the ground. With the RAF now ineffective at Akyab and Magwe, and the disorganization of the remaining British ground forces in Burma, Stevenson withdrew what little was left for the defence of Calcutta and Ceylon. The Japanese took Lashio on 29 April, Mandalay on 1 May and Myitkyina on 8 May.

Throughout the Japanese advances in Burma, units had been arriving gradually in India to provide some air defence of the

Royal Navy in Ceylon and the Bay of Bengal, where there was a serious threat from enemy warships. 30 Squadron on HMS *Indomitable* had arrived from Egypt at Ratmalana in Ceylon on 6 March with Hurricane IIbs. Also on board was 261 Squadron with Mk IIbs, which had arrived initially at Dum Dum, Calcutta at the end of February, and then moved on 6 March to China Bay in Ceylon. A totally new 258 Squadron was formed at Colombo from local resources, all part of Wavell's plan to defend the RN bases and ships against the Japanese threat to control the eastern part of the Indian Ocean.

Japanese naval forces were first reported in the Indian Ocean on 4 April. During the next five days, 23 Allied merchant ships were lost in the Bay of Bengal, 15 being sunk by carrier borne aircraft. Colombo harbour was attacked by some 125 aircraft on Easter Sunday, 5 April. Two patrolling Catalina flying boats radioed a warning of the approaching attack, allowing 36 Hurricanes of 30 and 258 Squadrons to take off, together with six FAA Fulmars, to intercept the raid. The escorting Japanese Zekes were effective in defending the bombers, losing three Zekes, two Kates and two Vals for the loss of 15 Hurricanes and four of the more vulnerable Fulmars. Fortunately, eight of the Hurricane pilots survived unhurt and replacement Hurricanes were supplied from local stocks.

On 9 April, the Japanese attacked Ceylon again with a force of 129 aircraft, concentrating this time on the airfields at Trincomalee and China Bay, and were met by 17 Hurricanes of 261 Squadron and six more Fulmars of 873 Squadron FAA. A total of 15 Zekes were shot down by the defenders, 12 by Hurricanes and three by Fulmars. Eight Hurricanes were shot down, but six pilots were uninjured, and three Fulmars destroyed. With most of the naval and merchant shipping moving away from the Bay of Bengal, the Japanese were able to concentrate attacks on Ceylon shore installations, creating widespread damage. The Japanese naval task force consisted of five aircraft carriers, four battleships, three cruisers and eight destroyers, which far outnumbered all the Allied warships in the Indian Ocean. Allied naval units suffered from inadequate air cover and as a result, in the first ten days of April, the carrier HMS *Hermes*, two cruisers and two destroyers were all lost.

The RN moved its main base facilities out of the immediate range of enemy forces, releasing the RAF from defence of naval assets. Hurricane squadrons re-equipped in eastern India to prepare for the air defence of Calcutta. The Buffalo and Mohawk equipped

146 Squadron was re-equipped with Hurricane IIbs at Dum Dum in May. 607 Squadron, which had left Britain in March, arrived at Alipore, near Calcutta, on 25 May, and in June received the first Hurricane IIcs in the Asia campaign.

Heavy summer rains that year prevented operations by either side on the Burma front. Allied forces were not yet strong enough to launch a major offensive against the Japanese in Burma as potential reinforcements were still tied-up in the Western Desert. Air Chief Marshall Sir Richard Peirse, Air Officer Commander-in-Chief, believed the next enemy move would be an attack on Calcutta. The task of the RAF during that autumn of 1942 was therefore to build up the air defence of Calcutta to prevent heavy damage from bombers and to demonstrate that the Allies still possessed a significant presence in the air. There was also the need to continue the air defence of Ceylon, and to deter further attacks by the Japanese Navy.

By December 1942, the air defence of Calcutta consisted of Hurricane IIcs of 17, 67, 135 and 146 Squadrons. Ceylon had 30 Squadron, equipped with Mk IIcs for air defence of the ports, and the Mk IIb equipped 258, 261 and 273 Squadrons. Elsewhere, Tac R IIbs of 28 Squadron provided tactical reconnaissance over the Burma front from Ranchi in Bihar, and in East Bengal were 79, 136, 607 and 615 Squadrons with mostly Mk IIcs providing further air defence of Calcutta and operations over Burma. In the event of the attack on Calcutta materializing, there were four operational day squadrons, and 146 Squadron by night, to provide air defence. When the first attack came, it was by night, and though involving only a small force, caused panic among the population. The non-radar equipped Hurricanes were unable to be effective; so, in January 1943, a flight of AI equipped Beaufighters was sent to put an end to the night threat.

28 Squadron flew Hurricane Tac R IIbs over Burma, including KZ353. (*Author's Collection*)

Early in December, Wavell had made an abortive attempt to return to the offensive with the object of establishing a landing ground on Akyab Island, which appeared lightly defended by the Japanese. However, the operation did not go according to plan. There were delays with supplies, the advance was held up, Akyab was reinforced by the enemy; and, in April, with the threat of some of the Commonwealth forces being cut off, a withdrawal was ordered back to Cox's Bazaar. Although the campaign failed, it provided valuable experience for the Hurricane pilots of 28, 67, 136, 607 and 615 Squadrons, who flew in total more than 150 sorties a day. Thanks to the effectiveness of the cannon armed Mk IIcs against surface transport on the roads and rivers, the Japanese were forced to move only under cover of darkness.

In addition to regular Hurricane combat squadrons, No 3 PRU operated a selection of unarmed photo reconnaissance Hurricanes. The unit had its beginnings in January 1942 when two Hurricanes being ferried to Singapore had not arrived before the surrender. The two pilots became based instead at Mingaladon, and flew some 25 sorties over Thailand and Malaya before the aircraft were written off. The pilots made their way to Calcutta, where they were joined by three others, one of whom, Flt Lt Alexander Pearson, had been flying with 2 PRU in Egypt and was tasked with forming 3 PRU. The first two Hurricane PR IIbs arrived at Dum Dum in April, with two more in May

Unarmed Hurricane PR IIb of 3 PRU equipped at Dum Dum in April 1942. (*IWM*)

Hurricane Mk IIcs replaced Blenheims with 34 Squadron in mid-1943, LB836 seen here with a USAAF P-47 taxiing behind. (*IWM*)

and four in June. Photo reconnaissance sorties commenced on 6 June 1942 over northern Burma, but without long-range fuel tanks the sortie radius was limited to 300 miles. When suitable 44 gal. drop tanks arrived in November 1942, the Hurricane PR Mk IIs could just reach Mandalay and Rangoon from Calcutta. In January 1943, 3 PRU became 681 Squadron and continued to undertake short-range reconnaissance with around six Hurricanes, until replaced by Spitfire XIs and long-range Mosquito XVIs in September 1944.

From February to June 1943, Hurricanes were involved in escort duties covering supply drops into the jungle. Brigadier Orde Wingate led Chindit commando-style operations behind enemy lines in northern Burma, supplied from the air by DC3 Dakotas. However, little Japanese air opposition was encountered, as the enemy were moving their aircraft to the Pacific Islands, where advancing US forces were causing a serious threat, so the Hurricane patrols were scaled down.

By mid-1943, Blenheim bombers were being retired from operations; and, during the monsoon season, Hurricane IIb and IIc bombers were issued to 11, 34, 42, 60 and 113 Squadrons. In addition, Hurricane IId anti-armour ground attack fighters had been delivered to India from the Middle East. Although they were issued to 5 and 20 Squadrons, ammunition for the 40 mm cannons did not arrive until the end of the year.

By December, up to 970 Hurricanes were available in India, including 46 Mk Is in use with 151 OTU on the North-West Frontier, pilots from all over the Commonwealth undergoing conversion training for the new Hurricane units. The Indian Air Force had been supplied with ex-RAF Hurricane IIas and IIbs, 1 Squadron being declared operational at the end of the year. Hurricanes, however, were being replaced in the air defence role by new Spitfire

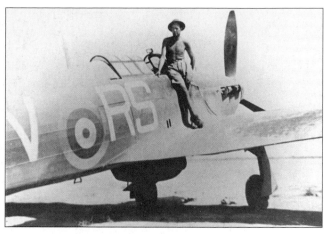

With the Allied return to the offensive, 30 Squadron operated Hurricane Mk II bombers from India on the Burma front. (*Author's Collection*)

squadrons, which were able to inflict heavy losses on the enemy when raids resumed against Calcutta in December.

20 Squadron were issued with anti-armour Hurricane IIds and operated from Hove airstrip at Arakan. (*IWM*)

By the end of the year, Admiral Mountbatten headed South-East Asia Command with Peirse in overall command of the Allied Air Forces, and the time was judged right for the launch of a further offensive operation. With the monsoon season over at the end of 1943, Allied forces were much better equipped, and prepared to forestall a Japanese threat aimed at Chittagong by once again attempting to capture Akyab in the Arakan.

The main thrust was led by the 7th Indian Division, setting out from Cox's Bazaar in November and capturing Sinzweya by 6 February. Japanese forces then cut the vital supply route, isolating and encircling the Allies, so that the only method of supply was by air, with RAF Dakotas and USAAF C-47s performing the air-drops, escorted by five squadrons of Hurricanes and two of Spitfires. The battle raged for a month until reinforcements arrived in the shape of the 5th Indian Division, which landed on the coast, allowing a break-out and encirclement of the enemy, who fought to the death rather than surrender.

Meanwhile, Japanese forces attacked on the central front in Burma with three divisions, planning to cut the main overland route supplying the air bridge to China, established after the loss of the Burma Road. The villages of Imphal and Kohima were surrounded, and most of Kohima was occupied. Once again, the only method of resupply was by air. Reinforcements of the 33rd Indian Corps were flown in to Dinapur with an escort provided by Hurricane IIc bombers, including 1 Squadron Indian Air Force. Close support was then given for the advance to relieve Kohima. With total air superiority, Hurricanes flew 2,200 sorties in 16 days, dropping some 2,500 bombs on the Japanese 31st Division.

At Imphal, the defenders were able to maintain a fairly large perimeter with room to prepare six airstrips within a horseshoe shaped valley. As troops of the 5th Indian Division were flown in aboard C-46 Commandos and C-47s, many non-combatant personnel were evacuated. Three Hurricane squadrons from Kohima joined 28 Squadron and two Spitfire units at Imphal, and in the first two weeks of April Hurricanes flew about 6,000 sorties out of a total of 10,000.

28 Squadron was flying a brand new batch of Hurricane Tac R Mk IIcs. Aircraft of one flight were fitted with a single vertical camera in the rear fuselage, the other flight being equipped with an oblique camera. The requirement of ground forces for continuous local reconnaissance over the rugged terrain kept at least one of the Hurricanes airborne during the hours of daylight. 28 Squadron also located targets for air attack, one example being a Japanese motorized battalion, which was spotted at dusk by an Indian pilot, moving towards Imphal. The resulting attack by 33 Hurricane bombers with the aid of landing lights, dropping bombs and firing cannons, stopped the advance and killed 220 enemy. Soon after this, a local tribesman brought details of an enemy HQ concealed in the jungle. He returned to the tribe, members of which surrounded the target and, at a pre-arranged time, laid out red blankets to guide a dozen 250 lb bomb carrying Hurricanes in to the attack. It was later learned that there were some 100 enemy casualties in this action.

The second Chindit expedition had been under way since December, supported by two Hurricane squadrons. The aim of the combined Ghurka, American and Chinese forces was to cut the Indaw to Myitkyina railway and capture Myitkyina and Mogaung. With the approach of the monsoon season, Japanese resistance strengthened, and it was not until early June that Imphal and Kohima were finally

60 Squadron Hurricane Mk IIs after replacing the older Blenheims. (*Author's Collection*)

A new 258 Squadron was formed at Colombo with Hurricane Mk IIbs on 1 March 1942. This formal line-up was taken later in India when the tension had eased. (*IWM*)

A 146 Squadron Hurricane ready for the next sortie while the pilot, Australian Sgt Douglas St John, poses for a photo. (*Author's Collection*)

60 Squadron was equipped with Hurricane Mk IVs for offensive operations against the Japanese, including LD993:MU-T. (*Author's Collection*)

Hurricane Mk IIc armed on the Arakan front in Burma. (*IWM*)

captured, followed by Mogaung on 20 June, just as the rains started. With the rains in Assam restricting Allied operations for two months, and the Japanese at a standstill, Myitkyina did not fall until 3 August.

By 1 July, Peirse had command of a total of 38 combat squadrons of which 21 were equipped with Hurricanes. Those units flying Mk IIc bombers based in India and operating on the Burma front were 30, 34, 42, 60, 113, 134, 146, 261, and 9(IAF) Squadrons. Mk IIds were operated by 20 Squadron on anti-armour duties in Burma until September 1945. Hurricane Tac R Mk IIcs were operated over the Burma front by 4 and 6(IAF) Squadrons, and 17 and 135 Squadrons were responsible for the defence of ports in Ceylon, although 17 Squadron was in the process of converting to Spitfires. The remaining 5, 11, 28, 79, 123, 258 and 1(IAF) Squadrons were mainly flying from Indian bases on ground attack, reconnaissance and bomber escort duties.

Even in the final campaign for the liberation of Burma, Hurricanes were the most numerous aircraft on the Allied side, used mainly to provide close air support. Their ease of maintenance made them readily available, and by now there was little sign of Japanese aircraft in the skies. The conquest was led by General Slim with IV, XV and XXXIII Corps representing the Fourteenth Army. American and Chinese forces occupied the northern Shan States. The plan was first to retake Mandalay, but the terrain was extremely rugged, making ground fighting difficult. Hurricanes and Thunderbolts operated using a 'cab-rank' tactic, waiting

Hurricane Tac R off Mandalay in support of the 14th Army flies past Aya Bridge over the River Irawaddy. (*Author's Collection*)

Tac R Hurricane Mk IIcs were operated over the Burma front by 6 (IAF) Squadron, often fitted with underwing LR fuel tanks. (*J.H.F. Cutler*)

Hurricanes in the Imphal Valley during 1944, amid near-desert conditions. (*Sqn Ldr Grossey*)

Hurricane Mk II is serviced in basic conditions at Palembang. (*Author's Collection*)

Hurricane Mk IIc BN872 fitted with LR fuel tanks at RAF Jodhpur in 1942. (*Aviation Heritage Museum of WA*)

17 Squadron was responsible for the defence of the port installations in Ceylon and was in the process of exchanging Hurricanes for Spitfires. This Hurricane has the fabric burned from the rear fuselage, but brought the pilot back safely. (*Author's Collection*)

Hurricane Mk IIc 40-hour inspection, Burma, March 1945. (*IWM*)

March, and the liberating forces also captured the strategic road, rail and river junction at Meiktila, 80 miles to the south.

General Slim's forces then consolidated for about two weeks while supplies of ammunition and fuel were replenished. Eight Hurricane squadrons were moved forward from Mandalay to within 20 miles of the advancing Allied troops, equipped with a total of 118 Mk IIc bombers and Tac R Mk IIcs. With the monsoon due to start again within six weeks, it was essential to capture Rangoon before then.

Equipped with tank-busting Hurricane Mk IVs, 20 Squadron, together with 28 Squadron on tactical reconnaissance, started operations from Thedaw airstrip on 13 April 1945, while the runways were still being repaired; the main targets being enemy motor and river transport. So rapid were the advances that, within two weeks, the front line was beyond the Hurricanes' endurance and a move was made to Tennant airstrip, bringing within range the main Japanese escape routes at Pegu and Sittang Ferry. Both squadrons became operational on arrival at the rudimentary strip on 28 April, the Mk IVs harrying river craft, while the Mk IIds attacked the bottleneck of fleeing motor transport. After four months of air support by Hurricane units, with the fall of Rangoon imminent on 30 April, it could indeed be said that the aircraft had made a major contribution to the final defeat of Japan in the jungles of Burma.

aloft to be called down wherever they were needed by the ground forces. They attacked any resistance, including enemy tanks. Mandalay fell according to plan, on 21

CHAPTER 9

FOREIGN AIR FORCES

Canada was a major contributor to the Allied effort during the Second World War, not only building aircraft, in many cases under licence, but also contributing combat units in Europe, the Middle East and Asia. Hurricanes were built under licence by the Canadian Car and Foundry Company for overseas and domestic use in Canada, 1 OTU being formed at Bagotville, Quebec on 6 June 1942 to undertake conversion and operational training. After successfully graduating 940 pilots out of a total intake of 1,012, the unit disbanded on 31 January 1945.

Five Canadian squadrons were formed with Hurricanes, as well as other types, for coastal air defence in Canada, 125 to 130 Squadrons on the East coast, and 133, 135 and 163 Squadrons on the West. 125 Squadron was formed on 20 April 1942 at Sydney, Nova Scotia, equipped from the outset with Hurricane Mk Is and XIIs, until May 1943. It was renumbered 441 Squadron at Digby in Britain on 8 February 1944 and equipped with Spitfires. 126 Squadron was formed at Dartmouth, Nova Scotia, on 27 April 1942 and operated Hurricanes Mk XIIs exclusively throughout its existence. The first mission was flown on 11 July 1942, the last on 13 May

Hurricane Mk XIIa BW150 of 126 Squadron RCAF, based at Dartmouth.
(*Public Archives of Canada*)

1945, the unit disbanding on 31 May 1945. 127 Squadron formed at Dartmouth on 1 July 1942 equipped with Hurricane Mk XIIs and became 443 Squadron at Digby on 8 February 1944 with Spitfires. 128 Squadron was formed at Sydney on 7 June 1942, equipped with Hurricane Mk Is and later Mk XIIs, until disbanded on 15 March 1944. 129 Squadron was formed at Dartmouth with Hurricane Mk XIIs on 28 August 1942 until disbanding at Gander on 30 September 1944, and 130 Squadron was formed at Mont Joli, Quebec on 1 May 1942 with a mixture of Hurricane Mk XIIs and Kittyhawks, disbanding at Goose Bay on 15 March 1944.

On the West coast of Canada 133 Squadron was formed at Lethbridge, Alberta on 3 June 1942 with Hurricane XIIs from July 1942 until March 1944, as well as Kittyhawks and Mosquitos. The squadron disbanded at Patricia Bay, Vancouver, on 10 September 1945. 135 Squadron was formed at Mossbank, Saskatchewan, on 15 June 1942, equipped with Hurricane XIIs from July 1942 until May 1944, as well as Kittyhawks. The first mission was flown on 9 November 1942 and the unit disbanded at Patricia Bay on 10 September 1945. The third unit was

Canada was a major contributor to the Hurricane programme with production by the Canadian Car & Foundry Company for domestic use in Canada and with the RAF. Mk XII 5658 of 127 Squadron was equivalent to RAF Mk IIa, armed with eight .303 in machine guns. The Hamilton Hydromatic propeller hub often lacked a spinner. (*Public Archives of Canada*)

163 Squadron formed for Army Co-operation at Sea Island, Vancouver, on 1 March 1943, with Bolingbrokes and Harvards. A conversion was made to the Hurricane XIIs in June 1943 and 163 was designated a fighter squadron on 14 October. Hurricanes were replaced by Kittyhawks during November 1943 and the squadron was disbanded at Patricia Bay on 15 March 1944.

The only other RCAF Hurricane unit in Canada was 123 Squadron, which formed for Army Co-operation training with Lysanders, Grumman Goblins and Hurricane Mk Is and XIIs at Rockcliffe on 22 October 1941. The

Hurricanes were operated from November 1942 until October 1943 and provided training in close support and reconnaissance for Canadian ground troops.

The major Canadian contribution to the air defence of Britain with Hurricanes was Digby Wing in Lincolnshire, consisting of 401 and 402 Squadrons. 401 Squadron had started life as 1 Squadron RCAF and was issued with Hurricanes in place of Siskins at Calgary in February 1939. It was mobilized at St Hubert, Quebec, in September and moved to Dartmouth, Nova Scotia, in November. It absorbed 115(Aux AF) Squadron in May 1940 and departed for

Canadian built Mk I 328 with the Test & Development Flight at Rockcliffe, Ontario, August 1939, fitted with a British supplied three-blade variable pitch propeller. (*Public Archives of Canada*)

Britain in June, joining 11 Group Fighter Command, and arrived at Middle Wallop on 21 June. Moves were made to Croydon in July and Northolt on 17 August, with the first victory against a Do 215 claimed on 26 August. Before moving to Digby, the unit claimed 30 destroyed enemy aircraft with eight probables and 34 damaged, for the loss of ten Hurricanes and three pilots killed. On 1 March 1941, the unit arrived at Digby and was renumbered 401 Squadron, equipped with Hurricane Is from March until May, which were then replaced by Mk IIs. The first claim was damage to a Ju88, and Spitfires replaced Hurricanes in September.

2 Squadron RCAF was formed from 112(Army Co-op) Squadron RCAF at Digby on 9 December 1940 and was renumbered 402 Squadron as a Hurricane fighter-bomber unit on 1 March 1941 alongside 401 Squadron. Moves were made to Martlesham Heath on 23 June 1941 when the first claim was made of damage to a Ju88 on 18 September. The squadron was initially equipped with Hurricane Is from March to May 1942, followed by IIas until July, and IIbs from June 1941 until March 1942, when Spitfires arrived. Moves were made to Ayr in July 1941 and Southend in August, from where three enemy aircraft were claimed destroyed and two damaged on 18

1 OTU was formed at Bagotville, Quebec, in June 1942 to undertake pilot conversion. A line-up of Hurricane Mk XIIs prepares for the day's training, November 1942. (*Public Archives of Canada*)

September. The final move with Hurricanes was made to Warmwell.

As part of the Allied support in the Middle East, 417 Squadron formed at Charmy Down in Britain on 27 November 1941, equipped with Spitfires. A move was made to Egypt in April 1942 and Hurricane IIcs were issued from September 1942 until January 1943 by which time they had been fully replaced by Spitfires.

Three other Canadian squadrons used Hurricane IVs non-operationally for training before equipping with Typhoons to cover D-Day and the invasion of Europe. These were 438, 439 and 440 Squadrons. 438 Squadron was originally formed as 118 Squadron RCAF at Rockcliffe on 13 January 1941 and arrived at Digby as 438 Squadron on 18 November 1943, operating Hurricanes from December 1943 to May 1944. 439 Squadron was originally formed as 123 (Army Co-op) Squadron on 15 January 1942 at Rockcliffe and became 439 Squadron at Wellingore on 31 December 1943. Hurricanes were used from January to April 1944. 440 Squadron formed as 111(F) Squadron at Rockcliffe on 1 November 1941 and was renumbered 440 Squadron at Ayr on 8 February 1944, operating Hurricanes for only a month, from February to March 1944. All three squadrons, equipped with Typhoons, were disbanded at Flensburg in Germany on 26 August 1945, their work having been completed.

Hurricane Mk XIIs of 1 OTU at RCAF Bagotville in July 1943 with 5470 nearest. (*Public Archives of Canada*)

A flight of Hurricane Mk XIIs of 127 Squadron at RCAF Gander on a typically cold December day in 1942. Coastal defence of Eastern Canada was shared between 125 to 130 Squadrons with Hurricanes. (*Public Archives of Canada*)

Hurricane Mk Is fitted with three-blade variable pitch propellers with 1 Squadron RCAF at Dartmouth, November 1939. The two nearest aircraft are 320 and 327. (*Public Archives of Canada*)

Hurricane Mk XIIs of 1 OTU taxi for take-off from RCAF Bagotville, November 1942. (*Public Archives of Canada*)

Hurricane Mk XII carrying RP and operating with 1 Naval Air Gunnery School, RCAF Yarmouth, November 1944. (*Public Archives of Canada*)

Mk I 313 of 1 Squadron RCAF flying over Vancouver on 3 April 1939. (*Public Archives of Canada*)

On arrival at Digby in March 1941, 1 Squadron RCAF was renumbered 401 Squadron as part of the Digby Canadian Hurricane Wing. Mk IIb Z3658 YO-N has its engine checked by ground crew, July 1941. (*Public Archives of Canada*)

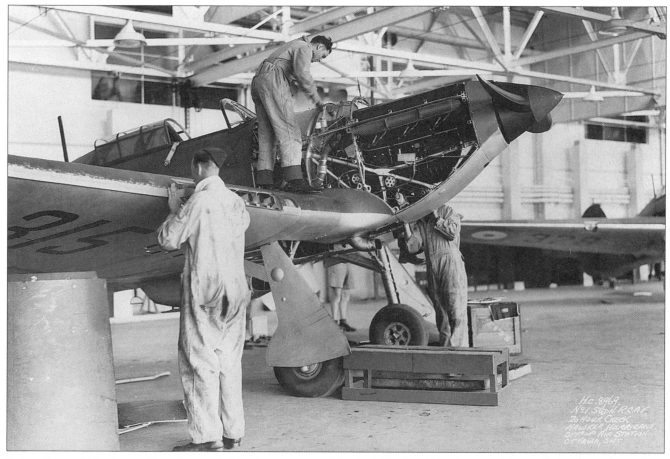

Hurricane Mk I 315 of 1 Squadron on a 24-hour check at RCAF Rockcliffe, September 1939. 1 Squadron RCAF exchanged Siskins for Hurricane Mk Is at Calgary in February 1939. (*Public Archives of Canada*)

402 Squadron RCAF Hurricane Mk IIb BE417 being loaded with bombs at Warmwell, early 1942. (*Author's Collection*)

Hurricane Mk IIb BE485 AE-W:402 Squadron carrying underwing bombs. (*IWM*)

1 Squadron RCAF Hurricane Mk I 315, ex-RAF L1878, engine start after 24-hour check at Rockcliffe in September 1939, fitted with a two blade fixed pitch Watts wooden propeller. (*Public Archives of Canada*)

In addition to early Hurricanes being exported to foreign air forces before the start of the Second World War, a number were transferred from RAF stocks or acquired by other means during the war. As already mentioned, the Belgian Hurricane Mk Is were wiped out in the German advances leading to the Allied withdrawal at Dunkirk. As covered in the chapter on FAA operations, many of the ships sailing around the North Cape were carrying dismantled Hurricanes as part of their cargo of war materials supplied from Britain to help keep the enemy occupied on a second front. To provide an air defence of the ports where ships were unloaded, and also to train Russian pilots and ground crews, two local squadrons were formed, equipped with Hurricane Mk IIs. On 29 July 1941, 81

Squadron was formed at Debden with Mk IIas and two days later 134 Squadron was formed at Acklington with Mk IIbs. The pilots and aircraft of the two squadrons were taken aboard HMS *Argus*, arriving at Vaenga near Murmansk on 1 September, the ground crews following in one of the first convoys to Russia. As further convoys arrived, additional stocks of Hurricanes were unloaded, making the ports prime targets for the Luftwaffe. The two squadrons were declared operational on 12 September, with 81 Squadron in action on the first day intercepting five Finnish Bf109s escorting a German Hs126 reconnaissance aircraft. Three Bf109s were claimed shot down and the Hs126 damaged for the loss of one Hurricane and pilot. That afternoon, a further three Bf109s were claimed, at the start of a busy period of action for both squadrons during the rest of the month.

By the end of the month, some 60 Hurricane IIs had been assembled for the Russian Air Force, allowing RAF pilots to begin training. On 28 October, 134 Squadron handed over its aircraft to the Russians before returning to Britain, and was followed by 81 Squadron in November. Information available suggests that some 2,952 Hurricanes were supplied to Russia from production lines in Britain and Canada, consisting mainly of all versions of the Mk II, together with 30 Mk IVs. Those which did not arrive directly from Britain were supplied from RAF MUs in the Middle East and transported by train through Persia. Details of operational service with the Soviet Air Force are minimal, but the aircraft with the two RAF squadrons were handed over to the 72nd Regiment of the Red Naval Air Fleet and a number were flown by a French volunteer regiment in the Soviet Union.

With a lack of spares due to logistics problems and the inexperience of the ground crews, there was a high wastage rate of Hurricanes, as with other aircraft supplied by the Allies to Russia. Many could have been fairly easily repaired, but were abandoned or dumped without any effort to salvage parts to help keep others operational. It is only in recent years, with the opening up of Russia, that it has been possible to discover some of these relics, a number of which are being restored to flying condition, in some cases using only a few original parts.

As already covered in the chapter on the Asia Campaign, the Indian Air Force received a number of Hurricanes and used them to great effect with other members of the Allied air forces in the recapture of Burma from the Japanese. They equipped eight squadrons with Hurricane Mk IIbs and IIcs from September 1942, until the last were withdrawn in August 1946. A number of the

pre-war deliveries to Egypt, Turkey and Yugoslavia had also survived to provide some modest combat capability to help keep the peace when the war was over. About 15 surplus Sea Hurricanes were acquired by the French Navy, probably from North Africa, and a few were still flying early in 1946. Neutral Eire managed to acquire at least 19 Hurricane Mk Is and IIs during the war, when RAF pilots had to force land on their territory, and the planes were impounded. There were sufficient aircraft eventually to equip 1 Squadron at Baldonnel near Dublin. Following lengthy negotiations with the Irish for the return of two Hurricanes, three early production aircraft were supplied in their place. An additional Hurricane was delivered from RAF Newtownards in 1943, followed by seven Mk Is and six Mk IIs during 1943 and 1944, the survivors remaining in service until 1947.

With hostilities over, Hawker Aircraft was able to start rebuilding its established pre-war export market, the first customer for Hurricanes being Portugal, as a result of a Government-to-Government agreement. This was in return for Portugal allowing Britain to use air and naval bases in the Azores, and 50 late series tropicalized Hurricane IIcs were released from RAF MUs. These aircraft were returned to Langley, where the engines were exchanged for Merlin 22s in 40 of the aircraft, while the remainder provided a large stock of spares. The Hurricanes were shipped to Lisbon and served with the Lisbon Fighter Defence Flight from Tancos until around 1951, when a number returned to Britain to fly from Kenley in the film *Reach for the Sky*, starring Kenneth More in the life story of air ace Douglas Bader, who lost both legs in a pre-war flying accident and went on to fly in the Battle of Britain.

An original Hurricane order from Persia had been interrupted by the war in 1940, and interest was again resumed at the end of

Hurricane scramble with 402 Squadron RCAF at Digby, early 1941. The photograph has been retouched for Propaganda purposes. (*Author's Collection*)

Lt Col B.F. Safanov was one of the earliest Russian aces to fly Hurricanes. He was killed in action in May 1942. (*Author's Collection*)

Substantial numbers of Hurricanes were supplied to Russia. Mk I Z5257 was an early presentation aircraft to the Russian Fleet Air Arm. (*IWM*)

Persia (Iran) also took delivery of a pair of Hurricane trainers with a second cockpit installed behind the front one. This aircraft was ex-RAF KZ232 and made its first flight from Langley on 27 September 1946. (*HSA*)

Persia (Iran) received Hurricanes from RAF Mid-East stocks during the hostilities and acquired 16 more Mk IIcs in 1946. (*RAF Museum*)

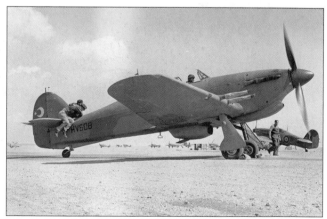

To supplement pre-war Hurricane deliveries to Turkey a number of tropical Mk IIcs were delivered in late 1942, including HV608, here being prepared for delivery. (*IWM*)

The first Hurricane export after the war was to Portugal with a batch of ex-RAF Mk IIcs which were refurbished by Hawker Aircraft. (*Author's Collection*)

The Indian Air Force operated Hurricanes on ground attack and bombing missions over Burma. An Indian Air Force Hurricane IIa with tropical filter and underwing LR fuel tanks runs up its engine prior to taxiing. (*IWM*)

351 and 352 (Yugoslav) Squadrons transferred with Hurricane Mk IVs from the RAF to the Balkan Air Force in August 1944. 351 Squadron prepares for another ground attack mission armed with RP. (*IWM*)

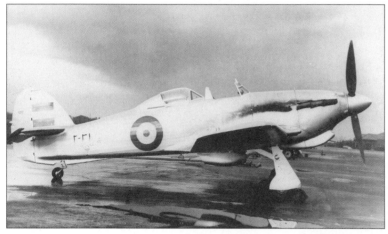

Owing to turbulence around the rear cockpit of the Hurricane trainer, a modified Tempest bubble canopy was fitted for the instructor. (*Author's Collection*)

In addition to providing air defence of the convoys around the North Cape, 81 and 134 Squadron also trained Russian air and ground crew to operate the aircraft, 134 Squadron handing over its Hurricanes at the end of October before returning to Britain. Despite the cold, the Hurricanes were fitted with tropical filters. (*Author's Collection*)

To provide air defence of northern Russian ports where war supplies including Hurricanes were being delivered by convoy, 81 and 134 Squadrons arrived at Vaenga near Murmansk on 1 September 1941 to form 151 Wing. Mk IIb Z3768 of 134 Squadron is seen at Vaenga with Hurricanes flying over. (*IWM*)

Operating conditions could become very demanding at Vaenga. Here, 134 Squadron aircraft prepare for another mission. (*Author's Collection*)

After completing the conversion of pilots and ground crews, 81 Squadron returned to Britain in November 1941, leaving their aircraft in the hands of the Russian Air Force who took over the defence of the convoys around the Northern Cape. (*Author's Collection*)

Sqn Ldr E.A. McNab, CO of 1 Squadron RCAF, after arrival in Britain at Northolt, September 1940. (*Public Archives of Canada*)

hostilities. In addition to ten Hurricanes which had been transferred to the Persian Air Force from RAF stocks during the war, a further 16 Mk IIcs and a pair of two seater trainers were delivered in 1946 and 1947. All were based with the Advanced Fighter Training Group of the Flying Training School at Doshan Teppeh and used as fighter trainers. The two seater Hurricanes originally had tandem open cockpits, with the second dual control cockpit inserted behind the original one in a cut down rear fuselage. However, early test flights indicated that at speeds above 280 mph, the rear occupant suffered considerable discomfort from turbulence around the front cockpit. The problem was solved by fitting an adaptation of the Hawker Tempest sliding canopy over the rear cockpit, leaving the front one open. The first of two such Hurricanes made its maiden flight on 27 September 1946, and both were delivered the following year. This version had an all-up weight of 8,140 lb without armament and could reach 320 mph at 21,500 ft.

CHAPTER 10

SUPPORT DUTIES

During the early part of the war, there were not enough aircraft available to enable the RAF to form operational training units (OTUs) for the conversion of new pilots to Hurricanes. New pilots would receive advanced training on Miles Masters or North American Harvards, passing through Group Pools to make the basic conversion, and then were sent to operational squadrons to learn how to use the aircraft as a fighting machine. This of course all took time, when the active pilots should have been in combat. By early 1940, sufficient aircraft became available to allow some to be allocated to advanced training, for which the first unit was 5 OTU, established at Aston Down in February 1940, equipped with Hurricanes, Defiants and Blenheims. This was followed in March by 6 OTU at Sutton Bridge, with Hurricanes, Masters and Battles; and 7 OTU at Hawarden, with Hurricanes, Spitfires and Masters. These OTUs were later renumbered 55, 56 and 57.

These training units were initially equipped with redundant Hurricane Is with fabric covered wings and Watts two blade fixed pitch wooden propellers. Trainees were given about 40 hours for conversion, basic combat tactics and operational procedures. The new pilots were therefore in a position of adapting to the operational aircraft with a good basic knowledge. Such was the shortage of pilots during the Battle of Britain, however, that many new arrivals had only about 20 hours on the type, putting a greater pressure on operational pilots. Hurricane operational training continued in Britain until 1944, when 55 OTU at Annan in Dumfriesshire closed.

In the Middle East, the two main OTUs were 71(ME) OTU based at Ismailia for fighter and fighter-bomber training, and later 74(ME) OTU at Aqir in Palestine for tactical training. Hurricane pilots also qualified with the Rhodesian Air Training Group from 1942 onwards as part of the Empire Air Training Scheme. In addition, there were up to three OTUs in India preparing pilots for the Burma campaign against the Japanese.

As well as training pilots, Hurricanes were also used for the training of air gunners, and even the pilots of RAF heavy bombers, in the skills of defending themselves against enemy fighters. Initially, this training tended to be by operational fighter squadrons on rest, but after a while Bomber Defence Flights were formed to provide more relevant training.

With the growing spread of global operations, knowledge of regional weather conditions became critical for successful planning of operations over enemy territory. A number of different types of aircraft were deployed on weather reconnaissance, depending upon the range required and the local conditions encountered. One of the critical areas was the Middle East, where violent tropical storms could develop very rapidly.

Hurricanes were first used for weather reconnaissance duties by 1413 Flight based at Lydda in Palestine from August 1943, replacing Gladiators. The initial aircraft were combat-worn Mk Is operating with detachments at Aqir, Damascus and Rayak, but with the expansion of the weather flights, specially adapted Hurricane Met Mk IIcs were issued. These aircraft were usually

Canadian Car & Foundry built Hurricane Mk X AG162 EH-W of 55 OTU, based at Aston Down. (*IWM*)

Before OTUs for the conversion of student pilots to the Hurricane, station flight aircraft were used for this purpose. Mk IIa Z2487:FC-T served with the Northolt Station Flight in 1941. (*RAF Museum*)

More aircraft were damaged in training accidents than were lost in combat. Hurricane Mk I R2680 of 56 OTU at Sutton Bridge became another training statistic on 20 June 1941. (*RAF Museum*)

A 'non-standard' arrival by Hurricane Mk I L1926, possibly with 55 OTU at Aston Down. (*H. Lees*)

unarmed and fitted with a psychrometer to measure humidity, mounted on a strut attached to the starboard side of the fuselage below the cockpit. Amongst other units were 1412 Flight at Khartoum, 1414 Flight at Mogadishu and Eastleigh in East Africa, and 1415 Flight at Habbaniya. Normal operations were two sorties a day, making ascents to between 30,000 and 35,000 ft. Hurricanes continued with this work until September 1945, when 1413 and 1415 Flights were issued with Spitfires and the other Middle East flights disbanded.

On the home front, Hurricanes were used for weather duties with 518 (Weather Calibration) Squadron based at Aldergrove from September 1945 until October the following year, and 521 (Weather Calibration) Squadron at Docking, Langham and Chivenor from August 1944 until February 1946. In addition, 520 (Weather Calibration) Squadron flew from Gibraltar from June 1944 to April 1946. New, specially equipped Hurricane Met Mk IIcs were issued to these units, making the testing, twice daily meteorological climb-ups a great deal easier to achieve.

Hurricanes were also allocated to the relatively mundane task of assisting in the calibration of ground defence equipment, particularly the AMES Type 1(CH) radar, which had a range in excess of 100 miles. Under certain atmospheric conditions this radar was prone to spurious signals, and a number of special calibration units were formed to help identify real targets.

The first of these units was 116 Squadron, formed at Hatfield on 17 February 1941. Initially equipped with Lysanders, the squadron moved to Hendon in April and began to receive Hurricane Mk Is in November. The Mk Is were eventually replaced by Mk IIas, flown until May 1945, when the Squadron disbanded. After a period assisting the Royal Observer Corps and anti-aircraft gun defences, the pilots began work to calibrate the early Chain Home Low (CHL) radars along the east coast, and continued later in 1942 with CHEL (Extra-low) and Type 7 radars. Following the Allied landing in Normandy in June 1944, the squadron provided mobile detachments in France to help with calibration of mobile Type 15 radars accompanying British and Canadian troops.

The other radar calibration unit was 527 Squadron, which formed at Castle Camps on 15 June 1943 with a selection of Hurricanes and Blenheim IVs, moving to Snailwell in February 1944, and Digby two months later. The Hurricane Mk Is and IIbs could be equipped with 44 gal. long-range fuel tanks and also flew detachments from Sutton Bridge and Coltishall to provide calibration of CH Type I radars located around Britain.

Before the outbreak of war, ground based anti-aircraft weapons were fairly elementary, any 'practice' required being provided by regular squadrons. One or two miscellaneous units had been formed in the latter 1930s to provide target aircraft and towed drogues for live firings. With the massive wartime expansion there was a continuous need to provide practice for Army and Navy guns on realistic targets, and a series of Anti-Aircraft

The Empire Air Training Scheme in Canada, India and Africa made an important contribution to the Allied war effort. This ex-Desert Air Force Canadian built Hurricane Mk X, AG244, was operated by the Central Flying School (CFS) in Southern Rhodesia (Zimbabwe). (*Author's Collection*)

Co-operation (AAC) Flights were formed. These flights were not only able to tow drogues for AA guns, but also flew simulated low level and dive bombing attacks on ground troops and defended installations, as well as providing any other services required by surface forces. By the end of 1941, the flights had expanded into squadron strength and were allocated numbers, although they were non-operational units. The units concerned were 285 to 290 (AAC) Squadrons, 286 to 289 Squadrons being formed in November and December 1941 at Filton, Croydon, Digby and Kirknewton with Hurricane IIcs. 290 Squadron was formed at Newtownards on 1 December 1943 and the final unit was 285 (AAC) Squadron at Woodvale in January 1944. As well as Hurricanes, later including Mk IVs, the units operated a variety of aircraft, including Lysanders, Hudsons, Defiants and Blenheims, along with other miscellaneous types. Many of the squadrons operated on detachment to other airfields according to the task required. The last of the Hurricanes on these duties was withdrawn by June 1945.

During enemy night raids in 1940, the relative ineffectiveness of Britain's night

Hawker built Mk I T9531, retired from combat duties with 317 and 80 Squadrons in North Africa, before being delivered to 33 Fighter Instructors School (FIS) with the CFS in Southern Rhodesia. It was one of three delivered to the FIS and, with no need for camouflage, was painted silver for better visibility. (*Author's Collection*)

Hurricanes were also used in the training of air gunners and pilots of heavy bombers. A Mk IIc with 1661 Conversion Unit at Lindholm, here fitted with a night fighter exhaust glare deflector. (*RAF Museum*)

Experienced pilots needed specialized combat training before being promoted to leadership. One of the units where combat skills could be developed was the Fighter Leaders School. Canadian built Hurricane Mk X AG111 flew with this unit. (*IWM*)

Hurricanes were used for weather reconnaissance flights in the Middle East and Britain. Mk IIc of 521 (Met) Squadron operated weather flights from Langham. (*J. Rounce*)

527 Squadron was one of two units in Britain used for the calibration of ground based radar systems. This Canadian built Hurricane XII JS290 served with 527 Squadron at Digby from 1944 to 1945. (*RAF Museum*)

defences had become obvious. Many schemes were tried to improve the situation before the use of Airborne Interception (AI) radar in heavily armed Blenheims, Beaufighters and, later, Mosquitos became widespread and effective. One idea which seemed to have some chance of success was to fit an airborne searchlight in the nose of a relatively large AI equipped aircraft, accompanied by a single seater fighter which would move in for the kill once the target had been illuminated. The aircraft most commonly fitted with this means of illumination were Turbinlite Douglas Havoc converted bombers, accompanied by Hurricanes. The Hurricane units allocated to this unusual task were 530

to 539 Squadrons, the first three, 532, 533 and 534 forming in July 1941 at Wittering, Colerne and Tangmere respectively. By the end of the year, these had been followed by 535, 536, 537, 538 and 539 Squadrons based at Honiley, Colerne, Middle Wallop, Hunsdon and Acklington; and 530 and 531 Squadrons at Hunsdon and West Malling in 1942.

The Turbinlite Havocs were fitted with formation keeping lights to assist the satellite or 'parasite' Hurricane to remain in visual contact. The Havoc would use its AI radar to home to within 3,000 ft of the enemy aircraft, passing the code word 'hot' to the Hurricane. When the target was firmly locked-on, the code word 'boiling' was passed and the parasite would drop 300 ft and open up to full power ahead of the Havoc. When the Hurricane was about 900 ft behind the target, the Havoc would illuminate it for the Hurricane to destroy. The problem was that, once a target was illuminated, it was hardly likely to continue to carry on flying straight and level. Violent evasive manoeuvres would ensue, by which time the Hurricane pilot would have lost his 'night vision' in the brilliance of the searchlight. Clearly, the ideal solution would be to arm the fighter itself with radar. With the entry into service of the more effective, dedicated AI equipped night fighters, the Turbinlite squadrons became redundant, and were disbanded in January 1943. Despite having made a considerable number of radar contacts during these operations, only one enemy aircraft was claimed as destroyed, with one probable and two damaged.

As part of the combat training role, 516 Squadron was formed from 1441 (Combined Operations) Flight at Dundonald on 28 April 1943 to provide simulated low-level attacks on ground troops training for combined operations assaults. Hurricane Mk IIs were delivered to the squadron in December 1943 to complement Mustangs, Lysanders and Blenheim IVs already in use. The aircraft participated in a number of assault exercises along the West coast of Scotland, laying smoke screens and making simulated strafing runs along the beaches. By March the following year, vertical and oblique cameras had been fitted to the Hurricanes in preparation for the D-Day landings. The training continued until the squadron disbanded on 2 December 1944, as there was little likelihood of any further major seaborne landings in Europe.

An important humanitarian task was the recovery of downed aircrews in the sea and survivors from sunken ships by Air Sea Rescue (ASR) squadrons. Four of these units included Hurricanes in their various specialized fleets of aircraft: 276 and 279 Squadron in the UK, and 283 and 284 Squadrons in North Africa.

276 Squadron was formed at Harrowbeer, north of Plymouth, on 21 October 1941. Hurricanes flew with the squadron from December 1941 to 1942 and were used in the search role until replaced by Defiants and Spitfires. 279 Squadron was formed at Bircham Newton on 16 November 1941, but Hurricane Mk IIcs and IVs did not arrive until April 1945, staying only until June. 283 Squadron formed at Algiers in February 1943 and is recorded as having at least one Hurricane II on the strength until its disbandment at Hal Far on 31 March 1946. 284 Squadron was formed at Gravesend on 7 May 1943 and received at least one Hurricane Mk II in September 1944 while stationed in North Africa and Italy. The squadron disbanded at Pomigliano on 21 September 1945, the last Hurricane having been withdrawn from the unit by March 1945.

A less predictable role for the single seater Hurricane was in Communications, not just for inter-station flights but also, as in the case of 173 Squadron at Heliopolis in Egypt, for the use of staff officers to make visits to the units under their command when conventional transport aircraft were not available. 173 Squadron formed on 9 July 1942 out of part of 267 Squadron and received Hurricane Mk Is from the outset, until they were withdrawn in 1943. Hurricanes were used in the Communications role with established squadrons to carry urgent items, such as films and prints to operational headquarters after reconnaissance sorties. In 1944, the Air Dispatch Letter Service was formed, equipped exclusively with Hurricanes, at Hendon. The squadron used about a dozen Mk IIcs to carry important despatches from Britain to France

Before the formation of Turbinlite flights, later to become squadrons, 245 Squadron co-operated early in 1941 on Turbinlite Havoc trials. (*W. Huntley*)

and Belgium following the invasion of Europe. The return loads were often press stories from war correspondents, the material usually being carried below the radio bay behind the cockpit; and, as the volume of traffic increased, in underwing containers adapted from drop tanks.

Once the Belgian capital had been liberated, the Belgian Communications Flight was formed in 1944, using RAF supplied Hurricanes to carry urgent documents between London and Brussels. Two of these aircraft survived the war and one is preserved in the Aviation Museum in Brussels.

Hurricane IV KZ706 fitted experimentally at Farnborough with two large underwing mounted Long Tom 500 lb (227 kg) RPs for tests in 1944, otherwise unarmed. (*BAe*)

APPENDIX 1 – SPECIFICATIONS

Mk	Type	Span	Length	Height	Wing Area	Engine	Power	Loaded Wt	Max Speed	Climb to 20,000ft	Ceiling	Range	Armament
Prot.	Fighter	40 ft/ 12.2 m	31.5 ft/ 9.6 m	13.5 ft/ 4.11 m	257.5sq ft	Merlin C	1,025 hp	5,672lb/ 2,578kg	312 mph/ 501 kph	12 min	33,000ft	500 miles	8 x .303 m/c guns
I/	Fighter	40 ft/ 12.2 m	31.33ft/ 9.6 m	13 ft/ 3.95 m	257.5sq ft	Merlin II/III	1,030hp	6,666lb/ 3,030kg	335 mph/ 536 kph	9 min	36,000ft	525 miles	8 x .303 m/c guns
1 Trop	Fighter	40 ft/ 12.2 m	31.33 ft/ 9.6 m	13 ft/ 3.95 m	257.5sq ft	Merlin II/III	1,030 hp	6,850lb/ 3,113kg	317 mph/ 509 kph	9.5 min	33,000ft	460 miles	8 x .303 m/c guns
Sea Ia	Naval Fighter	40 ft/ 12.2 m	31.33 ft/ 9.6 m	13 ft/ 3.95 m	257.5sq ft	Merlin III	1,030hp	6,780lb/ 3,082kg	302 mph/ 485 kph	11.6 min	31,000 ft	505 miles	8 x .303 m/c guns
Sea Ib	Naval Fighter	40 ft/ 12.2 m	31.33 ft/ 9.6 m	13 ft/ 3.95 m	257.5sq ft	Merlin III	1,030hp	6,800lb/ 3,091kg	296 mph/ 475 kph	12 min	30,000ft	505 miles	8 x .303 m/c guns
IIa	Fighter	40 ft/ 12.2 m	32.19 ft/ 9.83 m	13.08 ft/ 3.99 m	257.5sq ft	Merlin XX	1,185hp	7,014lb/ 3,188kg	340 mph/ 546 kph	7 min	41,000ft	468 miles	8 x .303 m/c guns
IIb/XI	Fighter	40 ft/ 12.2 m	32.19 ft/ 9.83 m	13.08 ft/ 3.99 m	275.5sq ft	Merlin XX	1,185hp	7,440lb/ 3,382kg	340 mph/ 546 kph	7.5 min	40,000ft	465 miles	6/8/12 x .303 m/c guns
IIb	Fighter-bomber	40 ft/ 12.2 m	32.19 ft/ 9.83 m	13.08 ft/ 3.99 m	275.5sq ft	Merlin XX	1,185hp	8,470lb/ 3,850kg	320 mph/ 514 kph	9.3/ 10.5 min	33,000/ 30,000ft	460 miles	6/8/12 x .303 m/c guns + 2 x 250/ 500lb bombs
IIc/	Fighter-Bomber	40 ft/ 12.2 m	32.19 ft/ 9.83 m	13.08 ft/ 3.99 m	275.5sq ft	Merlin XX	1,185hp	7,670lb/ 3,486kg	334 mph/ 536 kph	7.6 min	36,000ft	460 miles	4 x 20 mm cannon + 2 x 250/500lb bombs
IId	Anti-armour	40 ft/ 12.2 m	32.19 ft/ 9.83 m	13.08 ft/ 3.99 m	275.5sq ft	Merlin XX	1,185hp	7,850lb/ 3,568kg	322 mph/ 517 kph	12.4 min	32,100ft	420 miles	2 x 40 mm cannons + 2 x .303 m/c guns
Sea IIc	Naval Fighter	40 ft/ 12.2 m	32.19 ft/ 9.83 m	13.08 ft/ 3.99 m	275.5sq ft	Merlin XX	1,185hp	7,618lb/ 3,462kg	301 mph/ 484 kph	12 min	35,600ft	452 miles	4 x 20 mm cannon + 2 x 250/500lb bombs
IV	Ground Attack	40 ft/ 12.2 m	32.19 ft/ 9.83 m	13.08 ft/ 3.99 m	275.5sq ft	Merlin 27	1,185hp	8,462lb/ 3,846kg	280 mph/ 450 kph	12 min	29,100ft	450 miles	4 x 20mm/2 x 40mm cannons + 8 x RP or 2 x 250/500lb bombs
X	Fighter	40 ft/ 12.2 m	31.33ft/ 9.6 m	13 ft/ 3.95 m	275.5sq ft	Packard Merlin 28	1,300hp	7,160lb/ 3,251kg	330 mph/ 531 kph	9.9 min	35,000ft		8 x .303 m/c guns
XII	Fighter-bomber	40 ft/ 12.2 m	31.33ft/ 9.6 m	13 ft/ 3.95 m	275.5sq ft	Packard Merlin 29	1,300hp	7,360lb/ 3,341kg	330 mph/ 531 kph	9.9 min	36,500ft		12 x .303 m/c guns + 2 x 250/500lb bombs

APPENDIX 2 – PRODUCTION

Prototype
K5083 ordered under contract 357483/34 to Air Ministry Specification F.36/34 and first flown 6 November 1935

600 Hawker built Mk Is ordered 3 June 1936 to Spec. 15/36
L1547 – L2146. Contract No 527112/36, powered by R-R Merlin II with Watts wooden two-blade fixed pitch propeller and fabric covered wings, delivered between 15 December 1937 and 6 October 1939.
L1708, L1710 & L1711 to SAAF
L1751(1-205), L1752(2-206), L1837(3-291), L1838(4-292), L1839(5-293), L1840(6-294), L1858(7-312), L1859(8-313), L1860(9-314), L1861(10-315), L1862(11-316), L1863(12-317) to Yugoslavian Air Force – serials in brackets.
L2077, L2078, L2085, L2093 to L2097, L2104, L2112 to L2114 to Rumanian Air Force 8 to 9.39.
L1759(310), L1760(311), L1761(312), L1762(313), L1763(314), L1878(315), L1879(316), L1880(317), L1881(318), L1882(319), L1883(320), L1884(321), L1885(322), L1886(323), L1887(324), L1888(325), L1890(326), L2021(327), L2022(328), L2023(329) to RCAF
L1918(1), L1919(2), L1920(3), L1993(4), L1994(5), L1995(6), L1996(7), L1997(8), L2040(9), L2041(10), L2042(11), L2043(12), L2044(13), L2105(14), L2106(15), L2107(16), L2108(17), L2109(18), L2110(19), L2111(20) to Belgian Air Force.
L2048 to Poland 24.7.39
L2079(252) to Persia
L2024, L2025, L2027 – L2033, L2125 to L2139 to Turkey, delivered 14.9.39 to 6.10.39

300 Hawker built Mk Is
N2318 – N2367, N2380 – N2409, N2422 – N2441, N2453 – N2502, N2520 – N2559, N2582 – N2631, N2645 – N2729. Contract No 751458/38, powered by R-R Merlin III with de Havilland three blade variable pitch propeller. The first 80 aircraft had fabric covered wings and the remainder metal wings. Delivered 29.9.39 to 1.5.40.
N2718 – N2729 to Yugoslavia 3.40.

500 Gloster built Mk Is
P2535 – P2584, P2614 – P2653, P2672 – P2701, P2713 – P2732, P2751 – P2770, P2792 – P2836, P2854 – P2888, P2900 – P2924, P2946 – P2995, P3030 – P3069, P3080 – P3124, P3140 – P3179, P3200 – P3234, P3250 – P3264. Powered by R-R Merlin III with de Havilland or Rotol three blade variable pitch propeller, delivered 11.39 to 4.40. Contract No. 962371/38/C.23a.
P2968(107) to Ireland 11.43.

500 Hawker built Mk Is, plus 44 attrition replacements
P3265 – P3279, P3300 – P3324, P3345 – P3364, P3380 – P3429, P3348 – P3492, P3515 – P3554, P3574 – P3623, P3640 – P3684, P3700 – P3739, P3755 – P3789, P3802 – P3836, P3854 – P3903, P3920 – P3944, P3960 – P3984. Plus replacements P8809 – P8818, R2680 – R2689, T9519 – T9538, W6667 – W6670. Powered by R-R Merlin II with de Havilland or Rotol three blade variable pitch propeller, delivered 21.2.40 to 20.7.40 Contract No. 962371/38.
P3269 Prototype Mk II
P3416(108) to Ireland 11.43
P3620 to Sea Hurricane Mk Ia.
P3720 to Iran as 252 11.40.

100 Gloster built Mk Is

R4074 – R4123, R4171 – R4200, R4213 – R4132. Powered by R-R Merlin III with de Havilland or Rotol three blade variable pitch propeller, delivered 5.40 to 7.40. Contract No. 19773/39/23.
R4103, R4104 to SAAF 7.40.

500 Gloster built Mk Is

V6533 – V6582, V6600 – V6649, V6665 – V6704, V6722 – V6761, V6776 – V6825, V6840 – V6889, V6913 – V6962, V6979 – V7028, V7042 – V7081, V7099 – V7138, V7156 – V7195. Powered by R-R Merlin III with de Havilland or Rotol three blade variable pitch propeller, delivered 7 – 11.40. Contract No. 85730/40/C.23a
V6576(111), V7158(110), V7173(109) to Ireland.

500 Hawker built Mk Is

V7200 – V7209, V7221 – V7260, V7276 – V7318, V7337 – V7386, V7400 – V7446, V7461 – V7510, V7533 – V7572, V7588 – V7627, V7644 – V7690, V7705 – V7737, V7741 – V7780, V7795 – V7838, V7851 – V7862, AS987 – AS990. Powered by R-R Merlin III with de Havilland or Rotol three blade variable pitch propellers and metal wings, delivered 2.7.40 to 5.2.41. Contract No. 62305/39.
V7411(104), V7435(112), V7463(114), V7540(105) to Ireland.

200 Gloster built Mk Is

W9110 – W9159, W9170 – W9209, W9215 – W9244, W9260 – W9279, W9290 – W9329, W9340 – W9359. Powered by R-R Merlin III with de Havilland or Rotol three blade variable pitch propeller, delivered 11.40. Contract No. 85730/40/C.23a
W9209, W9215 – W9224 to Sea Hurricane I 11.40
W9314 to Mk IIc prototype.

1,000 Hawker built Mk IIs

Z2308 – Z2357, Z2382 – Z2426, Z2446 – Z2465, Z2479 – Z2528, Z2560 – Z2594, Z2624 – Z2643, Z2661 – Z2705, Z2741 – Z2775, Z2791 – Z2840, Z2882 – Z2931, Z2959 – Z2999, Z3017 – Z3036, Z3050 – Z3099, Z3143 – Z3187, Z3221 – Z3276, Z3310 – Z3359, Z3385 – Z3404, Z3421 – Z3470, Z3489 – Z3523, Z3554 – Z3598, Z3642 – Z3691, Z3740 – Z3784, Z3826 – Z3845, Z3885 – Z3919, Z3969 – Z4018. Powered by R-R Merlin XX with de Havilland or Rotol three blade variable pitch propeller, delivered 14.1.41 to 28.7.41. Contract No. 62305/39.
Z4015 to Sea Hurricane Mk Ic

400 Gloster built Mk Is

Z4022 – Z4071, Z4085 – Z4119, Z4161 – Z4205, Z4223 – Z4272, Z4308 – Z4327, Z4347 – Z4391, Z4415 – Z4434, Z4482 – Z4516, Z4532 – Z4581, Z4603 – Z4652. Powered by R-R Merlin III with de Havilland or Rotol three blade variable pitch propeller, delivered 12.40 to 3.41. Contract No. 85730/40/C.23a
Z4037(106) to Ireland 7.43.

600 Gloster built Mk IIas/IIbs

Z4686 – Z4720, Z4760 – Z4809, Z4832 – Z4876, Z4920 – Z4939, IIa Z4940 – Z4969, Z4987 – Z4989, IIb Z4990 – Z5006, Z5038 – Z5087, Z5117 – Z5161, Z5202 – Z5236, Z5252 – Z5271, Z5302 – Z5351, Z5376 – Z5395, Z5434 – Z5483, Z5529 – Z5563, Z5580 – Z5629, Z5649 – Z5693. Powered by R-R Merlin XX with de Havilland or Rotol three blade variable pitch propellers. 140 built as Mk IIas and remaining 341 as Mk IIbs delivered 3.9.41. Contract No. 85730/40/C.23a
Z5159, Z5210 – Z5213, Z5227, Z5236, Z5259, Z5262, Z5263, Z5480 to Russia 1941/'42.
Z4846, Z4847, Z4849, Z4851 – Z4854, Z4867, Z4873, Z4874, Z4876, Z4920 – Z4926, Z4929, Z4931, Z4933, Z4935 – Z4939, Z5440 converted to Sea Hurricane Mk Ia/Ib.

300 Austin Motors built Mk IIs

AP516 – AP550, AP564 – AP613, AP629 – AP648, AP670 – AP714, AP732 – AP781, AP801 – AP825, AP849 – AP898,

AP912 – AP936. Powered by R-R Merlin XX with de Havilland or Rotol three blade variable pitch propeller. Approximately 250 allocated to Russia 10.41, but some were allocated to RAF.

450 Gloster built Mk IIas/IIbs/IIcs
BG674 – BG723, BG737 – BG771, BG783 – BG832, BG844 – BG888, BG901 – BG920, BG933 – BG977, BG990 – BG999, BH115 – BH154, BH167 – BH201, BH215 – BH264, BH277 – BH296, BH312 – BH361. Powered by R-R Merlin XX with de Havilland or Rotol three blade variable pitch propeller, delivered 9.41 to 12.41.
400 shipped to Russia and remainder to Middle East.

1,350 Hawker built Mk IIs
BD696 – BD745, BD759 – BD793, BD818 – BD837, BD855 – BD899, BD914 – BD963, BD980 – BD 986, BE105 – BE117, BE130 – BE174, BE193 – BE242, BE274 – BE308, BE323 – BE372, BE394 – BE428, BE468 – BE517, BE546 – BE590, BE632 – BE651, BE667 – BE716, BM898 – BM936, BM947 – BM996, BN103 – BN142, BN155 – BN189, BN203 – BN242, BN265 – BN298, BN311 – BN337, BN346 – BN389, BN399 – BN435, BN449 – BN497, BN512 – BN547, BN559 – BN603, BN624 – BN654, BN667 – BN705, BN719 – BN759, BN773 – BN802, BN818 – BN846, BN859 – BN882, BN896 – BN940, BN953 – BN987. Powered by R-R Merlin XX with de Havilland or Rotol three blade variable pitch propeller and metal wings, delivered 24.7.41 to 18.3.42.
BD709, BD731, BD956, BE162, BE470, BN416, BN471, BN481, BN428 to Russia 1942.
BD787 to Sea Hurricane Mk Ia.

1,888 Hawker built Mk IIs
BN988 – BN992, BP109 – BP141, BP154 – BP200, BP217 – BP245, BP259 – BP302, BP316 – BP362, BP378 – BP416, BP430 – BP479, BP493 – BP526, BP538 – BP566, BP579 – BP614, BP628 – BP675, BP692 – BP711, BP734 – BP772, HL544 – HL591, HL603 – HL634, HL654 – HL683, HL698 – HL747, HL767 – HL809, HL828 – HL867, HL879 – HL913, HL925 – HL941, HL953 – HL997, HM110 – HM157, HV275 – HV317, HV333 – HV370, HV396 – HV445, HV468 – HV516, HV534 – HV560, HV577 – HV612, HV634 – HV674, HV696 – HV745, HV768 – HV799, HV815 – HV858, HV873 – HV921, HV943 – HV989, HW115 – HW146, HW167 – HW207, HW229 – HW278, HW291 – HW323, HW345 – HW373, HW399 – HW444, HW467 – HW501, HW533 – HW572, HW596 – HW624, HW651 – HW686, HW713 – HW757, HW779 – HW808, HW834 – HW881. Powered by R-R Merlin XX with de Havilland or Rotol three blade variable propeller, delivered 17.3.42 to 23.11.42. Contract No. 62305/39/B.
BP657, HL629, HL992, HL994, HV362, HV364, HV840, HV844, HV880, HW117, HW143, HW233, HW347, HW364, HW471, HW551, HW552, HW557, HW571 Mk IIcs shipped to Russia in 1943.
HL549 & HL665 shipped to Russia and converted to two seaters.
HV279, HV287, HV293, HV556, HV593, HW168, HW205, HW300, HW357, HW371, HW406, HW686, HW715, HW868, HW872, HW879 Mk IIds shipped to Russia in 1943.
HV513, HV551 tropical Mk IIcs to Turkey October/November 1942.
HL673 to Sea Hurricane Mk Ic.

1,200 Hawker built Mk IIs and Mk IVs
KW745 – KW777, KW791 – KW832, KW846 – KW881, KW893 – KW936, KW949 – KW982, KX101 – KX146, KX162 – KX202, KX220 – KX261, KX280 – KX307, KX321 – KX369, KX382 – KX425, KX452 – KX491, KX521 KX567, KX579 – KX621, KX691 – KX736, KX749 – KX784, KX796 – KX838, KX851 – KX892, KX922 – KX967, KZ111 – KZ156, KZ169 – KZ201, KZ216 – KZ250, KZ266 – KZ301, KZ319 – KZ356, KZ370 – KZ412, KZ424 – KZ470, KZ483 – KZ526, KZ540 – KZ582, KZ597 – KZ612, plus NF668 – NF703 Sea Hurricane Mk IIc conversions. Powered by R-R Merlin XX with de Havilland or Rotol three blade variable pitch propeller, delivered 20.11.42 to 19.4.43. Contract No. 62305/39/C.
KW770(NF668), KW774(NF671), KW791(NF669), KW792(NF670), KW799(NF672), KW800(NF673), KW804(NF674), KW807(NF677), KW808(NF675), KW809(NF678), KW810(NF676), KW816(NF679), KW817(NF680), KW827(NF681), KW828(NF682), KW849(NF683), KW850(NF684), KW860(NF685), KW862(NF686), KW868(NF687), KW870(NF688), KW878(NF689), KW880(NF690), KW897(NF691), KW899(NF692), KW908(NF693), KW909(NF694), KW910(NF695),

KW911(NF696), KW918(NF697), KW919(NF698), KW920(NF699), KW921(NF700), KW928(NF701), KW929(NF702), KW930(NF703) conversions to Sea Hurricane Mk IIcs with new serial numbers in brackets.
KW706, KW723, KX113, KX125, KX137, KX538, KX545, KZ234 Mk IIcs; KW777, KX177, KX181, KZ301 Mk IIds; KX813, KX865, KX888 Mk IVs; KZ509 Sea Hurricane Mk IIc all shipped to Russia in 1943.
KX405 & KZ193 converted to Mk Vs.

1,205 Hawker built Mk IIs & Mk IVs
KZ613 – KZ632, KZ646 – KZ689, KZ702 – KZ750, KZ766 – KZ801, KZ817 – KZ862, KZ877 – KZ920, KZ933 – KZ949, LA101 – LA144, LB542 – LB575, LB588 – LB624, LB639 – LB687, LB707 – LB744, LB769 – LB801, LB827 – LB862, LB873 – LB913, LB927 – LB973, LB986 – LB999, LD100 – LD131, LD157 – LD185, LD199 – LD219, LD232 – LD266, LD287 – LD315, LD334 – LD351, LD369 – LD416, LD435 – LD470, LD487 – LD508, LD524 – LD539, LD557 – LD580, LD594 – LD632, LD651 – LD695, LD723 – LD749, LD772 – LD809, LD827 – LD866, LD885 – LD905, LD931 – LD979, LD993 – LD999. Powered by R-R Merlin XX with de Havilland or Rotol three blade variable propeller, delivered 18.4.43 to 29.9.43. Contract No. 62305/39/C.
KZ858, LB991, LD205 to Russia 1943–4.
LB602, LB664, LB732, plus others to Indian Air Force.

1,357 Hawker built Mk IIs & Mk IVs
LE121 – LE146, LE163 – LE183, LE201 – LE214, LE247 – LE273, LE291 – LE309, LE334 – LE368, LE387 – LE405, LE432 – LE449, LE456 – LE484, LE499 – LE535, LE552 – LE593, LE617 – LE665, LE679 – LE713, LE737 – LE769, LE784 – LE816, LE829 – LE867, LE885 – LE925, LE938 – LE966, LE979 – LE999, LF101 – LF135, LF153 – LF184, LF197 – LF237, LF256 – LF298, LF313 – LF346, LF359 – LF405, LF418 – LF435, LF451 – LF482, LF494 – LF516, LF529 – LF542, LF559 – LF601, LF620 – LF660, LF674 – LF721, LF737 – LF774, MW335 – MW373, PG425 – PG456, PG469 – PG499, PG512 – PG554, PG567 - PG610, PZ730 – PZ778, PZ791 – PZ835, PZ848 – PZ865. Powered by R-R Merlin XX with de Havilland or Rotol three blade variable pitch propeller, delivered 29.9.43 to 24.5.44. Contract No. 62305/39/C.
LE529, LF463, LF470, LF473, LF481, LF509, LF510, LF592, LF595, LF596 to Russia 1944.
LF342, LF133, LF360, LF383, LF422, LF425, LF514, LF564, LF565, LF568, LF570, LF586, LF620, LF699, LF706, LF717, LF757, LF772, MW373, PG521, PG535, PG538, PG543, PG599, PG610, PZ735, PZ738, PZ745, PZ759 to Portugal 1945–46.
LF541(116), LF624(118), PZ796(120) to Ireland.

One Hawker built Mk V
NL255 prototype

TOTAL UK PRODUCTION – 12,952

CANADIAN PRODUCTION

160 Canadian Car & Foundry built Mk Is
P5170 – P5209, T9519 – T9538, Z6983 – Z7017, Z7049 – Z7093, Z7143 – Z7162 Powered by R-R Merlin II with de Havilland three blade variable pitch propeller, majority shipped to UK March to November 1940.
P5176(93) to Ireland 1942.

340 Canadian Car & Foundry built Mk Xs
AE958 – AE977, AF945 – AF999, AG100 – AG286, AG287 – AG344, AG665 – AG684. Powered by Packard Merlin 28 with Hamilton Hydromatic three blade propeller. Some 100 were completed with eight gun wing, and remainder with 12 gun wing.
AG287(1374), AG293 – 296(1377, 1368, 1375, 1376), AG299(1378), AG300(1380), AG302(1379), AG304 – 319(1372,

1363, 1366, 1367, 1371, 1363, 1362, 1365, 1361, 1356, 1358, 1354, 1357, 1353, 1355, 1352), AG323(1351), AG325 – 327(1359, 1373, 1369), AG330(1370), AG332(1360) all to RCAF
AE958 – AE962, AE964 – AE969, AE975, AE977, AF945 – AF947, AF949 – AF955, AF962, AF963, AF965, AF967, AF969, AF971, AF973, AF974, AF976, AF981, AF982 to Sea Hurricane IIbs.
AG672 – AG984 to Russia.

100 Canadian Car & Foundry built Mk Xs
AM270 – AM369, AP138. Powered by Packard Merlin 28 with Hamilton Hydromatic three blade propellers. Originally built with eight gun metal wing, but many converted to 12 gun or four cannon armament.
AM367 to Russia.

50 Canadian Car & Foundry built Mk XIIas
BW835 – BW884. Powered by Packard Merlin 28 with Hamilton Hydromatic three blade variable pitch propeller. To RCAF as Sea Hurricanes. Lend-Lease contract.

150 Canadian Car & Foundry built Mk XIs
BW885 – BW999, BX100 – BX134. Powered by Packard Merlin 28 with Hamilton Hydromatic three blade variable pitch propeller. Originally built with eight gun wing, but many converted to 12 gun or four cannon armament.
BW920, BW922, BW926, BW984, BX102, BX108 – BX111, BX119 – BX124 to Russia, with remainder to RAF.

248 Canadian Car & Foundry built Mk XIs & Mk XIIs
JS219 – JS371, JS374 – JS420 (12 gun wing), JS421 – JS468 (most converted in UK to four cannon armament. Powered by Packard Merlin 28 & 29 with Hamilton Hydromatic three blade variable pitch propeller.
JS219 – JS221, JS225, JS227 – JS229, JS232, JS233, JS235, JS237, JS240, JS241, JS256, JS257, JS300, JS309, JS317, JS391, JS396 – JS399, JS405 – JS412, JS415, JS419 shipped to Russia. Remainder to RCAF, RCN, RAF & FAA.

150 Canadian Car & Foundry built Mk XIIas
PJ660 – PJ695, PJ711 – PJ758, PJ779 – PJ813, PJ842 – PJ872. Powered by Packard Merlin 29 with Hamilton Hydromatic three blade variable pitch propeller, built with eight gun wings, and many converted to 12 gun or four cannon armament. Most of this batch were shipped to Russia or the Asia Campaign with a few retained in Canada for conversion to Sea Hurricane Mk XIIas.

200 Canadian Car & Foundry built Mk XIIs
5376 – 5775. Powered by Packard Merlin 28.29 with Hamilton Hydromatic three blade variable pitch propeller, built with eight .303 machine gun wings, all allocated to the RCAF.

TOTAL CANADIAN PRODUCTION – 1,398

TOTAL COMBINED PRODUCTION – 14,350 HURRICANES

APPENDIX 3 - HURRICANE UNITS

ROYAL AIR FORCE

Unit	Role	Code	Mk	Dates	Bases
1 Sq	F	NA	I	10.38 – 4.41	Tangmere, France, Northolt, Wittering, Kenley & Croydon.
	F	JX	I	4.42 – 7.42	Tangmere
	F	JX	IIa	2.41 – 6.41	Kenley, Croydon & Redhill
	F	JX	IIb	4.41 – 1.42	Croydon, Redhill, Kenley, Tangmere
	F	JX	IIb	6.42 – 9.42	Tangmere
	F	JX	IIc	7.41 – 9.42	Tangmere, Acklington
3 Sq	F	OP	I	3.38 – 7.38	Kenley
	F	OP	I	5.39 – 4.41	Biggin Hill, Hawkinge, Kenley, France, Wick, Castletown, Turnhouse, Skaebrae
	NF	QO	IIb	4.41 – 10.41	Martlesham Heath, Debden, Stapleford Tawney, Hunsdon
	NF	QO	IIc	4.41 – 2.43	Martlesham, Stapleford, Hunsdon
5 Sq	FB		IIc/d	6.43 – 10.44	Khangpur, Yelahanka, India/Burma
6 Sq	F	JV	I	3.41 – 7.41	Tobruk
	F		I	9.41 – 2.42	Egypt, Libya
	FB	JV	IIc	12.42 – 2.43	Egypt, Libya
	FB	JV	IId	5.42 – 9.43	Egypt, Libya, Tunisia
	FB	JV	IV	7.43 – 1.47	Egypt, Italy, Palestine, Cyprus
11 Sq	F		IIc	8.43 – 6.45	India, Burma
17 Sq	F	UV	IIc	6.39 – 2.41	North Weald, Croydon, Debden, Hawkinge, Kenley, France, Tangmere, Martlesham
	F	YB	IIa	2.41 – 4.41	Croydon & Martlesham
	F	YB	IIa	1.42 – 6.42	Asia
	F	YB	IIb	7.41 – 11.41	Elgin, Dyce, Tain, Catterick
	F	YB	IIb	6.42 – 8.42	Jessore Asia
	F	YB	IIc	8.42 – 6.44	Alipore, Agartala, China Bay, Minneriya
20 Sq	F		IId	3.43 – 9.45	Charra India/Burma
	FB		IIc	8.44 – 10.44	Sapan India/Burma
	FB		IV	11.44 – 9.45	Sapan India/Burma
28 Sq	Army Co-op		IIb	12.42 – 12.44	India, Burma
			IIc/IV	3.44 – 7.45	India, Burma, Malaya
29 Sq	F		I	8 – 12.40	Wellingore
30 Sq	F	RS	I	6.41 – 8.42	Alexandria, Ratmalana Ceylon
	F		IIb	8.41 – 8.42	Ceylon, Burma

Unit	Role	Code	Mk	Dates	Bases
	F	RS	IIc	8.42 – 9.44	Ceylon, Burma
32 Sq	F	KT	I	10.38 – '42	Biggin Hill, Gravesend, Manston, Wittering, Acklington, Middle Wallop, Ibsley, Pembrey, Angle, West Malling
	F	GZ	IIb	7.41 – 11.42	Angle, Manston, W Malling, Friston, Honiley, Baginton
	F	GZ	IIc	11.41 – 8.43	Manston, W Malling, Friston, Baginton, Algeria, Tunisia
33 Sq	F	NW	I	9.40 – 2.42	Egypt, Greece, Libya
	FB		IIb	3.42 – 6.42	Egypt, Libya
	FB		IIc	6.42 – 12.43	Egypt, Libya
34 Sq	FB	8Q	IIc	8.43 – 4.45	Burma, India
	FB		IIb	12.43 – 12.44	Burma, India
	AAC		IIc		Horsham St Faith
42 Sq	FB	AW	IV	10.43 – 6.45	Burma, India
	FB	AW	IIc	9.44 – 12.44	Burma, India and 4.45 – 6.45
43 Sq	F	NQ	I	11.38 – 7.41	Tangmere, Acklington, Wick, Northolt, Usworth, Drem, Crail
	F	FT	I	9.42 – 11.42	Kirton-in-Lindsey
	F	FT	IIb	4.41 – 9.42	Drem, Acklington, Tangmere
	F	FT	IIc	11.42 – 3.43	Algiers (Maison Blanche)
46Sq	F	RJ/PO	I	3.39 – 5.41	Digby, Acklington, Norway, Stapleford, N Weald, Church Fenton, Sherburn-in-Elmet
	F		IIc	6 – 7.41	Malta
56 Sq	F	LR/US	I	4.38 – 2.41	N Weald, Martlesham, France, Digby, Wittering, Boscombe Down, Middle Wallop
	F	US	IIb	2.41 – 3.42	N Weald, Martlesham, Duxford
60 Sq	FB	MU	IIc	7.43 – 6.45	Burma, India
63 Sq	Tac Recce	UB	IIc/IV	3.44 – 5.44	Turnhouse, Woodvale
			IIc	9.44 – 12.44	N Weald, Manston
67 Sq	FB	RD	IIb	2.42 – 6.42	Burma, India
	FB		IIc	6.42 – 2.44	Burma, India
69 Sq	Recce		I/II	4.41 – 2.42	Malta
71 Sq Eagle	F	XR	I	11.40 – 5.41	Church Fenton, Kirton-in-Lindsey, Martlesham
	F	XR	IIa	5.41 – 8.41	Martlesham, N Weald
73 Sq	F/NF	HV/ TP	I	7.38 – 1.42	Digby, France, Church Fenton, Castle Camps, Egypt, Libya
	NF		IIb	'41 – 2.42	Egypt, Libya
74 Sq	F		IIb	12.42 – 8.43	Persia, Iraq, Palestine, Egypt
79 Sq	F	AL	I	11.38 – '41	Biggin Hill, Manston, Digby, France, Hawkinge, Sealand, Acklington, Pembrey, Fairwood Common
	F	NV	IIb	'41 – 12.41	Pembrey, Fairwood Common
	FB	NV	IIc	6.42 – 9.44	Burma, India
80 Sq	F	AP	I	6.40 – 1.42	Egypt, Greece, Palestine, Syria
	F	AP	II	1.42 – 4.43	Egypt, Libya, Palestine
81 Sq	F		IIb	7.41 – 11.41	Leconfield, Russia

Unit	Role	Code	Mk	Dates	Bases
85 Sq	NF	NO/ VY	I	9.38 – 4.41	Aldergrove, Debden, France, Martlesham, Croydon, Castle Camps, Church Fenton, Kirton-in-Lindsey, Gravesend, Hunsdon, West Malling, Swannington
87 Sq	NF	PD/LK	I	7.38 – 9.42	Debden, France, Church Fenton, Colerne, Charmy Down
	NF	LK	IIc	6.41 – 3.44	Charmy Down, Algeria, Gibraltar, Morocco, Sicily
94 Sq	NF/FB	GO	I	5.41 – 12.41	Egypt, Iraq
	F		I	6.42 – 8.42	Egypt, Libya
	FB		IIb	12.41 – 1.42	Egypt, Libya
	FB	GO	IIc	6.42 – 5.44	Egypt, Libya
95 Sq	F		I	7 – 10.41	Sierra Leone
96 Sq	NF	ZJ	I/IIc	10.40 – 3.42	Cranage
98 Sq	F		I	6.41 – 7.41	Kaldarnes, Iceland
111 Sq 1st unit	F	TM/ JU	I	12.37 – 4.41	Northolt, Acklington, Drem, Wick, Digby, N Weald, Croydon, Debden, Dyce
113 Sq	FB		IIc	9.43 – 4.45	India, Burma
116 Sq	Calib	II	I/IIa	11.41 – 5.45	Hendon, Heston, Croydon, N Weald, Gatwick, Redhill, Hornchurch
121 Sq	F	AV	I	5.41 – 7.41	Kirton-in-Lindsey, Digby
Eagle	F	AV	IIb	7.41 – 11.41	Kirton-in-Lindsey, N Weald
123 Sq	FB		IIc	11.42 – 9.44	Persia, Egypt, Asia
126 Sq	F		IIa/b	28.6.41 – 4.42	Malta
127 Sq	F	BZ	I	29.6.41 – 7.41	Syria, Iraq
	F		I	2.42 – 6.42	Palestine
	F		IIb	6.42 – 10.43	Egypt
	F		IIb	8.43 – 4.44	Egypt, Palestine
128 Sq	F	WG	I/IIb	10.41 – 3.43	Sierra Leone
133 Sq Eagle	F	MD	IIb	29.8.41 – 12.41	Coltishall, Duxford, Colly Weston, Fowlmere, Eglington
134 Sq	F	GQ/ GA	IIb	31.7.41 – 10.41	Leconfield, Russia
	F	GV	IIb	1.43 – 10.43	Egypt, Libya
135 Sq	F		IIa	15.8.41 – '42	Baginton, Honiley, Burma, India
	F		IIb	2.42 – 10.43	Burma, India
	F		IIc	11.41 – '41	Burma, India
	FB		IIc	10.43 – 9.44	Ceylon
136 Sq	FB	HM	IIa	20.8.41 – 11.41	Kirton-in-Lindsey
	FB		IIb/c	3.42 – 10.43	India, Burma
137 Sq	FB	SF	IV	6.43 – 1.44	Rochford, Manston, Lympne
145 Sq	F	SO	I	3.40 – 2.41	Croydon, France, Filton, Tangmere, Westhampnett, Drem, Dyce
146 Sq	F		IIb	5.42 – 1.44	India, Burma
151 Sq	NF	GG/ DZ	I	12.38 – 6.41	N Weald, Martlesham, France, Stapleford, Digby, Bramcote, Wittering
	NF		IIc	4.41 – 1.42	Wittering
153 Sq	FB		IIc	8 – 9.44	Algeria

Unit	Role	Code	Mk	Dates	Bases
164 Sq	FB	FJ	IId IV	2.43 – 2.44	Middle Wallop, Warmwell, Manston, Fairlop, Twinwood Farm
173 Sq	Comms		I	7.42 – '43	Heliopolis
174 Sq	FB	XP	IIb	3.3.42 – 4.43	Manston, Fowlmere, Warmwell, Odiham, Chilbolton, Grove, Zeals
175 Sq	FB	HH	IIb	3.3.42 – 4.43	Warmwell, Harrowbeer, Gatwick, Odiham, Stony Cross, Lasham
176 Sq	AAC		IIc	5.43 – 1.44	India
181 Sq	FB	EL	I	1.9.42 – '43	Duxford, Snailwell
182 Sq	FB	XM	I	1.9.42 – '43	Martlesham, Sawbridgeworth
183 Sq	FB	HF	I	1.11.42 – '43	Church Fenton
184 Sq	Anti-tank	BR	IId	1.12.42 – '43	Colerne, Chilbolton, Eastchurch, Merston, Manston
	FB	BR	IV	'43 – '44	Merston, Manston, Detling, Odiham
185 Sq	F		I	12.5.41 – 6.42	Malta
	F		IIa	7.41 – 6.42	Malta
186 Sq	Army Co-op	AP	IV	8.43 – 11.43	Ayr
193 Sq	FB	DP	I/IIc	1.43 – 2.43	Harrowbeer
195 Sq	F		I	16.11.42 – 3.43	Duxford, Hutton Cranswick
208 Sq	Army Co-op		I	11.40 – '42	Egypt, Libya, Greece, Palestine
			IIa/b/c	5.42 – 12.43	Egypt, Libya, Iraq, Syria, Palestine
213 Sq	F	AK	I	1.39 – '42	Wittering, France, Biggin Hill, Exeter, Tangmere, Leconfield, Driffield, Nicosia, Egypt
	FB	AK	IIc	1.42 – 5.44	Egypt, Libya
225 Sq	FR	WU	I	1.42 – 6.42	Thruxton
	FR		IIb/c	2.42 – 4.43	Thruxton, Algeria, Tunisia
229 Sq	F	RE	I	3.40 – 5.41	Digby, Wittering, Northolt, Speke
	FB	HB	IIc	9.41 – 4.42	Egypt, Libya, Malta
232 Sq	F	EF	I	17.7.40 – 11.41	Sumburgh, Castletown, Skitten, Drem, Montrose, Abbotsinch, Ouston
	F		IIb	8.41 – 2.42	Ouston, Singapore
237 Sq	F		I	1.1.42 – 12.42	Egypt, Libya, Iraq, Persia
Rhodesia	F		IIc	2.43 – 12.43	Egypt, Libya
238 Sq	F	VK	I	6.40 – 3.41	Middle Wallop, St Eval, Chilbolton
	F	VK	I	2.42 – 5.42	Egypt, Libya
	F	VK	IIa	3.41 – 5.41	Chilbolton, Pembrey
	F		IIc	9.41 – 2.42	Egypt, Libya
	FB		IIc	10.42 – 9.43	Egypt, Libya
	Anti-Tank		IIb	5.42 – 10.42	Egypt, Libya
239 Sq	Army Co-op	HB	I/IIc	1.42 – 5.42	Hatfield, Gatwick
241 Sq	Army Co-op	RZ	IIc	10.42 – 1.44	Ayr, Algeria, Tunisia
242 Sq Canada	F	LE	I	2.40 – 4.41	Church Fenton, Biggin Hill, France, Coltishall,

Unit	Role	Code	Mk	Dates	Bases
					Duxford, Martlesham
	F	LE	IIb	2.41 – 3.42	Martlesham, Stapleford, N Weald, Manston, Valley, Singapore, Sumatra/Java
	FB		IIc	'41 – 9.41	Stapleford, N Weald, Manston
245 Sq	F	DX	I	3.40 – '41	Leconfield, Drem, Turnhouse, Aldergrove, Ballyhalbert
	FB	MR	IIb	8.41 – '42	Chilbolton, Warmwell, Middle Wallop
	NF		IIc	'42 – 1.43	Charmy Down
247 Sq	F	HP	I	12.40 – 6.41	Roborough, St Eval, Portreath
China -	F	HP	IIa	6.41 – 12.41	Predannack, Exeter
British	F		IIb	8.41 – 12.41	Predannack, Exeter
	NF		IIb	8.42 – 3.43	High Ercall, Middle Wallop
	NF	ZY	IIc	8.41 – 3.43	Predannack, High Ercall, Middle Wallop
249 Sq	F	GN	I	16.5.40 – '41	Church Fenton, Leconfield, Boscombe Down, N Weald
Gold	FB		I	5.41 – '42	Malta
Coast	FB		IIa	2.41 – '42	N Weald, Malta
	FB		IIb	'42 – 3.42	Malta
250 Sq Sudan	NF		I/IIc	2.42 – 4.42	Egypt
253 Sq	F	SW	I	1.40 – 9.41	Manston, Northolt, Kenley, Kirton-in-Lindsey, Turnhouse, Prestwick, Leconfield, Skeabrae
	NF		IIb	7.41 – 9.42	Skeabrae, Hibaldstow, Shoreham, Friston
	NF		IIc	1.42 – 9.42	Hibaldstow, Shoreham, Friston
	F		IIc	11.42 – 9.43	Algeria, Tunisia
255 Sq	NF		I	3.41 – 7.41	Kirton-in-Lindsey, Hibaldstow
256 Sq	NF	JT	I	3.41 – 5.42	Squires Gate
257 Sq	F	DT	I	6.40 – 6.41	Hendon, Northolt, Debden, Martlesham, N Weald, Coltishall
	Army Co-op	DT	I	4.42 – 7.42	Honiley, High Ercall
	F		IIc	4.41 – 8.41	Coltishall
	Army Co-op	FM	IIb	6.41 – 9.42	Coltishall, Honiley, High Ercall
258 Sq	F	ZT	I	12.40 – 4.41	Leconfield, Duxford, Drem, Acklington, Jurby
	F		I	3.42 – '43	Java, Ceylon
	F		IIa	4.41 – 2.42	Kenley, Redhill, Martlesham, Singapore
	F		IIb	1.3.42 – 12.43	Java, India
	FB		IIc	11.43 – 8.44	India, Burma
260 Sq	F		I	12.40 – 2.42	Castletown, Drem, Palestine, Egypt, Libya
261 Sq	F		I	2.8.40 – 5.41	Malta
	F		I	12.7.41 – 3.42	Iraq, Palestine, India
	F		IIb	3.42 – 11.43	Ceylon, India, Burma
	FB		IIc	10.43 – 6.44	India, Burma
263 Sq	F	HE	I	10.6.40 – 11.40	Drem, Grangemouth
273 Sq	F		I	8.42 – '42	Ceylon
	F		IIa/b	8.42 – '42	Ceylon
	F		IIc	12.43 – 5.44	Ceylon

Unit	Role	Code	Mk	Dates	Bases
274 Sq	F	YK	I	8.40 – '41	Egypt, Malta
	FB	NH	IIb	10.41 – 5.42	Greece, Egypt, Libya
	FB	NH	IIc	'42 – 11.43	Egypt, Libya, Cyprus
276 Sq	ASR		II	12.41 – '42	Harrowbeer
279 Sq	ASR		IIc/IV	4.45 – 6.45	Thornaby
283 Sq	ASR		II	'44 – '45	N Africa
284 Sq	ASR		II	9.44 – 3.45	Tunisia
285 Sq	AAC		IIc	1.44 – 6.45	Woodvale, Andover, N Weald
286 Sq	AAC		IIc/IV	17.11.41 – 5.45	Filton, Lulsgate, Colerne, Zeals, Locking, Weston Zoyland, Culmhead
287 Sq	AAC	KZ	IIb/IV	19.11.41 – 2.44	Croydon
288 Sq	AAC	RP	IIc/IV	18.11.41 – '44	Digby, Wellingore, Coleby Grange, Collyweston
289 Sq	AAC	YE	IIc/IV	12.41 – 6.45	Kirknewton, Turnhouse, Acklington, Eshott, Andover
290 Sq	AAC		IIc	1.12.43 – 1.45	Newtownards, Long Kesh, Turnhouse
291 Sq	ASR	8Q	IIc	3.44 – 6.45	Hutton Cranswick
302 Sq Polish	F	WX	I	13.7.40 – 3.41	Leconfield, Northolt, Westhampnett
	F		I	5.41 – 7.41	Jurby
	F		IIa	3.41 – 5.41	Westhampnett
	F		IIb	7.41 – 10.41	Jurby, Church Stanton, Warmwell
303 Sq Polish	F	RF	I	2.8.40 – 1.41	Northolt, Leconfield
	F		I	8.41 – 10.41	Speke
306 Sq Polish	F	UZ	I	28.8.41 – 7.41	Church Fenton, Tern Hill
	F	UZ	IIa	4.41 – 7.41	Northolt
308 Sq Polish	F	ZF	I	11.40 – 4.41	Baginton
309 Sq Polish	Army Co-op	WC	IIc/IV	4.44 – 10.44	Drem, Hutton Cranswick, Acklington, Peterhead
310 Sq Czech	F	NN	I	10.7.40 – 3.41	Duxford
	F		IIa	3.41 – 12.41	Martlesham, Dyce
	F		IIb	6.41 – 11.41	Dyce
312 Sq Czech	F	DU	I	29.8.40 – 5.41	Duxford, Speke, Valley, Jurby
	F		IIb	5.41 – 12.41	Kenley, Martlesham, Ayr
315 Sq Polish	F	PK	I	2.41 – 7.41	Acklington, Speke
316 Sq Polish	F	SZ	I	15.2.41 – 6.41	Pembrey, Colerne
	F		IIa/b	6.41 – 11.41	Colerne, Church Stanton
317 Sq Polish	F	JH	I	22.2.41 – 7.41	Acklington, Ouston, Colerne, Fairwood Common
	F		IIa/b	7.41 – 10.41	Exeter
318 Sq Polish	Tac Recce		I	20.3.43 – 8.43	Detling
			IIb	9.43 – 2.44	Palestine, Egypt
331 Sq Norway	F	FN	I	21.7.41 – 8.41	Catterick
	F	FN	IIb	8.41 – 11.41	Castletown, Skeabrae
335 Sq Greece	F	FG	I	10.41 – 9.42	Palestine
	FB		IIb	8.42 – 10.43	Egypt, Libya
	FB		IIc	10.43 – 1.44	Egypt, Libya
336 Sq Greece	F		IIc	2.43 – 8.44	Egypt, Libya
351 Sq Yugo	FB		IIc	1.7.44 – 9.44	Libya

Unit	Role	Code	Mk	Dates	Bases
	FB		IV	9.44 – 15.6.45	Italy, Yugoslavia
352 Sq Yugo	FB		IIc	22.4.44 – 6.44	Libya
401 Sq RCAF	F	YO	I	20.6.40 – 2.41	Middle Wallop, Croydon, Northolt, Prestwick, Castletown
	F		IIb	2.41 – 9.41	Driffield, Digby
402 Sq RCAF	F	AE	I	11.12.40 – 5.41	Digby
	F		IIa	5.41 – 8.41	Wellingore, Martlesham, Ayr
	FB	AE	IIb	8.41 – 3.42	Rochford, Warmwell
417 Sq	F	AN	IIb	9.42 – 10.42	Egypt
	F		IIc	9.42 – 1.43	Cyprus
438 Sq RCAF	FB	F3	IV	15.11.43 – 4.44	Digby, Wittering, Ayr, Hurn, Funtington
439 Sq RCAF	FB	5V	IV	1.1.44 – 4.44	Wellingore, Ayr, Hurn, Funtington
440 Sq RCAF	FB	18	IV	2.44 – 3.44	Ayr, Hurn
450 Sq RAAF	FB	OK	I	5.41 – 12.41	Egypt, Palestine, Syria
451 Sq RAAF	F		I	7.41 – 1.43	Egypt, Libya, Syria, Cyprus, Palestine
	Army Co-op		IIc	2.43 – 10.43	Egypt
486 Sq RNZAF	NF	SA	I/IIb	3.3.42 – 7.42	Kirton-in-Lindsey, Wittering, Hibaldstow
488 Sq RNZAF	F		I	1.42 – 2.42	Singapore
501 Sq RAuxAF	F	ZH/ SD	I	3.39 – 5.41	Filton, Tangmere, France, Croydon, Middle Wallop, Gravesend, Kenley, Colerne
504 Sq RAuxAF	F	TM	I	8.39 – 7.41	Hucknall, Digby, Debden, France, Wick, Castletown, Catterick, Hendon, Filton, Exeter
	F		IIb	7 – 11.41	Fairwood Common, Chilbolton, Ballyhalbert
516 Sq	COpsT		II	12.43 – 12.44	Dundonald
518 Sq	Met	Y3	IIc	9.45 – 10.46	Aldergrove
520 Sq	Met		IIc	6.44 – 4.46	Gibraltar
521 Sq	Met		IIc	8.44 – 2.46	Docking, Langham, Chivenor
527 Sq	Calib	WN	I/IIb	15.6.43 – 4.45	Castle Camps, Snailwell, Digby
530 Sq	Tblt		I	9.42 – 25.1.43	Hunsdon
531 Sq 1452 Flt	Tblt		IIc	5.42 – 31.1.43	West Malling, Debden
532 Sq 1453 Flt	Tblt		IIc/XII	10.7.41 – 1.2.43	Wittering, Hibaldstow
533 Sq 1454 Flt	Tblt		IIc/XIb	4.7.41 – 25.1.43	Colerne, Charmy Down
534 Sq 1455 Flt	Tblt		IIc/X	7.7.41 – 25.1.43	Tangmere
535 Sq 1456 Flt	Tblt		IIc	24.11.41 – 9.42	Honiley, High Ercall
536 Sq 1457 Flt	Tblt		IIc	15.9.41 – 9.42	Colerne, Predannack, Fairwood Common
537 Sq 1458 Flt	Tblt		IIc/XII	9.12.41 – 25.1.43	Middle Wallop
538 Sq 1459 Flt	Tblt		IIc	20.9.41 – 25.1.43	Hunsdon, Hibaldstow
539 Sq 1460 Flt	Tblt		IIc/X	15.12.41 – 25.1.43	Acklington
567 Sq	AAC	I4	IIc/IV	1.12.43 – 6.45	Detling, Hornchurch, Hawkinge
577 Sq	AAC		IIc/IV	1.12.43 – 7.45	Castle Bromwich
587 Sq	AAC	M4	IIc/IV	1.12.43 – 6.45	Weston Zoyland, Culmhead
595 Sq	AAC		IIc/IV	1.12.43 – 12.44	Aberporth
598 Sq	AAC		IIc	2.44 – 4.45	Peterhead, Bircham Newton
601 Sq RAuxAF	F	UF	I	2.40 – 9.40	Tangmere, France, Middle Wallop, Debden, Exeter, Northolt
	F	UF	IIb	9.40 – '41	Northolt, Manston, Matlaske, Duxford

Unit	Role	Code	Mk	Dates	Bases
605 Sq RAuxAF	F	UP	I	8.39 – 12.40	Tangmere, Leuchars, Wick, Hawkinge, Drem, Croydon
	F		IIa	11.40 – 8.41	Croydon, Martlesham, Tern Hill, Baginton
	F		IIb	8.41 – 3.42	Baginton, Kenley, Sealand, Sumatra
	F		IIb	1.42 – 2.42	Malta
607 Sq RAuxAF	F	AF	I	3.40 – 6.41	France, Croydon, Usworth, Tangmere, Turnhouse, Drem, MacMerry, Skitten
	FB		IIa	6.41 – 8.41	Skitten, Castletown
	FB		IIb	7.41 – 3.42	Castletown, Martlesham, Manston
	FB		IIb	2.43 – 12.43	India, Burma
	FB		IIc	6.42 – 2.43	India, Burma
	FB		IIc	7.43 – 9.43	India, Burma
610 Sq RAuxAF	F		I	9.39 – 9.39	Hooton Park
615 Sq RAuxAF	F	KW	I	4.40 – 2.41	France, Kenley, Prestwick, Northolt
	F		I	4.41 – 7.41	Valley
	F		IIa	2.41 – 4.41	Kenley
	F		IIb	7.41 – '42	Valley, Manston, Angle, Fairwood Common
	F		IIc	7.41 – 3.42	Valley, Manston, Angle, Fairwood Common
	F		IIc	6.42 – 9.43	India, Burma
631 Sq	AAC	6D	IIc	3.44 – 7.45	Towyn, Llanbedr
639 Sq	AAC		IV	8.44 – 4.45	Cleave
650 Sq	AAC		IV	4.44 – 6.45	Cark, Bordogan
667 Sq	AAC		I/IIc	6.44 – 12.45	Gosport
679 Sq	AAC		IIc/IV	1.12.43 – 6.45	Ipswich
680 Sq	PR		I/II	2.43 – 12.44	N Africa
681 Sq	PR		II	25.1.43 – 11.43	India
691 Sq	AAC	5S	I/IIc	1.12.43 – 8.45	Roborough, Harrowbeer
695 Sq	AAC		IIc	1.12.43 – 9.45	Bircham Newton

Commonwealth & Allied

Unit	Role	Code	Mk	Dates	Bases
3 Sq RAAF	F		I	2.41 – 7.41	Egypt, Libya, Palestine
2 Sq Egypt	FB		IIc	1.44 – 1.45	Egypt
1 Sq RCAF	F	NA/ YO	I	2.39 – 6.40	Calgary, Alberta
				6.40 – 2.41	Middle Wallop, Croydon, Northolt, Prestwick, Castletown, Driffield
123 Sq RCAF	Army Co-op	VD	I/XII	11.42 – 10.43	Rockcliffe, Ontario
125 Sq RCAF	F	BA	I/XII	4.42 – 5.43	Sydney, Nova Scotia
126 Sq RCAF	F	BV	XII	4.42 – 5.45	Dartmouth, Nova Scotia
127 Sq RCAF	F	TF	XII	7.42 – 12.43	Dartmouth, Nova Scotia
128 Sq RCAF	F	RA	I/XII	6.42 – 3.44	Sydney, Nova Scotia
129 Sq RCAF	F	HA	XII	8.42 – 9.44	Dartmouth, Nova Scotia
130 Sq RCAF	F	AE	XII	9.42 – 3.44	Mont Joli, Quebec
133 Sq RCAF	F	FN	XII	7.42 – 3.44	Lethbridge, Alberta
135 Sq RCAF	F	XP	XII	7.42 – 5.44	Mossbank, Saskatchewan/Patricia Bay, BC

Unit	Role	Code	Mk	Dates	Bases
1 Sq India	FB		IIb/IIc	9.42 – 3.46	India, Burma
2 Sq India	FB		IIb	9.42 – 2.46	India, Burma
3 Sq India	FB		IIc	11.43 – 11.45	India, Burma
4 Sq India	FB		IIc	8.43 – 8.46	India, Burma, Japan
6 Sq India	FB		IIb/IIc	2.43 – 1.45	India, Burma
7 Sq India	FB		IIc	11.44 – 3.46	India, Burma
9 Sq India	FB		IIc	1.44 – 5.45	India, Burma
10 Sq India	FB		IIc	4.44 – 4.45	India, Burma
1 Sq SAAF	F		I	12.40 – 4.41	E Africa, Egypt, Libya
	FB		IIb/IIc	4.41 – 11.42	Egypt, Libya
3 Sq SAAF	F		I	12.40 – 4.43	E Africa, Aden
	FB		IIb/IIc	4.43 – 3.44	Egypt, Libya
7 Sq SAAF	FB		IIb/IIc	5.42 – 8.43	Egypt, Libya
40 Sq SAAF	F		I	1.42 – 11.42	Egypt, Libya
	FB		IIb	11.42 – 5.43	Egypt, Libya, Tunisia
41 Sq SAAF	FB		IIb/IIc	5.43 – 5.44	Egypt, Libya

Role – abbreviations:

AAC	Anti-Aircraft Co-operation	FB	Fighter-bomber
Army Co-op	Army Co-operation	FR	Fighter Reconnaissance
ASR	Air Sea Rescue	NF	Night Fighter
Calib	Calibration	PR	Photo Reconnaissance
COpsT	Combined Operations Training	Recce	Reconnaissance
Comms	Communications	Tac Recce	Tactical Reconnaissance
F	Day Fighter	Tblt	Turbinlite

Bases – the list covers the main locations for the units, which are in the overall order, but to reduce space no mention is made of any return to an airfield.

RAF Training & Miscellaneous Units

Many of the training and support units operated other aircraft types as well as Hurricanes. The aim here has been to identify dates and bases when Hurricanes were in operation, many of the units being concerned with conversion and operational training to remove the load from operational squadrons, which were generally busy fighting a war.

Unit	Role	Code	Mk	Dates	Bases
AFU	Ops T		IIb/c	7.43 – 3.44	Setif, Mediterranean
7 AFU	Ops T		I	2.44 – 10.44	Peterborough
9 AFU	Ops T		I/II	4.42 – 8.42	Hullavington
				1.45 – 6.45	
11 AFU	Ops T		IIc	12.44 – 6.45	Shawbury
1 Air Arm School	Weapons Training		I/IV	9.43 – 10.44	Manby
1321 Flt	Bomber defence		IIc	9.44 – 11.44	Bottesford
1342 Flt	RP training		II/IV	2.45 – 11.45	Shallufa
1344 Flt	Fighter control		IIc/d/IV	1.45 – 6.45	Gujrat

Unit	Role	Code	Mk	Dates	Bases
401 Flt	Met	TE	I	10.41 – 2.42	Bircham Newton
402/1402 Flt	Met	DQ	IIc	12.44 – 10.45	Ballyhalbert
1411 Flt	Met		II	7.43 – 8.43	Almaza
1412 Flt	Met		IIb/c	6.43 – 6.45	Khartoum
1413 Flt	Met		I,IIb/c	7.43 – 7.45	St Jean
1415 Flt	Met		IIb/c	4.44 – 7.45	Baghdad
418 Flt	Malta defence		I	7.40 – 8.40	Abbotsinch
421 Flt	Recce		IIa	10.40 – 11.40	Gravesend
1423 Flt	Defence of Iceland		I	6.41 – 12.41	Kaldadarnes
1432 Flt	PR		X	9.42 – 4.43	Kaduna
1441 Flt	Combined ops		I,X	1942 – 4.43	Dundonald
1449 Flt	Fighter defence	VD	I,IIb,X	4.42 – 9.44	St Mary's, Scilly Isles
1565 Met Flt	Met		IIb/c	9.44 – 8.45	Cyprus
1566 Met Flt	Met		IIb/c	3.44 – 8.45	Aden
1567 Met Flt	Met		I,IIb,X	6.43 – 7.45	Khartoum
1568 Met Flt	Met		IIb/c	2.44 – 1.46	Diego Suarez
1569 Met Flt	Met		IIb/c	3.44 – 7.45	Eastleigh
1681 Bomber (Defence) Training Flt	Bomber defence	LT	IIc	3.44 – 8.44	Long Marston
1682 Bomber (Defence) Training Flt	Bomber defence	UH	IIc	2.44 – 8.44	Enstone
Air Del. Letter Service Flt	Document delivery	DR	IIc	3.44 – 12.44	Northolt
MSFU	Camships	KE/LU	Sea Ia	5.41 – 9.43	Speke
1 ME T School	Conversion		I,IIc/d,X	4.42 – 7.42	Ballah
5 OTU	Conversion		I	3.40 – 11.40	Aston Down
6 OTU	Conversion		I,X	3.40 – 11.40	Sutton Bridge
7 OTU	Conversion		I	6.40 – 8.40	Hawarden
52 OTU	Conversion		I	11.40 – 9.41	Debden & Aston Down
55 OTU	Conversion	EH/PA	I,IIa/b,X	11.40 – 12.43	Aston Down & Usworth
56 OTU	Conversion	FE	I,IIa/b,X	11.40 – 10.43	Sutton Bridge
59 OTU	Conversion		I,IIb,X	12.40 – 1.44	Crosby
70 ME OTU	Conversion		I,II	12.40 – 4.41	Ismailia
71 ME OTU	Air fighting & ground attack		I,II,X	6.41 – 5.45	Ismailia
73 OTU	Conversion		I,IIa/b/c	1.42 – 11.42	Aden
74 OTU	Army Co-operation		I,II	10.41 – 7.45	Aqir
151 Fighter OTU	Conversion		II	7.42 – 4.46	Risalpur
1 OTU India	Conversion		I	6.42 – 7.42	Risalpur
2 PRU	Recce		I,IIa/b	3.41 – 3.42	Heliopolis

Unit	Role	Code	Mk	Dates	Bases
Fleet Air Arm					
700 Sq	MTPTS		IIc	5.45	Worthy Down
			S IIb	8.45 – 9.45	Worthy Down
702 Sq			S IIb	5.42 – 7.42	Belfast
727 Sq	FRU		IIc	8.43 – 8.44	Brawdy
728 Sq	FRU		IIc	5.44 – 1.45	Malta
731 Sq	DLCOT		S Ib	12.43 – 6.44	East Haven
748 Sq	F Pool		S Ib	2.43 – 7.43	St Merryn
			S IIc	6.43 – 2.44	St Merryn
759 Sq	Fleet F School	Y1	S Ib	6.41 – 3.44	Eastleigh
	1 NAFS	Y1	S II	2.43 – 8.43	Eastleigh
760 Sq	F Pool	W7/8	I	9.42 – 12.42	Yeovilton
		W9	S IIb	10.41 – 12.42	Yeovilton
			S IIc	5.44 – 1.11.44	Yeovilton
761 Sq	F Pool		S IIc	9.43 – 5.44	Gosport
762 Sq	AFTS		S Ia	9.42 – 9.6.43	Yeovilton
			S Ib	9.42 – 9.6.43	Yeovilton
766 Sq	NOTU	K1	S IIc	11.44 – 3.45	Inskip
768 Sq	DLTS	M2	S Ib	9.41 – 3.44	Arbroath, Machrihanish
			S IIc	12.43	Machrihanish
769 Sq	DLTS		S Ib	3.42 – 4.44	Arbroath, East Haven
770 Sq	FRU		IIc	6.44 – 4.45	Drem
771 Sq	FRU		FBIIc	5.44 – 4.45	Twatt
772 Sq	FRU		IIc	6.44 – 4.45	Machrihanish, Ayr
774 Sq	AT Sq		S Ib	7.44 – 9.44	St Merryn
			FBIIc	12.44 – 2.45	Rattray
775 Sq	FRU		II	5.44 – 1.45	Gibraltar
776 Sq	FRU		Ib	3.44 – 4.45	Speke
			IIc	10.44	Speke
		R7	FBIIc	4.44 – 7.45	Speke, Woodvale
778 Sq	S T Unit		S Ib	8.41 – 6.43	Arbroath, Crail
			S IIC	'43 – 10.43	Crail
779 Sq	FRU		S Ib	2.42	Gibraltar
			IIc	6.44 – 4.45	Gibraltar
781 Sq	Comms		S Ib	11.42 – 2.45	Lee-on-Solent
			S IIc	10.43	Lee-on-Solent
787Z Flt	FFDU		S Ia	11.43 –	Wittering
		YO	S IIc	11.43	Wittering
788 Sq	FRU		S Ib	'42	Mombasa
			IIb	8.42 – 11.42	Mombasa
791 Sq	ATTU		S Ia	12.43 – 1.44	Arbroath
			S Ib	4.42	Arbroath
			S IIc	10.43	Arbroath
792 Sq	ATTU		S Ia	5.44	St Merryn
794 Sq	NAFU		S Ib	8.43 – 9.43	Angle
			IIb	9.43 – 10.43	Dale

Unit	Role	Code	Mk	Dates	Bases
795 Sq	EFFP		S Ib	12.42 – 6.43	Tanga, Mackinnon Road – Combat
800 Sq	F		S Ib	6.42 – 10.42	St Merryn
			S IIb	9.42 – 10.42	HMS *Indomitable* – Indian Ocean
			S IIc	10.42 – 11.43	HMS *Biter* – N Africa
801 Sq	F		S Ia	8.41 – 11.41	Yeovilton, St Merryn, Skeabrae
			S Ib	8.41 – 8.42	Yeovilton, St Merryn, Skeabrae, Tain, Turnhouse, Abbotsinch, HMS *Argus*, Gibraltar, HMS *Eagle* – sunk 11.8.42
802 Sq	F		S I	5.41 – 6.41	Donibristle
			S Ib	2.42 – 9.42	Yeovilton, St Merryn, Peterhead, Donibristle, Machrihanish, Hatson, HMS *Avenger*
			S IIb	9.42 – 11.42	Hatson, HMS *Avenger* – sunk 15.11.42
803 Sq	F		I	6.41 – 3.42	Ramat David & N Africa
			S II	6.42 – 8.42	HMS *Formidable*
804 Sq	F – Camships	S7	S Ia/ S Ib	2.41 – 9.41	Yeovilton, Belfast, HMS *Pegasus*, HMS *Ariguani*, HMS *Springbank* – sunk 17.7.41, HMS *Mapen*
	F		S IIb	9.41 – 10.42	Belfast, HMS *Argus*, Gibraltar, HMS *Furious*
			S IIc	10.42 – 6.43	HMS *Dasher* – N Africa
805 Sq	F		I	5.41 – 6.41	Egypt
806 Sq	F		I	5.41 – '42	Western Desert
807 Sq	F		S II	11.41	Gibraltar, HMS *Argus*
811 Sq	TBRSq		S II	7.41 – 9.41	Lee-on-Solent
813 Sq	Anti-sub		S Ib	1.42 – 8.42	HMS *Eagle*, Gibraltar
824 Sq	Convoy Escort		S IIc	8.43 – 6.44	Machrihanish, Ayr, HMS *Striker*, Hatson
825 Sq	Convoy Escort		S IIc	8.43 – 9.44	Lee-on-Solent, Yeovilton, HMS *Vindex*, Machrihanish
835 Sq	Convoy Escort		S IIc	6.43 – 9.44	HMS *Battler*, Ayr, HMS *Argus*, HMS *Ravager*, Eglinton, HMS *Chaser*, HMS *Nairana*, Burscough
877 Sq	Fleet F Sq		IIb	1.4.43 – 30.12.43	Tanga East Africa, Port Reitz
880 Sq	Fleet F Sq		S Ia	3.41 – 7.41	Yeovilton, HMS *Furious*,

Unit	Role	Code	Mk	Dates	Bases
			S Ib	7.41 – 8.42	St Merryn HMS *Indomitable* – Indian Ocean, Stretton
882 Sq	Fleet F Sq		S Ib	15.7.41 – 4.42	Donibristle, St Merryn, Yeovilton, Gosport, HMS *Illustrious*
883 Sq	Fleet F Sq		S Ib	10.10.41 – 9.42	Yeovilton, St Merryn, HMS *Avenger*
			S IIb	9.42 – 11.42	Hatston, HMS *Avenger*
885 Sq	Fleet F Sq		S Ib	1.12.41 – 8.42	Yeovilton, HMS *Victorious*
889 Sq	F		IIc	10.42 – 28.2.43	Egypt
891 Sq	F		S Ib	1.7.42 – 10.42	Lee-on-Solent, HMS *Argus*, HMS *Dasher*
	F		S IIc	10.42 – 5.4.43	HMS *Dasher* – N Africa, Donibristle, Machrihanish, Hatston
895 Sq	F		S Ib	15.11.42 – 3.43	Stretton
897 Sq	F		S Ib	1.12.42 – 3.43	Stretton

Role: abbreviations;   Mk: S – Sea Hurricane

AFTS	Advanced Flying Training School	FRU	Fleet Requirements Unit
AT Sq	Armament Training Squadron	MTPTS	Maintenance Test Pilots Training Unit
ATTU	Air Target Training Unit	NAFS	Naval Air Fighter School
Comms	Communications	NAFU	Naval Air Fighting Unit
DLCOT	Deck Landing Control Officers Training	NOTU	Naval Operations Training Unit
DLTS	Deck Landing Training School	ST Unit	Service Trials Unit
EFFP	Eastern Fleet Fighter Pool	TBR Sq	Torpedo Bomber Squadron
F	Fighter		

Foreign Service

Country/Unit	Role	No.	Mk	Dates	Bases & Remarks
Belgium					
2e Esc	F	15	I		
Finland					
LeLv 22	F	12	I	1.40	
Free French					
Esc 1 & 2	F		I/II		
Ireland					
IAC	F	12	I	1942	
	FB	6	IIc	1943	

Country/Unit	Role	No.	Mk	Dates	Bases & Remarks
Persia					
	F	2	I	1939	
	FB	16	IIc	1946	
Poland					
	F	10	I	1939	Only one delivered
Portugal					
Esq BA2	FB	15	IIb	8.43	Ota
Esq BA3	FB	50	IIb/IIc	1945	Tancos, Lisbon
Romania					
	F	12	I	8.39	
Russia					
Air Force	FB	210	IIa		
	FB	1557	IIb/XI/XII		
	FB	1009	IIc		
	FB	100	IV		
Turkey					
	F	15	I	1939	
	FB		IIc	1942	
Yugoslavia					
51st Sq	F	24	I	1939	Also 33rd & 34th Sq

APPENDIX 4 – PRESERVED HURRICANES

Not many years ago there seemed to be a finite number of Hurricanes preserved mainly in Europe and Canada, a small number of them airworthy, all of which could be easily identified from various sources. However, with the pulling back of the Iron Curtain, access into Russia improved and a number of wrecks have been recovered from remote areas around the Kola Peninsula where, thanks to the difficult terrain, they have remained for up to 60 years undisturbed.

A number of these Hurricanes were probably force-landed and not seriously damaged and are now candidates for restoration to flying condition. Others are in a poorer state and are generally donating parts to other rebuilds, but such are the skills available that even a small number of parts can result in a full restoration.

Therefore the following list may have omissions, and the author would appreciate any feedback on airframes missed, the confirmation of identities and prior histories, and any relevant illustrations.

Identity	Mk	History	Location
L1592	I	To 56 Sq, 17 Sq, 87 Sq, 43 Sq, 17 Sq, 152 Sq, 43 Sq, 615 Sq, SDF, 9 AOS, 5 PAFU, 9 RAFU Damaged in forced landing near Croydon 18.8.40. Repaired & stored for preservation. RAF Air Historical Branch 1954. Science Museum 1962.	Science Museum, London – KW-Z:615 Sq
N2394	I	To Finnish Air Force as HU452/HC452 1940, allocated to Finnish AF Museum 1969 & stored at Vesivehmaa AB.	Aviation Museum of Central Finland. Luonetjarvi AB 1972
P2617 AF-F	I	To 615 Sq, 607 Sq, 1 Sq, 9 SFTS, 9 FTS, RAF Historical Branch, RAF 1955, 8373M at 71MU Bicester as travelling exhibit 1965.	RAF Museum, Hendon – AF-F:607 Sq
P2902 DX-X G-ROBT	I	Crashed Dunkirk 3.5.40 & hulk recovered 1988. To Richard Roberts, Billinghurst & restoration to fly 1994.	Hawker Restorations, Sudbury
P3175	I	Shot down by Bf110 near N Weald 31.8.40. Recovered as wreck & unrestored.	RAF Museum, Hendon, Nov 1972
P3351 ZK-TPL	I IIa	Crashed Prestwick 21.7.40 & rebuilt as Mk IIa DR393. To Soviet AF 5.41 & crashed near Murmansk 1943. Recovered 9.92 to Hawker Restorations UK 1993 for Alpine Fighter Collection NZ 9.95.	Alpine Fighter Collection, Wanaka, NZ
P3717	I II	To 238 Sq, 253(Polish) Sq, 257 Sq, damaged 23.9.40, 43 Sq, 55 OTU, heavy landing 25.6.41. Repaired as Mk II & sent to Russia. Static	Hinckley, Leics

Hurricane Mk I L1592 preserved in the London Science Museum as KW-Z:615 Squadron. (*Science Museum*)

RAF Hurricane tropical Mk IIc LD619 used by the SAAF as 5285 and allocated for preservation at the South African Museum of Military History in Johannesburg, May 1950. (*Author's Collection*)

Hurricane Mk I P2617 on Horse Guards Parade when on the charge of the RAF Historical branch in the markings AF-T:607 Squadron. (*Author's Collection*)

In the Battle of Britain Museum at Hendon, Hurricane Mk I P2617 now AF-F:607 Squadron displayed in a replica anti-blast pen alongside Spitfire Mk I X4590 in 609 Squadron colours. (*Author's Collection*)

Hurricane PZ865 was allocated the civil registration G-AMAU for entry in a number of air racing events, here under starter's orders. (*Flight*)

Hurricane Mk IIc LF363 was the last on RAF charge with the Biggin Hill Station Flight. It joined the Battle of Britain Memorial Flight (BBMF) as a founder member in June 1957 and was at Horsham St Faith, Norwich, in May 1962.

Identity	Mk	History	Location
		restoration by S. Milnthorpe from parts from Russia.	
V6846	I	To India AF June 1944, & preserved 1966.	Palam, India
Z2389	II	To 249 Sq, 71 Sq, 247 Sq, 136 Sq, 253 Sq, Russian AF. Recovered St Petersburg.	Brooklands Museum, Weybridge.
Z3055	IIa	Recovered from the Sea off Malta 19.9.95 & under restoration.	Malta Aviation Museum, Ta'Qali
Z5053 G-BWHA	IIb	To Soviet AF Jan 1942 & shot down Archangel Aug 1943. Recovered from crash site in 1994 & to Historic Flying, Audley End, UK 23.8.95.	Richard Roberts, Billinghurst, Kent, 1996.
Z5207	IIb	Shipped to Russia as part of 151 Wing, flew off HMS Argus 7.9.41 & to Russian AF 17.10.41. Crashed Kola Peninsula & recovered 7.94 to Historic Flying.	Richard Roberts 1996, Cam, SW Stroud
Z5227	IIb	Shipped to Russia as part of 151 Wing, flew off HMS Argus 7.9.41 & to Russian AF 72 IAP 17.10.41. Crashed Murmansk & recovered 1995.	Greg Herrich, USA
Z5252	IIb	Shipped to Russia as part of 151 Wing 8.41, assembled & test flown Archangel 13.9.41. Presentation aircraft to General Kouznetzoff 25.9.41. To UK 1996.	H Taylor 1996
Z7015 G-BKTH	Sea. Ib	To 880 Sq, 759 Sq, VL & soc. Loughborough Tech College 11.43, Old Warden 21.2.61 – 1975. Restoration to fly, Staverton 1975, Duxford 1981. Shuttleworth Trust/IWM 24.5.83, & flew Duxford 16.9.95.	Shuttleworth Trust, Old Warden/ IWM Duxford.
AE977 G-TWTD	Sea. Ib	To 759 Sq, 760 Sq, crashed 5.12.42. Recovered from crash site in SW England 1988 & acquired by Alpine Fighter Collection NZ 1994. Hawker Restorations & flown 21.4.94.	Sudbury/Wanaka NZ – LE-D:242 Sq
BH229	IIc	To Soviet AF & recovered from crash site 9.92. To Alpine Fighter Collection 1993.	Wanaka NZ
BH238	IIb	Wreck recovered from Russia 26.8.98.	Sandown, I of W
BW841	Sea XIIa	To RCAF 18.12.41 & soc 16.10.42. Derelict on farm in Ont. To Jack Arnold, Brantford Ont 1990 & restoration to fly.	Jack Arnold, Titusville, Fl 1993
BW853 G-BRKE	Sea XIIa	To RCAF 17.12.41 & soc 12.10.44 after crash at Bagotville Que 1.8.44. Hawker Restorations 1988 & restored to fly.	AJD Engineering, Sudbury, Suffolk

Identity	Mk	History	Location
BW862	Sea XIIa	To RCAF 30.12.41, forced landing Lac St Jean Que 6.7.44 & soc 12.10.44. To LaValler Cultural & Aero Collection 1980. Canadian Museum of Flight & Transportation, Surrey BC.	Stored Langley BC
BW873	Sea XIIa	To RCAF 19.1.42 & soc 15.8.44. To Jack Arnold, Brantford Ont 1988 as restoration project with parts of RCAF5301/5381.	Jack Arnold, Titusville, Fl 1993
BW881 G-KAMM	Sea XIIa	To RCAF 22.1.42 and soc 28.9.44. Derelict on farm & recovered by Jack Arnold 1988. Hawker Restorations 12.88 & restored to fly 23.2.95.	M. Hammond, Eye, Suffolk
KX829	IV	To 137 Sq, 1606 Flt, 631 Sq, Loughborough Tech College 7.3.46 & to Birmingham 1961 as JV-I, later P3395.	Museum of Science & Industry – JX-B:1 Sq
KZ191	IV	To AFDU, 1695 Flt, 351 Sq & Israel AF. Robs Lamplough, Duxford 1983 from scrap yard in Jaffa, Israel. Under restoration.	North Weald
KZ321 G-HURY	IV	To Yugoslav & Israel AF, wreck recovered from Jaffa 1983 by Warbirds of GB & restoration at Biggin Hill 1989. To Fighter Collection 1991 & restored to fly.	Fighter Collection, Duxford
LD619	IIc	To SAAF as 5285 4.44 and preserved May 1950.	SA National Museum of Military History, Saxonwold, Jo'burg
LD975	IV	To Yugoslav AF and preserved 1968.	Yugoslav Aviation Museum, Belgrade
LF363	IIc	To 63 Sq, 309 Sq, 63 Sq, 26 Sq, 62 OTU, 41 OTU, 61 OTU, M Wallop Stn Flt, FCCS, Biggin Hill Stn Flt, RAF Air Historical Branch 1954, BBMF 6.57. Repaired at Historic Flying after crash at Wittering 11.9.91.	BBMF at Coningsby
LF658	IIc	To Belgian AF 2.9.46 and preserved 1968 as LF345:ML-B & ZA-P.	Musée R de l'Armée, Brussels
LF686	IIc	RAF Bridgnorth 1962, RAF Colerne Museum 1965, NASM Silver Hill Md.	NASM Silver Hill Md, USA
LF738	IIc	22MU 9.42, 1682 BDTF Enstone 3.43, 22 OTU Wellesbourne Mountford 1944 to 7.45. RAF Biggin Hill 1954, Rochester 1984 & restored to static display for RAF Museum 1993 to June 1995.	Cosford Aerospace Museum 1996 – UH-A:682 BDTF
LF751	IIc	To 1681 BDTF, 27 OTU, RAF Waterbeach as 5466M & Bentley Priory 1954. To	Manston Memorial Museum 4.88

Identity	Mk	History	Location
		Rochester for static restoration 21.3.85 as BN230:FT-A.	
PZ865 G-AMAU	IIc	Last built, f/f Langley 27.7.44, to Hawker Aircraft Ltd 8.44 & stored 1946 –'50. Restored to fly 13.5.50 for Hawkers at Dunsfold & to BBMF 29.3.72.	BBMF Coningsby
RCAF5380	IIb XII	To RCAF 16.6.42, crashed 29.9.42 & soc 11.2.43. Under restoration 1988.	Ontario, Canada
RCAF5389	IIb XII	To RCAF 23.6.42 & soc 20.8.46. To Air Museum of Canada, Calgary 1969.	Calgary Air & Space Museum 1988
RCAF5390	IIb XII	To RCAF 30.6.42, crashed into sea 7.2.44 & soc 4.4.44. To RRS Av, Hawkins Tx 1988, static restoration as RAF Z3174.	USAFM Wright Paterson AFB, Oh 9.90
RCAF5400	IIb XII	To RCAF 18.1.44 & soc 3.7.47. To Don Bradshaw, Saskatoon 1985 & Weeks Air Museum 1985.	Weeks Air Museum, Tamiami Fl, USA
RCAF5409	IIb XII	To RCAF 20.7.47 & soc 20.8.46. To Neil M. Rose, Vancouver for restoration 1989.	Vancouver Wa, Canada
RCAF5418	IIb XII	To RCAF 5.8.42 & soc 20.8.46. To Reynolds Aviation Pioneer Museum, Wetaskiwin 1973 & restored – engine runs 12.88.	Reynolds Aviation Museum, Wetaskiwin 1987
RCAF5424	IIb XII	To RCAF 18.8.42 & soc 15.8.46. Air Museum of Canada, Calgary 1969, then under restoration by Rem Walker.	Regina, Sask. Canada
RCAF5447	IIb XII	To RCAF 29.9.42 & soc 20.8.46. Acquired by Harry Whereatt 1988.	Assiniboia Sask. Canada
RCAF5455	IIb XII	To RCAF 12.9.42, crashed 28.1.44 & soc 30.5.44. Derelict on farm & recovered by Harry Whereatt 1972.	Assiniboia Sask. Canada
RCAF5461	IIb XII	To RCAF 12.9.42 & soc 30.6.47. To Commonwealth Air Training Plan Museum 1988.	Brandon Man. Canada
RCAF5481 G-ORGI N678DP	IIb XII	To RCAF 7.10.42, with 125 Sq RCAF & soc 29.11.44. Derelict on farm less wings & recovered by Jack Arnold 1984. To Charles Church, Sandown 6.86 & restored to fly, f/f 8.9.91. Sold to Liberty Aero/Museum of Flying, Santa Monica Ca 2.91 as P2970:US-X.	Chino, Ca, USA
RCAF5584	IIb XII	To RCAF 6.11.42 & stored for preservation 1946. To Canadian Nat Aero Collection, Rockcliffe AB Ont 1964.	Nat Aviation Museum, Rockcliffe 9.82. Canada
RCAF5589 G-HURR	IIB XII	To RCAF 6.11.42 & soc 1.10.46. Derelict on farm & recovered by Harry Whereatt.	Real Aeroplane Co. Breighton, Yorks

Identity	Mk	History	Location
		To Autocraft Brooklands 1988 & restored to fly as BE417:AE-K.	
RCAF5590	IIb XII	To RCAF 6.11.42 & soc 3.7.47. Under restoration 1989.	Ontario, Canada
RCAF5625	IIb XII	To RCAF 26.1.43 & soc 26.10.46. Surplus 19.10.46 to Reid's Flying Service Ont. & derelict for scrap Guelph 1956. Parts to Rem Walker for restoration of RCAF5711 1980.	Regina Sask. Canada
RCAF5627	IIb XII	To RCAF 18.11.42 & soc 2.2.44. Restoration Ontario.	Ontario, Canada
RCAF5666	IIb XII	To RCAF 3.2.43, crashed 29.10.44 & soc 20.12.44. Scrap & incomplete hulk recovered by LaVallee Cultural & Aero Collection, passed to Ed Zalesky 1980.	Surrey BC, Canada
RCAF5667 N2549	IIb XII	To RCAF 3.2.43 & soc 1.10.46. Derelict on farm Saskatchewan & recovered by Neil Rose 6.65. Restored to fly Vancouver 10.5.94 but damaged on landing 22.5.94.	Vancouver
RCAF5711 G-HURI	IIb XII	To RCAF 8.1.43 & soc 3.7.47. To Air Museum of Canada, Calgary 1970 & Rem Walker for composite rebuild. To BJS Grey 12.82 for the Fighter Collection, Duxford 9.6.83. Restored to fly 1.9.89 as Z7381 XR-T:71(Eagle) Sq.	Fighter Collection, Duxford
"AP832"	IIb	India AF Museum 1967.	Palam AB, New Delhi
N68RW	IIb XII	Ex RCAF & crashed in swamp near Gander. To Len Tanner Ct for restoration & Lone Star Flight Museum 8.91.	Lone Star Flight Museum, Fort Collins, Galveston, Tx.

SELECTED BIBLIOGRAPHY

Barker, Ralph, *The Hurricats*, Stroud, Tempus Books, 2000

Bruce, J.M., *British Aeroplanes 1914–18*, London, Putnam, 1957

Chapman, John & Geoff Goodall, *Warbirds Worldwide Directory*, 1996

Cull, Brian & Bruce Lander, with Heinrich Weiss, *Twelve Days in May*, London, Grub Street, 1999

Ellis, Ken, *Wrecks & Relics*, 17th Edition, Midland Counties, 2000

Flypast Magazine, various issues, Stamford, Lincs.

Fozard, Dr John W., *Sydney Camm and the Hurricane*, Shrewsbury, Airlife Publishing, 1991

Franks, Richard A., *The Hawker Hurricane*, SAM, 1999

Jacobs, Peter, *Hawker Hurricane*, Ramsbury, The Crowood Press, 1998

Jane's All the World's Aircraft 1938 & 1945/6, London

Kostenuk, S. & J. Griffin, *RCAF Squadrons and Aircraft*, SSHC, 1977

Mason, Francis K., *Hawker Aircraft Since 1920*, London, Putnam, 1961

Mason, Francis K., *Hawker Hurricane*, Aston, 1987

Molson, K.M. & H.A. Taylor, *Canadian Aircraft since 1909*, Canada's Wings, 1982

Rawlings, J.D.R., *Coastal Support & Special Squadrons of the RAF & their Aircraft*, London, Jane's, 1982

Rawlings, J.D.R., *Fighter Squadrons of the RAF and their Aircraft*, London, McDonald, 1969

Robertson, Bruce, *Sopwith – the Man and his Aircraft*, Hayleyford, 1970

Shores, C. & B. Cull with N. Malizia, *Malta: The Hurricane Years 1940–41*, London, Grub Street, 1999

Sturtivant, Ray, John Hamlin & James Halley, *RAF Training & Support Units*, Air Britain

Sturtivant, Ray, *Squadrons of the Fleet Air Arm*, Air Britain, 1984.

INDEX